Voices from the
BATTLE OF
TRAFALGAR

Peter Warwick

David and Charles

To Tom
for suffering Nelson!

A DAVID & CHARLES BOOK
Copyright © David & Charles Limited 2005, 2006

David & Charles is an F+W Publications Inc. company
4700 East Galbraith Road
Cincinnati, OH 45236

First published in the UK in 2005
Reprinted 2005
First paperback edition 2006

Copyright © Peter Warwick 2005, 2006

Peter Warwick has asserted his right to be identified as author of this work
in accordance with the Copyright, Designs and Patents Act, 1988.

ISBN-13: 978-0-7153-2000-6 hardback
ISBN-10: 0-7153-2000-9 hardback

ISBN-13: 978-0-7153-2556-8 paperback
ISBN-10: 0-7153-2556-6 paperback

Printed and bound by Creative Print & Design Group,
Ebbw Vale, Wales, UK
for David & Charles
Brunel House   Newton Abbot   Devon

Commissioning Editor   Ruth Binney
Desk Editor   Lewis Birchon
Head of Design   Alison Myer
Designer   Jodie Lystor
Production Controller   Kelly Smith

Visit our website at www.davidandcharles.co.uk

David & Charles books are available from all good bookshops; alternatively
you can contact our Orderline on 0870 9908222 or write to us at FREEPOST
EX2 110, D&C Direct, Newton Abbot, TQ12 4ZZ (no stamp required UK only);
US customers call 800-289-0963 and Canadian customers call 800-840-5220.

CONTENTS

FOREWORD

On 2 November 1805, 29-year-old George Hewson, then serving as a lieutenant in the battleship HMS *DREADNOUGHT*, sat down to write a letter to a friend. He began, 'I have no doubt but that you will be pleased to hear that the fleet in which I serve has obtained over the enemies of our Country a Victory which was never equalled in the brightest periods of history, an account of which I shall give you in the best manner I can.'

Hewson's account was discovered only recently, and so it has never been published. But, in fact, his opening words are strikingly similar to others that were, even then, being penned by his comrades in arms. For all those who took part in the great victory at Trafalgar were conscious that they had witnessed an event of very special significance, and a large number of them set out to record it, usually in letters home. Moreover, those who received the letters appreciated their importance and many of them were carefully preserved. As a result, we have more participants' accounts of Trafalgar than of any other battle of the sailing era.

Some of these personal accounts have found their way into the large body of books about the battle that have been published since 1805 – but by no means all. Indeed, as so often happens, the same passages have been repeated from book to book, so that they have become almost hackneyed in the process.

One of the most pleasing aspects of the bicentenary of Trafalgar is that it has already prompted some important new original research. Unpublished Nelson letters have been discovered; details of every man who served at the battle unearthed and tabulated; and research in French and Spanish sources has greatly increased our understanding of the battle from the point of view of our former opponents. All these developments are refreshing the familiar narrative, and enabling historians to retell the story in new and exciting ways.

This splendid retelling of the Trafalgar story by Peter Warwick is also a product of painstaking and ground-breaking research. As a result, one of the strengths of the book is that, rather than being simply a roundup of the 'usual suspects', it includes a number of hitherto little-known accounts, or even completely unknown ones. Its other strength is that it allows the ordinary men of Trafalgar – the unsung heroes – to find their voice. The famous names are present of course – but here they take second place to the ordinary participants: junior officers, sailors and Royal Marines. These eyewitnesses struggle, often with moving success, to express some of the emotion they feel about the cataclysmic event in which they have just –taken part.

'The human mind cannot form a grander or more noble sight,' wrote George Hewson, remembering the moment just before the battle, when the two great fleets were spread out in full sight of each other. This fine book helps us to recapture the sights of Trafalgar, and to relive the experiences of those who fought there.

Dr Colin White

INTRODUCTION

On Monday 21 October 1805, off Cape Trafalgar, Vice Admiral Lord Nelson, with 27 ships of the line, attacked the 33 ships of the combined French and Spanish fleets under the command of Vice Admiral Villeneuve. Firing started close to midday and by tea-time the most famous sea battle in British history was over. Napoleon's fleet had been virtually annihilated with 17 ships captured. In round figures 50,000 had taken part. The British lost 450 men killed and 1,250 wounded, while the allies suffered more than 4,400 killed and 3,300 wounded. Many more were drowned during the storm that followed. The British had not lost a single ship, but their hero and most celebrated naval commander was dead.

The Battle of Trafalgar was the last major naval engagement of the Napoleonic Wars. While its consequences were not immediately apparent, the legacy was profound. Trafalgar undermined any future French invasion plans, paved the way for the downfall of Napoleon, established Britain as the dominant global maritime power up until the Second World War, and ushered in a long period of economic prosperity and political authority that blossomed into the British Empire – the largest the world has ever known.

The enormous significance of Trafalgar, coupled with the death of Nelson at the moment of his greatest triumph, helps to explain the enduring interest in the battle. Rarely, after 200 years, has five hours of history been so closely studied, and had so much written about it. I hope that, in this bicentenary year, this enduring fascination justifies a book that explores the first-hand experiences of the participants, ordinary sailors and officers alike.

Inevitably their accounts and perceptions are influenced by the chaotic nature of battle, the recipients of their stories – parent, wife, sibling, friend or senior officer – and by the effects of the passage of time on memories. We live in an age of immediate mass media, visual news coverage, live and recorded voices. In the case of Trafalgar, contemporary letters, diaries, Admiralty records, drawings and paintings are all we have to relive the immediacy of the battle. They are none the worse for that, given that whatever the media, being there is the only way anyone can truly experience war's terrible and brutal reality.

Attempts to establish what actually happened at the battle and the sequence of events are fraught with complications. Writing a few days after the battle, one observer remarked, 'The disorder and confusion which reigned throughout this fearful Battle, have rendered it almost impossible for the Commanders themselves to know what occurred on board their own Ships.'

In 1913 the British government commissioned a report to inquire into the tactics of Trafalgar. The expectation was that some elegant formula would explain the execution of Nelson's plan. Although it contains relevant extracts from all available logs and journals of the British ships involved, it was an attempt made in vain. For instance, timekeeping in 1805 was not an exact science and, combined with the inevitable distractions caused by the battle itself, ships' logs can vary by more than two hours. The difficulties of signalling and ship identification brought about by the lingering dense smoke and damage to masts contribute to the confusion. Moreover, the eye-witness accounts themselves do not always agree with one another. Consequently, this book tries to capture the atmosphere of the battle, focusing on its main elements, rather than attempting a blow-by-blow analysis of the battle and the role of every ship involved in it. It is not an academic study.

To help identify the nationality of the ships involved in the battle the British appear in italicized upper case – for example, *NEPTUNE* – and the French and Spanish ships are shown in lower case italics, for example, *Neptune*. The bracketed number after the name indicates the number of guns and is included only the first time the ship is mentioned.

I have mixed selected parts of the most famous British, French and Spanish eye-witness stories with less well-known accounts, some appearing in print for the first time, such as 'Reflections on Fortitude' by Captain John Cooke. Inevitably there is more reference to Nelson than others present. He is central to the story. He shaped the battle. The success was his.

Nelson demonstrated that with bold tactics it was possible to annihilate an enemy fleet. After hundreds of years of naval conflict this was a relatively new experience. Almost all of the great battles fought by wooden sailing ships before the Battle of the Saintes in 1782 had proven to be inconclusive. Admiral Rodney secured a decisive victory at the Saintes, as did Admiral Howe at the Glorious First of June in 1794 and Admiral Duncan at the Battle of Camperdown in 1797. Nelson refined elements of their tactics, added innovations of his own, and, infused with his personal chemistry and aggressive spirit, delivered total victory. Naval warfare had been transformed.

This is a personal book. I have been interested in Trafalgar, Nelson and the eighteenth century for virtually the whole of my life. The spark was struck in March 1957 while reading of Nelson's funeral in *Eagle*, the great boys' comic. For this book I have drawn heavily on my own library and papers, amassed over the past 40 years or so. However, a great number of people have contributed to the manuscript, many unwittingly: school teachers like John Jackson, friends at university, family, especially my father and uncle, and those whom I have met as a result of the Nelson Decade and through the 1805 Club. I am grateful to them all.

Others have had a much more direct influence on this book. I am indebted to my publisher for having the courage to commission yet another book on Trafalgar and for their guidance and kindness since the project started a year ago. In particular my thanks go to the commissioning editor, Ruth Binney, and to my dedicated researcher Mike Paterson, who has spent many hours on my behalf in the Caird Library at the National Maritime Museum, the Royal Naval Museum library, the Colindale Newspaper Library, the National Archives, and the London Library.

However, I would not have a publisher without the help of my dear friend Colin White. He both recommended me and encouraged me to write this book. I am eternally grateful to him and delighted that as one of the world's authorities on Nelson he has done me the great honour of writing the foreword.

I am grateful for the help I have received with research, finding illustrations and reading and commenting on the manuscript. Captain Peter Hore was an inspiration, made his own research available and guided me to many valuable accounts of the battle; Tim Clayton, the accomplished author of *Trafalgar: the Men, the Battle, the Storm*, shared his insights with me. The following made valuable contributions: Matthew Sheldon at the Royal Naval Museum; Andrew Davies at the National Maritime Museum archive; Tony Gray and the Inshore Squadron (a marvellous group of naval historians who use computer technology to reconstruct historic naval engagements); Margaret Peacock and the Orlando Oldham Estate for the Cooke letters; Anthony Cross at Warwick Leadlay Gallery; Sim Comfort; Susan Conyers; Simon Gerratt; Géraldine Guibert; Agustin Guimerá; Liz and Ronnie Kopas; and Paul and Sally Birkbeck (for all those breakfasts!). I owe you all a considerable debt.

I should like to single out Dr Ian and Dr Pat Grimble. Without them this book would not have been written on time – it might not have been written at all! They offered their wonderful Devon home as an author's retreat. Their friendship, advice and support were simply fantastic.

Finally, thanks to my son, Tom. His encouragement, patience and good humour has been a tonic throughout.

Kerswell, Devon
21 February 2005

1

'WE HAVE GAINED A GREAT VICTORY!'

A thick blanket of sulphurous fog enveloped the centre of Georgian London. It was so dense that drivers were forced to alight from their carriages to literally feel for the road. Every ten or twenty yards they felt for the doors of houses in order to check where they were. The flames from their coach lamps were barely visible and people not at all, although their muffled shouts and helloing conveyed their anxieties. It was a frightful night and it took hours for those unfortunate enough to be out in it to travel even the shortest of distances.

Royal Navy Lieutenant John Richards Lapenotiere, a 35-year-old Devonian of Huguenot descent, had travelled far. He had sailed from the south-western tip of Spain in command of His Majesty's Schooner *PICKLE* (10) and after landing at Falmouth had been driven by post chaise to London, covering a distance of 257 miles and changing horses 21 times along the way. Now, as he approached his journey's end he, too, was slowed by the impenetrable mist. His final destination was the Admiralty in Whitehall. The Falmouth correspondent of *Trewman's Exeter Flying Post* recorded that on Monday 4 November the wind was southerly and that, 'The *PICKLE* Schooner arrived off harbour this day from which an officer landed and went off express for London with dispatches.' It was now the first hour of 6 November 1805. The dispatch from Vice Admiral Cuthbert Collingwood contained momentous news.

William Marsden, the First Secretary to the Board of the Admiralty, had been working late that night at the huge boardroom table in the

light of a few candles and was preparing to go to bed at 1 a.m. when
the 35-year-old lieutenant arrived and stunned him with the news:

> In accosting me, the officer used these impressive words,
> 'Sir, we have gained a great victory, but we have lost Lord
> Nelson!' The effect this produced, it is not my purpose to
> describe, nor had I time to indulge in reflections, who was
> at that moment the only person informed of one of the
> greatest events recorded in our history, and which it was
> my duty to make known with the utmost promptitude.
> The First Lord had retired to rest, as had his domestics,
> and it was not until after some research that I could
> discover the room in which he slept. Drawing aside his
> curtain, with a candle in my hand, I awoke the old peer
> [the greatly talented and indefatigable Admiral Lord
> Barham] from a sound slumber; and to the credit of his
> nerves be it mentioned, that he showed no symptom of
> alarm or surprise, but calmly asked: 'What news, Mr. M.?'
> We then discussed in few words, what was immediately
> to be done, and I sat up the remainder of the night, with
> such of the clerks as I could collect, in order to make the
> necessary communications.

The Second Secretary to the Board, Sir John Barrow, remembered
the impact of the news when he arrived at the Admiralty, 'Never can I
forget the shock I received on opening the Boardroom door . . . when
Marsden called out – 'Glorious news! The most glorious victory our
brave navy ever achieved – but Nelson is dead!'

The clerks made copies of Collingwood's dispatch. One was quickly
delivered to the Prime Minister, William Pitt, at 10 Downing Street,
and another messenger was sent to King George III at Windsor Castle.
They were first published later the same day in a *Gazette Extraordinary*,
a special edition of *The London Gazette*, the government's official
communiqué, which was normally published twice weekly. This was
too late to catch *The Times*, which printed the dispatch on its front

page the following day, although 3,000 copies were dispatched to the continent. For anyone with access to a newspaper these were the first official voices of the Battle of Trafalgar they would have seen.

EURYALUS, off Cape Trafalgar, October 22, 1805
Sir,
The ever-to-be-lamented death of vice-Admiral Lord Viscount Nelson, who, in the late conflict with the enemy, fell in the hour of victory, leaves to me the duty of informing My Lords Commissioners of the Admiralty, that on the 19th instant, it was communicated to the Commander-in-Chief, from the ships watching the motions of the enemy in Cadiz, that the Combined fleets had put to sea; as they sailed with light winds westerly, His Lordship concluded their destination was the Mediterranean, and immediately made all sail for the Straits' entrance, with the British squadron, consisting of twenty seven ships, three of them sixty-fours, where His Lordship was informed by Captain Blackwood (whose vigilance in watching, and giving notice of the enemy's movements, has been highly meritorious), that they had not yet passed the Straits.

On Monday 21st instant, at daylight when Cape Trafalgar bore E. by S. about seven leagues, the enemy was discovered six or seven miles to the eastward; the wind was west, and very light; the Commander-in-Chief immediately made the signal for the fleet to bear up in two columns, as they are formed in order of sailing; a mode of attack His Lordship had previously directed, to avoid the inconvenience and delay in forming a line of battle in the usual manner. The enemy's line consisted of thirty-three ships (of which eighteen [in fact it was 17] were French, and fifteen [16] Spanish), commanded-in-chief by Admiral Villeneuve: the Spaniards, under the direction of Gravina, wore, with their heads to northwards, and formed their line of battle with great closeness and correctness; but as the mode of attack

was unusual, so that, in leading down to their centre, I
had both their van and rear abaft the beam; before the fire
opened, every alternative ship was about a cable's length to
windward of her second ahead and astern, forming a kind
of double line, and appeared, when on their beam, to leave a
very little interval between them; and this without crowding
their ships. Admiral Villeneuve was in the *Bucentaure*, in the
centre, and the *Principe de Asturias* bore Gravina's flag in the
rear, but the French and Spanish ships were mixed without
any apparent regard to order of national squadron.

As the mode of our attack had been previously
determined on, and communicated to flag officers, and
captains, few signals were necessary, and none were made,
except to direct the close order as the lines bore down.

The Commander-in-Chief, in the *VICTORY*, led the
weather column, and the *ROYAL SOVEREIGN*, which bore
my flag, the lee.

The action began at twelve o'clock, by the leading ships
of the columns breaking through the enemy's line, the
Commander-in-Chief about the tenth ship from the van,
the Second-in-Command about the twelfth from the rear,
leaving the van of the enemy unoccupied; the succeeding
ships breaking through in all parts, astern of their leaders,
and engaging the enemy at the muzzles of their guns;
the conflict was severe; the enemy's ships were fought
with a gallantry highly honourable to their officers; but
the attack on them was irresistible, and it pleased the
Almighty Disposer of all events to grant His Majesty's arms
a complete and glorious victory. About three pm many of
the enemy's ships having struck their colours, their line
gave way; Admiral Gravina, with ten ships joining their
frigates to leeward stood towards Cadiz. The five headmost
ships in their van tacked, and standing to the southward,
to windward of the British line, were engaged and the
sternmost of them taken; the others went off, leaving to

15

His Majesty's squadron nineteen ships of the line (of which two are first rates, the *Santissima Trinidad* and the *Santa Ana*), with three flag officers, viz. Admiral Villeneuve, the Commander-in-Chief, Don Ignatio Maria D'Alava, Vice-Admiral; and the Spanish Rear-Admiral, Don Baltazar Hidalgo Cisneros.

After such a victory it may appear unnecessary to enter into encomiums on the particular parts taken by the several commanders; the conclusion says more than I have language to express; the spirit which animated all in their country's service, all deserve that their high merits should stand recorded; and never was high merit more conspicuous than in the battle I have described.

The *Achille* (a French 74), after having surrendered, by some mismanagement of the Frenchmen, took fire and blew up; two hundred of her men were saved by the tenders.

A circumstance occurred during the action, which so strongly marks the invincible spirit of British seamen, when engaging the enemies of their country, that I cannot resist the pleasure I have in making it known to Their Lordships; the *TEMERAIRE* was boarded by accident or design, by a French ship on one side, and a Spaniard on the other; the contest was vigorous, but, in the end, the combined ensigns were torn from the poop, and the British hoisted in their places.

Such a battle could not be fought without sustaining a great loss of men. I have not only to lament, in common with the British navy, and the British Nation, in the fall of the Commander-in-Chief, the loss of a hero, whose name will be immortal, and his memory ever dear to his country; but my heart is rent with the most poignant grief for the death of a friend, to whom, by many years intimacy, and a perfect knowledge of the virtues of his mind, which inspired ideas superior to the common race of men, I was bound by the strongest ties of affection; grief to which even the glorious occasion in which he fell, does not bring the consolation which, perhaps, it ought: His Lordship received a musket ball in his left breast, about the middle of the action, and sent an officer to me immediately with his last farewell; and soon after expired.

I have also to lament the loss of those excellent officers, Captains Duff, of the *MARS*, and Cooke, of the *BELLEROPHON*; I have yet heard of none others.

I fear that the numbers that have fallen will be found very great, when the returns come to me; but it having blown a gale of wind ever since the action, I have not yet had it in my power to collect any reports from the ships.

The *ROYAL SOVEREIGN* having lost her masts, except the tottering foremast, I called the *EURYALUS* to me, while the action continued, which ship lying within hail, made my signals – a service Captain Blackwood performed with great attention; after the action, I shifted my flag to her, that I might more easily communicate any orders to, and collect the ships, and towed the *ROYAL SOVEREIGN* out to Seaward. The whole fleet were now in a very perilous situation, many dismasted, all shattered, in thirteen fathoms of water, off the shoals of Trafalgar; and when I made the signal to prepare to anchor, few of the ships had an anchor to let go, their cables being shot through; but the same good Providence which aided us through such a day preserved us in the night, by the wind shifting a few points, and drifting the ships off the land, except four of the captured dismasted ships, which are now at anchor off Trafalgar, and I hope will ride safe until those gales are over.

Having thus detailed the proceedings of the fleet on this occasion, I beg to congratulate Their lordships on a victory which, I hope, will add a ray to the glory of his Majesty's crown, and be attended with public benefit to our country. I am, &c.,

(signed) C. COLLINGWOOD.

Collingwood included *The Order in which Ships of the British Squadron attacked the Combined Fleets on 21 October 1805.*

Van	Rear
VICTORY	ROYAL SOVEREIGN
TÉMÉRAIRE	MARS
NEPTUNE	BELLEISLE
CONQUEROR	TONNANT
LEVIATHAN	BELLEROPHON
AJAX	COLOSSUS
ORION	ACHILLE
AGAMEMNON	POLYPHEMUS
MINOTAUR	REVENGE
SPARTIATE	SWIFTSURE
BRITANNIA	DEFENCE
AFRICA	THUNDERER
	DEFIANCE
	PRINCE
	DREADNOUGHT
Frigates	
EURYALUS	NAIAD
SIRIUS	PICKLE Schooner
PHOEBE	ENTREPENANTE
	Cutter

William Pitt had to be woken. Bizarrely, before he had gone to bed he had been writing a long letter to Nelson. He liked and respected him, had consulted him before the battle, and had even escorted him personally to his carriage after one of their meetings. James Harris, 1st Earl of Malmesbury, recorded his feelings:

> I shall never forget the eloquent manner in which he
> described his conflicting feelings when roused in the night
> to read Collingwood's despatches. Pitt observed that he had
> been called up at various hours in his eventful life by the

arrival of news of various hues; but that whether good or
bad he could always lay his head on his pillow and sink into
a sound sleep again. On this occasion, however, the great
event announced brought with it so much to weep over, as
well as to rejoice at, that he could not calm his thoughts,
but at length got up, though it was three in the morning.

The news was announced to the King at 6.30 a.m. He was so deeply
affected that a profound silence of nearly five minutes ensued before he
could give utterance to his feelings. He, the Queen and the princesses
'shed tears to the memory of Lord Nelson' and went to St George's
Chapel 'to return thanks to Almighty God on the success of His
Majesty's arms'. The King's private secretary, Colonel Taylor, wrote to
Marsden, 'I have not on any occasion seen His Majesty more affected.'

By now the news was spreading through the capital like wildfire.
The demand for more information was voracious. Crowds gathered
outside the Admiralty and newspaper offices, hoping to gain more
information. While they were not satisfied straight away, it was not
long before some of the early eye-witness accounts appeared, passed
on by word of mouth from Lapenotiere, sailors aboard the PICKLE
and soon afterwards in the form of private letters to families at home.
Many of these early accounts added colour to the story but the details
were patchy and often contradictory. Not that this really mattered
to the majority of people, because the main storyline was sound:
England had won another great naval victory, which was perceived
to have removed the threat of invasion by Napoleon Bonaparte, the
personification of all their fears since the resumption of the war in
1803, and their beloved Nelson had died a hero.

The speed with which the unofficial word-of-mouth news and
hearsay appears to have followed in Lapenotiere's wake is illustrated
by an article that appeared in *Trewman's Exeter Flying Post*, published
on the same day as *The Times* (7 November) but dated 'Exeter,
Wednesday, November 6th'. Whereas *The Times*' report is based on fact
and is full of detail, the *Flying Post*'s article is a splendid example of
journalistic puffery:

GLORIOUS and DECISIVE VICTORY over the Combined Fleets of France and Spain, On the 21st of October. Enemy 34 sail of the line – Lord Nelson's fleet 26 sail.

It is with pride and exultation we again lay before our readers the first intelligence of another glorious Victory, obtained by our naval heroes over the Combined Fleet of France and Spain! A victory unequalled in the annals of any country! – But whilst we rejoice in this further proof of the superior prowess of British seamen – our joy is checked at the consideration, that we have lost in the conflict many brave fellows, and most particularly a man adored by those under his command, idolised by his grateful country, and whose very name struck terror on his enemies – in a word, we have lost – NELSON; than whom a braver, never inhabited this terraqueous globe – and whose whole life has been dedicated to the service of his country. But, he fell in the arms of victory – for while life yet quivered on his lip, his gallant companions were decking his brow with never fading laurels! – Yet, he will live forever in the hearts of his countrymen; and the details of his naval exploits off Cape St Vincent – at the Nile – at Copenhagen – and off Cadiz, will adorn the annals of his native country, Great Britain, till time shall be no more. Altho' we cannot suppress the tear which the loss of this hero has drawn from us, we feel confident that our navy will convince our enemies that tho' NELSON is dead, the same invincible courage he possessed still lives in the breast of every True British Tar.

However, a broadsheet printed and published the day before in Plymouth, is allegedly the first printed account of the battle to have been seen anywhere in Britain. It is based on the word of mouth of some of the *PICKLE*'s eye-witness crew, is remarkably detailed and often quite accurate:

An account of the victory over the Combined Fleets of France
and Spain; and the death of Lord Nelson.

Plymouth, Nov. 5, 1805

Messrs. T. and W. Earle and Co.

Gentlemen,

The *PICKLE* arrived here this morning. Captain Sykes of
the *NAUTILUS*, went off express for London. On the 21st of
October, the fleet under the command of LORD NELSON,
consisting of 27 sail of the line, engaged the combined
fleets of Cadiz, consisting of 33 sail of the line, *nineteen Line
of Battleships of the enemy, of the number of four flags, taken, one
sunk, and one blown up.*

Villeneuve is aboard the *ROYAL SOVEREIGN*: Gravina
with 9 sail got back to Cadiz.

A gale of wind came on soon after the action, right on
shore, and 'tis said that two sail which had struck, got back
to Cadiz, that the large four-decker, *Santissimo Trinidad*,
was in tow, but sunk; the *ROYAL SOVEREIGN, VICTORY,
REVENGE, BELLEISLE, TÉMÉRAIRE, BELLEROPHON*, and
MARS, suffered most. The *TÉMÉRAIRE* engaged two ships
and took them, as did the *NEPTUNE* two three-deckers,
which struck to her. The *ROYAL SOVEREIGN*, it is said, had
400 men killed.

Great as this victory has been, the country has to mourn
the loss of LORD NELSON, who was killed by a Musket
Ball in the breast from the tops of a three-decker, *Santissima
Trinidad*, with whom the *VICTORY* was engaged, and actually
lashed together. His Lordship was, at the moment he received
his wound, expressing his delight at the conduct of the
Second in Command Admiral Collingwood. Before he died,
he made the signal, *that England expected every man would do
his duty*. This, I understand, he was enabled to do, by having
brought his telegraph signals to such perfection, We have
also to lament the loss of Capts. Duff and Cook, and Lord
Nelson's Secretary. Capt. Tyler wounded but not dangerously.

No other particulars of the loss have reached us. On the 24th, the *PICKLE* and *DONEGAL* were at anchor off Cadiz, in charge of the captured ships. Six sail are said to have sunk.

I write in great haste,

And am yours, &c.

P.S. 'Tis said by some of the crew of the *PICKLE* that they saw 14 sail in tow; the *NAUTILUS* is also arrived with duplicate dispatches.

But the paper that had the real scoop of the century was not published in England at all. The *Gibraltar Chronicle, Extraordinary*, edited at that time by a Frenchman, was the first newspaper to carry the story. Moreover, its story was based on a letter from Collingwood to the Governor of Gibraltar, General Henry Fox. It therefore summarized events with reasonable accuracy, only going awry in its editorial, which appeared in French alongside Collingwood's letter:

Thursday October 24th 1805.

(Copy)

EURYALUS at Sea, October 22, 1805

Yesterday a Battle was fought by His Majesty's Fleet, with the Combined Fleets of Spain and France, and a Victory gained, which will stand recorded as one of the most brilliant and decisive, that ever distinguished the BRITISH NAVY.

The Enemy's Fleet sailed from Cadiz, on the 19th, in the morning, Thirty Three sail of the Line in number, for the purpose of giving Battle to the British Squadron of Twenty Seven and yesterday at Eleven A. M. the contest began, close in with the Shoals of Trafalgar.

At Five P.M. Seventeen of the Enemy had surrendered and one (*L'Achille*) burnt, amongst which is the *Sta. Ana*, the Spanish Admiral DON D'ALEVA mortally wounded, and the *Santisima Trinidad*. The French Admiral VILLENEUVE

is now a Prisoner on board the MARS; I believe THREE
ADMIRALS are captured.

Our loss has been great in Men; but, what is irreparable,
and the cause of Universal Lamentation, is the Death of the
NOBLE COMMANDER IN CHIEF, who died in the arms of
Victory; I have not yet any reports from the Ships, but have
heard that Captains DUFF and COOKE fell in the action.
I have to congratulate you upon the Great Event, and have
the Honor to be, &c. &c.
(Signed) C. COLLINGWOOD

In addition to the above particulars of the late glorious
Victory, we are assured that 18 Sail of the Line were counted
in our possession, before the Vessel, which brought the
above dispatches, left the Fleet; and that three more of the
Enemy's Vessels were seen driving about, perfect wrecks, at
the mercy of the waves, on the Barbary Shore, and which
will probably also fall into our hands.

Admiral COLLINGWOOD in the DREADNOUGHT,
and the van of the British Fleet most gallantly into action,
without firing a shot, till his yard-arms were locked
with those of the Santisima Trinidad; when he opened
so tremendous a fire, that in fifteen minutes, she was
completely dismasted, and obliged to surrender.

Lord NELSON on the VICTORY, engaged the French
Admiral most closely; during the heat of the action, his
Lordship was severely wounded with a grape shot, in the
side, and was obliged to be carried below. Immediately
on his wound being dressed, he insisted upon being again
brought upon deck, when, shortly afterwards, he received
a shot through his body; he survived however, till the
Evening; long enough to be informed of the capture of the
French Admiral and of the extent of the Glorious Victory he
had gained. – His last words were, "Thank God I outlived this
day, and now I die content!!!"

The French press was subject to heavy censorship by the government and it appears that only one other newspaper, the *Journal du Commerce*, made any mention of the battle, and that only fleetingly and inconclusively. Even at the end of the Napoleonic Wars in 1815, many of the French people were found to be completely oblivious to the fact that there had even been a Battle of Trafalgar. Those who lived on the other side of the world were better informed. The news had reached Australia by the spring of 1806 and appeared in the *Sydney Gazette and New South Wales Advertiser* on 13 April. Meanwhile, any observant French person would have had to put up with either the *Moniteur* or the *Journal du Commerce*, and given the former's account of a French victory may have wondered why their Emperor had not made anything of such an important triumph, to complement his success at Ulm the day before Trafalgar and Austerlitz in December. As it was, these great military victories allowed him to hide the truth.

It has been rumoured on the authority of private letters, for some days, that there has been a battle off the coast of Spain, between the combined fleets of France and Spain and the English squadron. According to these accounts, the French squadron, commanded by admiral Villeneuve, and the Spanish by admiral Gravina, came out of Cadiz, on the 18th or 19th of last month, when they fell in with the English fleet under the command of Admiral Nelson. A most bloody action took place, in which both fleets fought with the greatest determination, and each suffered most severely. Towards the end of the engagement a violent storm came on, which dispersed the ships. It is reported that one Spanish and one English ship were blown up. It is also reported that some of the commanders were killed or dangerously wounded. But as these private letters are not from an authentic source, it would be imprudent to spread alarm, for which perhaps there is no foundation; and it would be proper to suspend judgement until the official intelligence gives some positive information respecting this important event.

In Spain there was much more openness and the news spread rapidly from Cadiz and across the peninsula. The French Ambassador in Madrid was even able to send a dispatch to Admiral Decrès, the French Minister of Marine in Paris, within 24 hours. The above inconclusive account is probably based on it. A further dispatch arrived on the 25th, from which it was clear that the Combined Fleet had been beaten. Villeneuve's own account was much delayed, since he was an English prisoner of war.

So much for the message; what of its author, Cuthbert Collingwood? This 'dry and caustic man' had settled himself in the undamaged cabin of the frigate *EURYALUS* (36) under the command of Captain Henry Blackwood, within a few hours of the end of the battle. His is an erudite first-hand account, but it is also an open expression of his personal grief for the loss of a dear friend. Moreover, it is a carefully composed document, as the changes he made to his first draft prove. For instance, in the final version he commended Captain Blackwood, by adding 'whose vigilance in watching, and giving notice of the enemy's movements, has been highly meritorious'. He specified, wrongly, the number of Spanish and French ships involved, and highlighted that two of the prizes were first-rates: the *Santissima Trinidad* and the *Santa Ana*. He also deleted passages, notably his justification for not having collected reports from the British ships:

> . . . and when their Lordships consider that I have 23
> infirm ships, 18 of them hulks, without a stick standing,
> and scarce a boat in the fleet, I am sure that they will
> have due consideration for the slowness with which all
> that kind of duty must necessarily be done, but as I feel
> the great importance of these reports to the Service, and
> to individuals, they may trust that I shall leave nothing
> undone to obtain them speedily.

The full story of how the first voices of Trafalgar reached England is an extraordinary one. Blackwood had always hoped that he would be entrusted with the delivery of these dispatches, and if Nelson had lived the honour would have probably fallen to him, but Collingwood favoured the obscure Lapenotiere instead, probably in order to repay an outstanding service. He is reported as saying, 'Now take these dispatches to England; you will receive £500 and your Commander's commission. Now I have kept my word.' Another more prosaic reason would have been because *PICKLE*, which was the second smallest ship in the fleet with 12 guns, was a newly designed topsail schooner described as 'a clever fast schooner – coppered – and every respect suited to the service', and therefore more likely to make a fast passage back to England.

She made sail on 26 October, close to the site of the battle, and soon met with the brig-sloop *NAUTILUS* (18). Her captain, John Sykes, received the news from Lapenotiere, who had been told by Collingwood 'not to stop for any vessel'. Sykes made an effort to deliver his version of the news to Mr Gambier, the British Consul in Lisbon, before he, acting on his initiative, also made for England. The possibility that the *PICKLE* might not have made it home safely was Sykes's only justification for leaving his station. Both ships had to avoid the enemy and cross the Bay of Biscay, which for sailing ships in wintry weather was never easy. *PICKLE*'s log records repeated making and reefing of sail. At one stage in a heavy gale and gigantic seas her frame was so strained that the oakum caulking was squeezed from between the planks of her hull, and she was taking on water too fast for her pumps to cope. As the ship was top heavy, Lapenotiere had to order four 12-pounder carronades, each weighing six hundredweight, to be cast overboard in order to lighten her, while George Almy, the Second Master, was resorting to guesswork and dead reckoning to find his course. Within a day's sail of the Lizard the wind fell away altogether and Lapenotiere had to set the crew to work with sweeps – large oars – with three or four men to each, to keep some steerage. It is unlikely that at night the *PICKLE* would have attracted the attention of any other boats close in shore, and the newspaper report of an officer landing at Falmouth with dispatches but without a reference to Trafalgar strongly suggests that Lapenotiere respected their confidentiality. The PICKLE's log for 4 November 1805 recorded:

> At 9.45 shortened sail and hove to. Out boat. Our commander landed at Falmouth with his dispatches at noon. Moderate breezes and cloudy. Pendennis Castle NNW 2 or 3 miles.

Lieutenant Lapenotiere came ashore at Fishstrand Quay rather than Custom Quay in order to avoid quarantine, and set about finding post chaise transport to London, the usual travel for naval officers delivering dispatches, otherwise they would have to wait for the daily mail coach and be delayed for more than a day. Lapenotiere got away a little after 12 noon and changed horses at Truro, Fraddon, Bodmin, Launceston, Okehampton and Crockernwell. At about this stage of his journey, late on Monday night, the NAUTILUS, which had narrowly escaped capture a hundred miles south-west of Ushant, hove to off Plymouth, and Captain Sykes went ashore by boat, reported to the port admiral and also took a post chaise for London. Meanwhile, Lapenotiere was racing on to Exeter, Honiton, Axminster and Bridport.

His post chaise passed through Bridport at first light on Tuesday morning. Mr J Kenway of Burton Bradstock, a village close by, described the occasion in a letter dated 7 December to his 20-year-old friend, Richard Francis Roberts, a midshipman in VICTORY (100) at the time. They both knew her captain, another Dorset man, Thomas Masterman Hardy.

> We first heard of the engagement on the morning of the 5th November. The account was sent by Mr J. Hounsell to Burton soon after Lieutenant Lapinature [sic] passed Bridport, it informed us of the death of Lord Nelson, and that nineteen ships were taken, and one blown up; our feelings were extremely racked; all deploring the loss of the hero – all immeasurably pleased the Victory was so

decisively in our favour; but at the same time our minds
were much distressed on your account, for my own part I
never experienced such incoherent emotions in my life; one
minute hoping you were safe; the next doubting it, from
the dreadful carnage that was inevitable in such a situation.
From this dilemma nothing could relieve me, but hearing
immediately from you. Every post was looked for with
indescribable anxiety; our disappointment was great in not
hearing the particulars of your ship in the first gazette, and
the impracticability of it did not appear till other dispatches
arrived. During the interval (which was extremely tedious)
every means was used by all your friends to obtain
the earliest information. Captain Blakwell [*sic*] of the
EURYALUS desired Mrs. Fish to present his compliments
to Mr Hardy's family and your father, saying Captain
Hardy was safe, and he had no doubt you were likewise.
This was some consolation – but nothing equal to what we
experienced when your name was not to be found amongst
the list of killed or wounded. The news flew like lightning
through the village, the bells rung and everybody seemed
actuated by one general sentiment of joy, but this however
was not the positive intelligence I wanted, for afterwards
a doubt crept in whether your name might not have been
omitted, and this was not dispelled till the receipt of your
very acceptable letter dated October 22nd (to your father)
which he received in Bridport, and immediately sent by Mr.
Fish to Burton. The bells rang again till several of the ropes
broke – they were repaired next morning. Your father's
colours were hoisted on the Tower and continued flying
several days. I was really astonished to find you were so
collected the day after the Action as to be able to write such
a letter, it gave me great pleasure and it does you infinite
credit. Your favour to me of the 27th came at the same
time. I should have written you sooner, but did not know
where to direct, as we expected the *VICTORY* home some

time past. I should have thought you would have been so much agitated by the transactions of the 21st that it would have been impossible to collect your ideas on paper; it is not to be wondered at that at the time you did not know the particulars of the Action. This has been pretty well supplied by the public prints, which is astonishing.

After Bridport, Lapenotiere stopped at Dorchester, Blandford Forum, Woodhayes, Salisbury, Andover, Overton Basingstoke, Hartford Bridge, Bagshot, Staines, Hounslow and finally fog-bound Piccadilly at 1 a.m., when his post chaise clattered into the cobbled courtyard of the Admiralty and stopped in front of the elegant colonnade. He had covered the 271 miles in about 37 hours and his travelling expenses later submitted to the Admiralty amounted to £46 19s 1d; an enormous sum for the time, equivalent to a lieutenant's pay for a year, but fitting given the weight of the news. Lapenotiere, who had had an uneventful naval career, enjoyed his moment of fame. He also received his promotion to Commander and a Lloyd's Patriotic Fund sword, but had to petition for the £500 bounty, which he received only when Barham wrote on the application, 'Let him have it!'

Captain Sykes, who had experienced an equally arduous journey, was close behind with his unofficial dispatch. He is believed to have arrived at the Admiralty a short while, maybe only a few minutes, after Lapenotiere. One imagines his disappointment at finding he no longer had any news to give.

2
THE TRAFALGAR CAMPAIGN
1803–1805

'I WILL PUT AN END TO THE FUTURE AND VERY
EXISTENCE OF ENGLAND'

Trafalgar was not an isolated battle fought on an autumn afternoon but the endgame of a two-year-long campaign by Britain to contain France's aggrandisement and forestall its serious ambitions to invade England. The self-crowned Emperor, Napoleon Bonaparte, was determined: 'With God's help I will put an end to the future and very existence of England.'

Britain could not support its European allies on land by fielding a large army like those of Austria or Russia, but it could deploy the Royal Navy to blockade French and Spanish ports, and use its growing economic power – Britain was the richest and most powerful trading nation on earth – to fund military coalitions against Napoleon. Nevertheless, the French Revolutionary War had taken a heavy toll, militarily, financially and politically, on both nations, and they were content to negotiate a peace at Amiens in October 1801. Napoleon had no enthusiasm for a lasting settlement but was surprised when Britain declared war again in May 1803. The declaration was premeditated so as to allow the Royal Navy to capture as many French ships at sea as possible, an initiative that was particularly successful. The campaign that culminated in Trafalgar had started.

The French decided that the quickest way to end the war was to invade Britain before it could effect an alliance with Russia and

Austria. Success with this strategy carried a bonus: control of Britain's valuable overseas possessions. France would then flourish as the world's greatest power and in western Europe Napoleon could emerge as a new Charlemagne.

The British campaign was about preventing that invasion. Napoleon became the very personification of the people's fears. He was epitomized as the incarnation of evil. Wives and daughters would be ravished, and children were warned that 'the bogeyman' would take them away if they did not behave. Before these fears could be realized, however, Napoleon had to create a *Grande Armée*, a flotilla of boats to transport it and its *matériel* to England's shores, and a strategy for clearing the Channel of the Royal Navy. 'Let us be masters of the Straits but for six hours, and we shall be masters of the world,' Napoleon declared in July 1804.

The Emperor hatched no fewer than nine successive plans between 1801 and 1805. The details differed but the overall strategy was the same. It required his Atlantic and Mediterranean fleets to break the British blockade and to attack British possessions in the West Indies and elsewhere. He believed this would force the Admiralty to weaken its blockade, particularly of Brest, allowing the squadron there to escape and land an army in Ireland. At this juncture all the French ships would return to their home waters, converge on the Channel and secure an overwhelming supremacy for long enough to allow his invasion flotilla to cross. The ships of Napoleon's new Spanish ally increased his chances of achieving this. Napoleon's strategy inside the Mediterranean was a combination of land and sea activity designed to hold down and unsettle Nelson, who was stationed there to protect British interests.

By the spring of 1805 Napoleon had spent vast sums of money on the enterprise. L'*Armée d'Angleterre* consisted of over 1,000 officers, 163,800 soldiers, nearly 24,000 horses and a stockpile of three million rations. The flotilla consisted of 2,300 specially built landing barges, which were berthed in a host of newly created ports along the Channel coast clustered around Boulogne. In reality this was not as impressive as it may first appear. It is estimated that it would have taken at least two days to row the army across the Channel. Moreover, to do so would require calm conditions. The smallest British warships and gunboats, and there were plenty of them, would have wreaked havoc on the defenceless barges. They would also have had to contend with William Congreve's latest rockets. It is hard to imagine how they would have survived. Admiral Ganteaume could see the problem and expressed his belief on 14 July to Rear Admiral Denis Decrès, Napoleon's Minister of Marine, that the Channel would need to be held for two weeks, during which time his ships would inevitably be challenged. Venturing . . .

> . . . into the Channel with no more than twenty-two vessels which compose our fleet, it would not be long before we were observed, or before the vessels we had eluded would get contact. To these they would not fail to join the whole of the force at their disposal on the coasts and in the ports of England, and then it seems to me the chances would be against us.

Napoleon refused to see the difficulty. This ignorance of the sea undermined his finely tuned and detailed plans. As late as August 1805 the only concession he seems to have made to the practical problems besetting his grandiose venture was a doubling of the time needed for the crossing. Writing to Decrès, he claims, 'If we are masters of the crossing for twelve hours then England will have had its day.'

Close blockade of the ports and arsenals of Brest, Rochefort and Toulon was the lynchpin of Britain's defensive campaign. Her strategy was to force her enemies to keep their fleets divided. The presence of a British fleet demanded that France and Spain divide their own forces. Ironically, there was now a shortage of ships to maintain it, a problem caused largely by the demobilization of the fleet after the Peace of Amiens. In July 1804 Nelson wrote:

> The French Navy is daily increasing, both at Toulon and Brest, whilst ours is as clearly going down-hill. It will

require all of Lord Melville's abilities to get our fleet ahead
of that of the French. We made use of the peace, not to
recruit our navy, but to be the cause of its ruin.

However, Henry Dundas, 1st Viscount Melville, First Lord of the
Admiralty in 1804–5, had little time to apply his abilities because he
was also implicated in an investigation into irregularities concerning
prize money that was to throw him out of office. As a stop-gap
replacement William Pitt, the youngest prime minister in British
history, appointed the 79-year-old Sir Charles Middleton, Lord
Barham. It proved to be an inspired choice, for not only did Barham
have an appetite for detail and hard work; he understood strategy and
his experience was vast. He also recognized that he should appoint an
officer in the Mediterranean who by force of personality alone might
intimidate the French. He chose Nelson.

'NELSON WILL NEVER BE FIT FOR AN INDEPENDENT COMMAND.'

By August 1805 Nelson had sought for more than two years to
bring the French to battle without success and it looked to some as
if he was guilty of misjudgement, since he seemed to have allowed
Villeneuve to escape from the Mediterranean and link up with
Spanish warships. On his return to Portsmouth he could not be
confident that either the public or the Admiralty would still favour
him. As always when things went wrong, Nelson became ill with
worry. Writing to Emma Hamilton he fretted, 'Your poor Nelson is
very unwell. After two years hard fag it has been mortifying not to
get at the enemy.'

Meanwhile, Barham was considering his choice very carefully. He
had studied and analysed Nelson's sea journals, orders, commands
and correspondence over the last two years to understand the vice
admiral's intellect and reasoning, and to determine why he had
not brought the French to battle. Barham needed to confirm in his

own mind that Nelson was not just a risk-taking maverick prone to making mistakes. Nelson had every reason to feel uncertain about the octogenarian's scrutiny. Ever since he had come to public notice doubts had been raised about his discipline and judgement, with incidents such as his action at the Battle of Cape St Vincent in February 1797, when as Commodore Nelson he had left the line, attacked the whole of the Spanish fleet single-handed and subsequently dashed, sword in hand, across two enemy decks. Nelson had acted according to the spirit but not the letter of his orders, and although Admiral Sir John Jervis privately approved, his official dispatch ignored Nelson's exploits.

Barham had time to consider the man and his career as a whole. Nelson had been born 46 years earlier on 29 September 1758 at Burnham Thorpe in north Norfolk. His father was rector of the parish and his background was lower middle class. There were seven other children in the family. Life was not easy, especially when his generous and strong-willed mother, Catherine, died on Boxing Day 1767. Her death left the nine-year-old Nelson emotionally insecure and vulnerable, but three years later he decided he'd like to go to sea, and his father wrote to his brother-in-law, the brave and urbane Captain Maurice Suckling, asking him whether he would take the boy. Suckling wrote back, 'What has poor little Horatio done that he should be sent to rough it at sea? But let him come, and if a cannon ball takes off his head he will at least be provided for.'

During the course of his naval career Nelson would see action on more than 120 occasions and sail to many parts of the world, including the Arctic, India, West Indies, North America, Central America and the Mediterranean. However, the opportunities that allowed him to secure success and fame came after 1793, when war broke out with Revolutionary France. At the siege of Calvi in 1794 he lost the sight in his right eye, which was afterwards only able to distinguish light from dark. It was not an unsightly wound and Nelson never wore an eye patch. In February 1797 his bold action at the Battle of Cape St Vincent, which resulted in the capture of two Spanish ships, made him a popular hero. In May of the same year he led from the front once again, this time in a desperate small boat fight in Cadiz harbour that left all his Spanish opponents either killed or wounded.

However, Barham was aware that Nelson's hunger for glory and over-confidence often put others at risk. In July 1797 Nelson received one of the worst defeats of his career at Santa Cruz de Tenerife, costing not only his right arm but also more killed and wounded than at the Battle of Cape St Vincent. Nelson had planned the attack very carefully, but the weather hindered the first assault. He ordered and led the second assault himself, knowing it to be, in his own words, 'a forlorn hope'. It was a humbling experience that might have ended his career, but after a long convalescence he rejoined Lord St Vincent's fleet in May 1798. His mission was to find and destroy a large French expeditionary force under the command of Napoleon Bonaparte. The level of responsibility he had been given surprised other admirals but on 1 August at the Battle of the Nile he demonstrated emphatically that he not only took risks but could bring them off as well. His leadership communicated the sense to his captains that they could do things without waiting for orders from him. This was very unusual among admirals in the eighteenth century, who rarely shared their ideas with fellow officers. Nelson had agreed the battle plan with his captains some time before and so even though night was falling he was able to attack at once, knowing he could rely on their initiative to follow through. Moreover, his captains also knew he would support their risk taking afterwards. This was the essence of Nelson the commander. It made him special.

The Battle of the Nile is generally regarded as Nelson's finest and most decisive. Only two of the 13 French ships escaped, one of them under the command of Rear Admiral Villeneuve, the man destined to command the Combined Fleet at Trafalgar.

Nelson was soon known throughout Europe as 'The Hero of the Nile'. However, its legacy was also the prelude to the darkest episode in his life, one that caused him to neglect his duty. This would have weighed heavily on Barham's mind. Not only had Nelson been swept off his feet by Lady Hamilton, probably the most beautiful woman in Naples, but he had also allowed himself to become embroiled in the sordid politics of the Kingdom of Naples. He described it as 'a country of fiddlers and poets, whores and scoundrels', and believed it to be 'a dangerous place and we must steer clear of it', but failed to heed his own advice. His role in the trial and execution of Commodore Prince Francesco Carraciolo, the former commander-in-chief of the Neapolitan Navy, was a controversial affair. The shabby interlude was brought to an end by a brusque letter from Lord Spencer, the First Lord of the Admiralty at the time:

> . . . you will more likely recover your health and strength in England than in an inactive situation at a foreign court, however pleasing the respect and gratitude shown to you for your services may be.

After a rapturous overland journey of feasting and jollities through Austria and Germany with the Hamiltons, Nelson had expected to be met by a British frigate to carry them back to England, but none was there. He wrote to the Admiralty. Waited. No ship came. Finally they made their own way home, where his scandalous relationship with Emma was being lampooned. General Sir John Moore described him 'as more like the prince at the opera than the conqueror of the Nile', and his old friend Earl St Vincent wrote, 'Poor man, devoured with vanity, weakness and folly strung with ribbons and medals.' So serious were his doubts that he placed Nelson second in command of the fleet he was ordering to the Baltic to break up the Armed Neutrality of the North, believing, 'Nelson will never be fit for an independent command.'

War, as ever, offered Nelson the chance to salvage his career. At Copenhagen in April 1801 his aggressive determination, speed of thought and resourcefulness secured another major victory and also revealed his humanity, since as soon as he recognized that the centre of the Danish line was collapsing he sent a message to the Danish Crown Prince offering a truce. He returned home in early July 1801 with his reputation restored.

When Britain declared war on France in May 1803 Nelson was given the important command of the Mediterranean Fleet. He hoisted his flag as Vice Admiral of the Blue in *VICTORY* on 18 May 1803 and for the next two years played 'cat and mouse with these fellows', including the talented and distinguished Vice Admiral Louis-René de Latouche-Tréville, who had repulsed Nelson's well-planned attack on Boulogne in 1801. However, Latouche died in August 1804 and command of his squadron at Toulon passed to the very different Vice Admiral Villeneuve, 'a tallish thin man, a very tranquil, placid English-looking' French aristocrat who had been rapidly promoted because of his willingness to serve the Republic. They were a long two years, but Barham would have concluded from all the correspondence he had examined that Nelson possessed a superb ability to manage a fleet at sea, maintaining it at peak fighting efficiency without recourse to dockyard refits; to play the role of diplomat with the many rulers and allies whose countries bordered the Mediterranean; to watch over the activities of pirates on the north African coast, and to cleverly gather and assess valuable intelligence from all quarters.

Weighing Nelson's strengths against his weaknesses Barham concluded that there could be no doubt that he was a great fighting admiral. He was controversial, but his rare abilities and approach to leadership and command expressed the complexity of a naval battle in a manner that those serving under him could easily understand. Moreover, he could see that Nelson did not visualize a battle as an end in itself, but as a means of achieving wider strategic, political and commercial aims. In this light his pursuit of the Combined Fleet across the Atlantic had not been an error of judgement but a piece of strategic brilliance and fine seamanship. Nelson was using naval power to ensure that France could not reach out beyond the European mainland, preventing any attempt its fleets might make to command the oceans and in so doing securing trade for Britain with the rest of the world at a time when trade with most of Europe was frustrated by the war.

After a little over three weeks rest ashore at Merton, Nelson, backed by Barham and with his confidence fully restored, rejoined the *VICTORY* in mid-September 1805 and sailed to join Collingwood off Cadiz. The *VICTORY* was the fifth ship of the Royal Navy to bear this name. She was one of the great wooden warships of the day and represented the peak of development after hundreds of years of experience and craftsmanship building seaworthy gun platforms that could also absorb the impact of the solid shot thrown at them. Her hull contained 300,000 cubic feet of timber, equivalent to 100 acres of woodland. Her full complement was 850 officers and men, but when she sailed from St Helens Roads, Isle of Wight, she was nearly 50 short.

'THE SQUADRON UNDER MY COMMAND IS IN PERFECT STATE OF READINESS'

In 1804, after more than a year at sea, Nelson was able to write to Earl St Vincent, 'I have the pleasure to acquaint you that the squadron under my command is in perfect state of readiness to act as the exigency of the moment may determine.' This was written at a time when Nelson was short of men, outnumbered by the enemy and having to refit and victual at sea.

William Robinson, known as 'Jack Nastyface', a landsman who served in the REVENGE (74) at Trafalgar, gave an insight into the daily life on board a ship of the line:

> Our crew were divided into two watches, starboard and larboard. When one was on deck the other was below: for instance the starboard watch would come on at eight o'clock at night, which is called eight bells; and half past is called one bell, and so on; every half hour is a bell, as the hour glass is turned, and the messenger sent to strike the bell, which is generally affixed near the fore-hatchway. It now becomes the duty of the officer on deck to see that the log line is run out, to ascertain how many knots the ship goes an hour, which is entered in the log-book, with any other occurrence which may take place during the watch. At twelve o'clock, or eight-bells in the first watch, the

boatswain's mate calls out lustily, 'Larboard watch, a-hoy.'
This is called the middle watch and when on deck, the other
watch go below to their hammocks, till eight-bells, which is
four o'clock in the morning. They then come on deck again,
pull off their shoes and stockings, turn up their trousers
to above their knees, and commence holy stoning the deck,
as it is termed. Here the men suffer from being obliged
to kneel down on the wetted deck, and a gravelly sort of
sand strewed over it. To perform this work they kneel with
their bare knees, rubbing the deck with the stone and the
sand, the grit of which is very injurious. In this manner
the watch continues till about four-bells, or six o'clock;
they then begin to wash and swab the decks till seven bells,
and at eight-bells the boatswain's mate pipes to breakfast.
This meal consists of burgoo, made of coarse oatmeal and
water; others will have Scottish coffee, which is burnt bread
boiled in some water, and sweetened with sugar. This is
generally cooked in a hook-pot in the galley, where there
is a range. Nearly all the crew have one of these pots, a
spoon, and a knife; for these are things indispensable; there
are also basons, plates, &c. which are kept in each mess,
which generally consists of eight persons, whose berth is
between two of the guns on the lower deck, where there is
a board placed, which swings with the rolling of the ship,
and answers for a table. It sometimes happens that a lurch
will dash all the crockery to pieces; they are then obliged
to eat out of wooden or tin utensils, until they come into
harbour, where they get another supply. At half-past eight
o'clock, or one-bell in the forenoon watch, the larboard goes
on deck, and the starboard remains below. Here again the
holy-stones or hand-bibles as they are called by the crew, are
used, and sometimes iron scrapers. After the lower deck has
been wetted with swabs, these scrapers are used to take the
rough dirt off. Whilst this is going on, the cooks from each
mess are employed in cleaning the utensils and preparing

for dinner, at the same time the watch are working the ship, and doing what is wanting to be done on deck.

About eleven o'clock, or six-bells, when any of the men are in irons, or on the black list, the boatswain or mate are ordered to call all hands; the culprits are then brought forward by the master at arms, who is a warrant officer, and acts the part of John Ketch, when required; he likewise has the prisoners in his custody, until they are put in irons, under any charge. All hands being now mustered, the captain orders the man to strip; he is then seized to the grating by the wrists and knees; his crime is then mentioned, and the prisoner may plead, but, in nineteen cases out of twenty, he is flogged for the most trifling offence or neglect, such as not hearing the watch called at night, not doing any thing properly on deck or aloft, which he might happen be sent to do, when, perhaps, he has been doing the best he could, and at the same time ignorant of having done wrong, until he is pounced on, and put in irons. So much for the legal process.

After punishment, the boatswain's mate pipes to dinner, it being eight-bells, or twelve o'clock; and this is the pleasantest part of the day, as at one-bell the fifer is called to play 'Nancy Dawson', or some other lively tune, a well known signal that the grog is ready to be served out. It is the duty of the cook from each mess to fetch and serve it out to his messmates, of which every man and boy is allowed a pint, that is, one gill of rum and three of water, to which is added lemon acid, sweetened with sugar.

A ship's routine was part of the discipline of the service and every officer and seaman knew his role, his place and what was expected of him. Flogging captains could still be found but many more officers believed in keeping this form of brutality to a minimum and since the mutinies at the Nore and Spithead in 1797 a more enlightened approach to discipline, which respected the seaman's professional abilities as well as his intelligence and self-respect, was evident. Nelson and Collingwood displayed a deep sense of duty to their men.

One of the frequent causes of mutiny was the poor range and quality of the seamen's food and drink. Examples included grog 'as thin as muslin and quite unfit to keep out the cold' and lean beef. However, the provisioning of ships at sea was seen as the most vital of all the processes necessary to make a fighting navy. The need for a balanced diet and fresh water was understood and during wartime the Navy made strenuous efforts to ensure that it bought healthy food. Preservation was the main difficulty. Working a sailing ship was a physically demanding job and seamen required and usually got around 5,000 calories per day.

Re-mobilization in 1803 was held up by a shortage of men, and even by the time of Trafalgar many ships were still below complement. The shortages necessitated impressments, the eighteenth-century form of conscription. The infamous press gangs looked for skilled seafarers who accepted conscription as an occupational hazard. They collected volunteers in significant numbers. The skills required were most likely to be found on merchant ships. Lieutenant Dillon had experience of recruiting by this method:

I told the Master that I should take away some of his men. This intention caused a terrible hubbub amongst the seamen; so I got up upon the quarter netting, hailed my schooner and demanded if the gun were loaded . . . Then I addressed the Master . . . 'You see I am all ready, and if you do not deliver up some of your men, I shall order my men in the schooner to fire into you. I do not mind the consequences myself. I care not for my own life. But here I am, and will not quit you until I have at least 10 or 12 seamen out of this vessel.'

The noise on board my schooner of moving the gun was heard; the lighted matches were seen; the muskets too were visible. A dead pause of some moments ensued; then I spoke to the Master again and asked what he would do. At last one seaman was brought aft, and I questioned him. As he was a stout able-bodied man, I accepted him, and as soon as he brought up his bag he went into the little dinghy and was taken to the schooner. I now had the Muster roll brought up, and called over the seamen by their names. I had to contend against every species of obstruction, the details of which I shall not enter into.

I remained on board *The Four Brothers* until 2 o'clock in the morning, and finally succeeded in taking from her 13 stout fellows; some capital seamen, one a Pilot of six feet. In fact most of them were not under 5 feet 10 inches. The Master requested me to give him a certificate of my having taken so many men, as it would, he hoped, prevent more being taken from him by other ships of war. I readily complied with that wish, and stated how courteously he had conducted himself towards me . . . I then left him. When I reached my own schooner, I found that my Padroon had placed all the pressed men in the hold. He had given them grog, then put them in irons, 'as,' he said, 'I became alarmed at having such stout men about me on deck. I thought they might have taken the schooner from me, with my 12 lads.' I was highly satisfied with the tar's good management and complimented him accordingly . . . I could not help feeling overjoyed at having performed one of those acts by which I had obtained some useful men to serve the Country, without any unpleasant result.

Impressment went hand in hand with desertion, a factor Nelson seems to have obscured in his mind given that he knew his crews recognized that he did more for them than he needed to, particularly the way he sought 'plenty of the very best provisions, with every comfort that can be thought of for them'. For a lot of pressed men a supply of fresh vegetables and a Bible, which Nelson obtained from the Society for Christian Knowledge, could not compensate for their loss of freedom and the long separation from their wives and families.

In spite of the Navy's brutal reputation, many boys and young men were attracted to the service. At Trafalgar all 54 seamen in *VICTORY* aged between 12 and 19 were volunteers. Their reasons for joining were multifarious but included the attractions of prize money, adventure, family tradition and even romance, as a small boy from Oxfordshire described.

> We had another source of relief in the antics of a
> hairbrained sailor. From spinning yarns, which looked
> amazingly like new inventions, he would take to dancing on
> the roof of the coach; at the foot of the hill he would leap
> off, and then spring up again with the agility of a monkey,
> to the no small amusement of the passengers. The more I
> saw of this reckless thoughtless tar, the more enamoured I
> became with the idea of sea life.

Men who had been forcibly taken by the press gangs were often given the chance to 'volunteer', as this then entitled them to a bounty. This practice may have exaggerated the true number of volunteers as shown in the muster books.

Notwithstanding their varied backgrounds, pressed merchant seamen were impressed by how efficient and smoothly the crews worked together, in particular by the way they handled sails with a dispatch unknown in the merchant service:

> . . . 'all hands make sail' followed, and instantly the
> shrouds on either side were filled with men like
> swarming bees. No voice was heard but his who gave
> command, and a noble voice it was; but his words
> were repeated in the outpoured shrillness of the silver
> calls of the boatswain and his mates; and when every man
> had set his foot in the rigging, with hands grasping the
> ratlines. 'Away aloft!' – away the swarm rushed with an
> upward rapidity, as if the life of each depended on his
> being first.

Samuel Leech, a Napoleonic veteran of the lower deck, observed that:

> In a merchantman the sails are spread, and set stragglingly
> and partially, portions tumble down, flap about, and
> slowly, creepingly spread at intervals, and from the several
> points; but with the words I have quoted, the instant
> flashing effect is magical and magnificent; the minute-ago
> naked masts, beams, and yards, the whole of the towering
> scaffolding and beautiful skeleton is clothed in fifteen
> thousand feet of graceful drapery, so perfectly fitted and
> so admirably put on; then out it swells, and curves in the
> wind: it is beauty itself.

At sea, captains were all-powerful. Apart from there being no one to interfere with their regime, the Navy reflected the morals and values of British society generally, notably the class system. Furthermore they had at their command the resources of many experts. These ranged from their fellow officers, who had passed exams as opposed to buying their commissions, to the petty officers and ordinary seamen. Together they sailed the ship. But the complement also included experienced gunners, skilled craftsmen such as the carpenter and his crew, coopers, tailors, armourers, the caulkers and sailmakers, clerical and administrative staff, a medical team under the surgeon, a chaplain and a schoolmaster, and a unit of disciplined marines commanded by an officer. The captain was accountable to the Admiralty for his actions and was required to keep journals and logs.

The Royal Navy was effective at the time of the French Revolutionary and Napoleonic Wars because it was not only blessed with an abundance of outstanding naval officers, but it also possessed a complex and well-organized naval administration that reported to Parliament. The Royal Navy was also at the leading edge of the technology of the day, and on average Britain spent £30 million per annum on the Navy during the 22 years of war after 1793.

British seamen were masters of their trade. Neither the French nor the Spanish could match their record of action and sea service;

they had spent too much time bottled up in harbour. Some crew members lacked sea service altogether. Moreover, for all their military and maritime lineage, the French and Spanish officers could not match as a whole the dedication and sea following of their British peers. Nor were they backed by the same quality of administration. However, they did build fine ships, which the British had made a habit of capturing and using themselves. The French built the fastest and most manoeuvrable big warships. Villeneuve's two-deck flagship *Bucentaure* (80) was a typical example. Weighing almost as much as a three-decker, the two-decker 80-gun ships were faster and less cumbersome than the giant three-deckers, which is why they were preferred as flagships, and their upper-deck 24-pounders made them significantly more powerful than the British 74-gun third-rate ships of the line. They could also be crewed by as few as 600 men.

'GOD SEND THAT I MAY FIND THEM!'

At the beginning of 1805 there was an increase in naval activity by the French and Spanish as they sought to execute Napoleon's plans for invasion of England. In January Nelson was at Agincourt Sound, his favourite sheltered anchorage at La Maddalena Islands off north-east Sardinia, when the frigates *Active* and *Seahorse* brought news that the French had escaped from Toulon 250 miles away. Concurrently, Rear Admiral Missiessy had managed to break Admiral Sir Thomas Graves' blockade of Rochefort during a damaging blizzard, but even under jury rig got clean away to the West Indies. However, believing that no more French ships were going to join him, he returned to Rochefort on 20 May, just one week after Villeneuve – on his second attempt to play his part in Napoleon's grand strategy – had arrived in Martinique with 11 sail of the line and seven frigates to reinforce him.

Meanwhile, Nelson, with his 11 ships and frigates, was looking frantically for evidence of Villeneuve's movements. 'I am in a fever. God send that I may find them! I have neither ate, drank or slept with any comfort since last Sunday.' On 19 February, off Malta, he learned that the French had been driven back into Toulon by storm damage. 'These Gentlemen,' said Nelson, 'are not accustomed to a Gulf of Lyon gale.' With this weight off his mind he revictualled and resumed his blockade off Toulon. His more relaxed mood is revealed in this overtly sexual letter to Emma Hamilton, dated 16 March.

The Ship is just parting and I take the last moment to renew my assurances to My Dearest beloved Emma of My eternal love affection and adoration, you are ever with me in my Soul, your resemblance is never absent from my mind, and my own dearest Emma I hope very soon that I shall embrace the substantial part of you instead of the Ideal, that will I am sure give us both real pleasure and exquisite happiness, longing as I do to be with you yet I am sure under the circumstances in which I am placed, you would be the first to say My Nelson try & get at those french fellows and come home with Glory to your own Emma, or if they will not come out then come home for a short time and arrange your affairs which have long been neglected, don't I say my own love what you would say. Only continue to love me as affectionately as I do you and we must then be the happiest couple in the World. May God bless you Ever prays yours and only your faithful Nelson & Bronte

(Nelson used various signatures throughout his life. 'Nelson & Bronte' was one of them. Bronte referred to the title Duke of Bronte, conferred on him by King Ferdinand of Naples in August 1799. With the title came an estate at Bronte in Sicily.)

Even though Villeneuve had been able to give Nelson the slip he found that his seamen were too inexperienced after months in port to cross the Atlantic. On his return to Toulon he appealed to Napoleon to relieve him of his command. Napoleon refused his request and on the morning of 30 March Villeneuve put to sea for the second time with 11 ships of the line, eight frigates and thousands of soldiers. He successfully passed through the Straits of Gibraltar and after joining up at Cadiz with six Spanish ships of the line (all they could muster) under the command of Admiral Gravina, got clean away to the West Indies. Nelson was at Palma Bay, and based on intelligence and a process of elimination sailed on 11 May, three days before Villeneuve arrived at Martinique. The Great Chase had begun.

In the West Indies, a junior French officer complained that, 'We have been masters of the sea for three weeks with an army of 7,000 and have not been able to attack a single island.' The only success was the recapture of 'HMS' *Diamond Rock*, off Martinique. The day the British garrison surrendered Villeneuve was startled to hear that Nelson was now only two days behind him and contrary to orders decided to return to Europe immediately. After he had made his decision fresh orders from Napoleon arrived, instructing him to sail to Ferrol and Brest so that all the available allied forces could concentrate in the Channel to support the invasion attempt.

Nelson searched the West Indies 'as far as Trinidad'. He was expecting to find and fight Villeneuve, but after analysing true and false intelligence 'sailed in pursuit of the enemy' once again. In a postscript to a letter he added,

> The French Fleet passed to the leeward of Antigua on
> Saturday last, standing to the northward. All their troops
> and stores which they took from Guadeloupe are re-landed
> there: therefore I am pushing for the anchorage of St.
> John's, to land the troops and hope to sail in the morning
> after them for the Straits' Mouth.

For Nelson the Great Chase had been a frustrating and fruitless episode. 'I am very, very unwell, and vexed . . . What a race I have run these fellows; but God is just, and I may be repaid for all my moments of anxiety.' Anticipating reinforcements, but realizing the theatre was moving back to the Bay of Biscay, he wrote to Rear Admiral Alexander Cochrane, Commander in Chief in the Leeward Islands:

> . . . should the expected reinforcements when they arrive
> be found unnecessary to be kept, and you determine upon
> sending them home I venture to suggest that it may be
> advantageous to His Majesty's service if the Squadron or
> some part of them called off St Vincent or Lisbon to know
> if their assistance might not be wanted off Cadiz or in the
> Mediterranean as the Combined fleet in that quarter will be
> full thirty Sail of the Line.

Moreover, he dispatched all his fast-sailing frigates to warn the British squadrons off Ushant, Ferrol, Gibraltar and Tangier. He also dispatched a fast brig, the CURIEUX (18), to England. She overtook Villeneuve's fleet, and Captain George Bettesworth reported its size and course to the Admiralty.

At 11 a.m. on 8 July, Lord Barham received his dispatch and acted immediately to adjust the disposition of the waiting squadrons, in particular the Western Squadron, which was under the command of one of his most trusted and experienced admirals, William Cornwallis. He sent a decisive order to Admiral Sir Robert Calder to raise his blockade of Ferrol and to cruise between Ushant and Cape Finisterre.

The situation appeared critical. It looked as if at last Napoleon's grand strategy was working. At Ferrol five French and nine Spanish ships of the line were ready to put to sea. Sir Robert Calder, with his blockading squadron of ten, to be increased to 15, would be in great danger when, as expected, Villeneuve arrived with his 20. Rochefort had five sail of the line waiting to break out and Vice Admiral Ganteaume at Brest had a fleet of 21. Meanwhile, Nelson had left the West Indies only three days after Villeneuve, overtaken him, but headed back towards the Mediterranean. After 3,459 miles he wrote, 'Cape Spartel in sight, but no French Fleet nor any information about them: how sorrowful this makes me, but I cannot help myself!' Lieutenant William Clarke, second in command of the marines in the ACHILLE (74), was also feeling the uncertainty of Villeneuve's whereabouts:

In the month of July Lord Nelsons fleet passed us on their
return from the West Indies in chase of the French fleet,
but I think we only communicated by signals. We were
however kept on the qui vive knowing the French fleet was
at sea, and uncertain where they might make for on their
return to Europe.

However, on 22 July Villeneuve ran straight into Calder's squadron
some 120 miles off Cape Finisterre. Barham's cunning and strategic
instinct had paid off. At 11 a.m. the French emerged from a fog bank
and Calder's inferior force ran down on them as fast as the light and
baffling winds would allow. The action did not start until 5.15 p.m.
and lasted four hours. The fog, failing light and gun smoke meant
that neither side could see each other clearly. Nevertheless, Calder
captured the Spanish *San Rafael* (80) and *Firme* (74), and so badly
mauled the French *Atlas* (74) and three more Spanish ships that they
took no further part in the campaign. The Spanish suffered 650
casualties, three times as many as the British.

Two of Calder's ships were so badly damaged that they had to
return to England. The following day he decided, with the opposing
fleets 17 miles apart, that discretion would be the better part of valour
and did not renew the engagement. Villeneuve saw no reason to renew
the battle either and was relieved to get his fleet into Vigo. He was
down to four days' water and had as many as 1,700 sick, many with
scurvy, because unlike the Royal Navy the French Marine failed to
issue lemon juice.

However, before the year was out Sir Robert Calder faced a Court
Martial and received a severe reprimand for not continuing the action.
After Trafalgar Villeneuve wrote, 'I wish Sir Robert and I had fought it
out that day. He would not be in his present position, nor I in mine.'
Captain Infernet of the French *Intrépide* (74) exclaimed in amazement
to his British captors:

It is very well for you gentlemen that you feel justified in
finding fault with an Admiral who, when in command of

> fifteen sail of the line, fights a battle with twenty, because
> he only makes two of them prizes!

There can be no reservations about the strategic success of Calder's action – it has never been given a name. His attack on the returning Combined Fleet, and not Trafalgar, put an end to Napoleon's grand invasion plans. However, he would not have been in the right place to attack if it had not been for Lord Barham's specific order. It is to this remarkable old man, far removed from all the hazards, at the centre of the Royal Navy's web in Whitehall, that the true credit belongs. The psychological impact of the action was decisive, for whatever confidence Villeneuve had in his fleet evaporated forever on 22 July. Two weeks later he wrote, 'In the fog our captains, without experience of an action or fleet tactics, had no better idea than to follow their second ahead, and here we are the laughing stock of Europe.'

'WE ARE ANXIOUSLY AWAITING YOU'

Napoleon's nerves were strained by the long wait at Boulogne. He had been ready for the invasion to begin since 3 August. All that was needed were allied sails to secure the Channel. His impatience with Villeneuve was mounting:

> Start now, there is not a moment to lose. Sail up the
> Channel with my squadrons united. England is ours! We
> are all ready: embarkation is complete. Show yourself for
> twenty-four hours and our business is done! . . . we are
> anxiously awaiting you. If you have not done this yet,
> do it now.

Villeneuve was less enthusiastic. He was obsessed with the idea that the English were always on his heels and when he sighted Allemand's squadron on the 14th he presumed it to be English. Confused further by mysterious sightings and false intelligence, Villeneuve made the critical decision to sail for Cadiz, putting an end to the invasion of England. Once safely there he wrote to Decrès to justify his decision:

I could feel no confidence in the state of my fleet's armament, in their sailing ability, or their co-ordination of manoeuvre. In addition, the enemy was concentrating his forces and had full knowledge of all my movements after I had reached the Spanish coast. All these circumstances have combined to crush my hopes of achieving the great task to which my force has been assigned. If I had continued to struggle against the head winds, I should have suffered irreparable damage and my units would have become separated. The Spanish man-of-war *San Francisco de Asis* has already lost her topmast. I am convinced that there has been a radical change in the situation since His Imperial and Royal Majesty issued his orders. No doubt his object in sending the greater part of his naval forces to the colonies was to divide those of the enemy. The attention of the English was to be diverted to their distant possessions, so that our own navy could spring a surprise and deal them a mortal blow by returning suddenly to Europe and combining in a united force. I am further convinced that this plan has failed, as it has been disclosed to the enemy by the passage of time, and by the calculations the movements of our ships have enabled him to make; further, the enemy is in any case now in a position to defeat it, for the concentration of his forces is at this moment more formidable than ever before – superior even to our combined squadrons of Brest and Ferrol. I am therefore unable to envisage any possibility of success in the present circumstances, and consequently, in accordance with Your Excellency's dispatch of July 16, I made the decision at nightfall on August 15, the third day after my departure, to make course for Cadiz, being at that time in a position 80 leagues west-north-west of Cape Finisterre.

Privately, he added:

> I cannot deceive myself. Whatever decision the Emperor
> comes to, nothing can lift me from the pit of misfortune into
> which I have fallen. But ever since my departure from Toulon
> I have been prepared for this, and I was never able to foresee
> any good coming of the operations I was to undertake.

In part, Villeneuve recognized that the stunning success of the
British blockade had left his crews at best only 'harbour trained',
whereas the Royal Navy, at sea from year to year, was 'trained to
storms'. Additionally, as an officer on board the *Bucentaure* put it,
'Admiral Villeneuve was haunted by the spectre of Nelson' and '*le
souvenir d'Aboukir*'.

On hearing from Decrès that Villeneuve was very possibly in
Cadiz, Napoleon saw red, called him a coward and even a traitor. The
Emperor declaimed to Decrès:

> Your precious Villeneuve is not even fit to command a
> frigate! What can you call a man who loses his head and
> throws his plans overboard just because a few seamen
> fall sick on two of his ships, or the end of a bowsprit is
> broken, or a few sails are torn, or there is a rumour that
> Nelson and Calder have joined forces? But if Nelson had
> joined Calder, they would be at the very entrance of Ferrol
> harbour, ready to catch the French as they came out, and
> not on the high seas. All this is as clear as crystal to anyone
> not blinded by fear!

Within an hour of their meeting, Napoleon, whose passion for
invading England remained undiminished, insisted that Decrès order
Villeneuve to proceed to the Channel. This made the Minister of
Marine so anxious that he plucked up the rare courage to question the
Emperor's orders. His words were delivered late at night to Napoleon's
residence at the Castle of Pont-de-Briques, Boulogne.

If Villeneuve's fleet is at Cadiz, I implore Your Majesty
to consider this circumstance as a mere setback which
will preserve it for other operations. I implore you on
no account to make the fleet come from Cadiz into the
Channel, because at the present moment that would bring
nothing but misfortune on the great enterprise.

3
COUNTDOWN TO BATTLE

'HOISTED THE FLAG OF THE RIGHT HONOURABLE LORD VISCOUNT NELSON'

There was grim reality to life in the Royal Navy during the Napoleonic Wars blockade. Ships could be tacking back and forth in front of an enemy port for as many as six months, and even then only the barest minimum of time was allowed for them to re-victual at a home port. Blockade was both hazardous, boring and a test of endurance. Few could stand the strain for long.

Cuthbert Collingwood, who had been promoted to Vice Admiral of the Blue in April 1804, was on blockade off Cadiz. He had been obliged to shift his flag from ship to ship, to ensure that he was always on station in a sail of the line fit for instant service. He frequently bemoaned his situation. 'When I sailed,' he said on one occasion, 'I had not time to make a coat, and I have only two, one of which is very old, but I did not suspect I should have been so long without the means of getting one.' On another occasion he complained that he had 'not seen a leaf on a tree' since leaving Portsmouth in June 1803, and declared 'Nothing but a sense of it being necessary for the safety of the country could make us support such a deprivation of everything which is pleasurable.' His thoughts were forever with his home and daughters in Morpeth.

Very little happened until 20 August. At ten o'clock in the morning the crowded canvas of the Combined Fleet of 29 ships of the line, accompanied by frigates and corvettes, hove into sight. Lieutenant William Clarke in the *ACHILLE* described the scene:

The morning of the 20th of August was very foggy, we were
pretty close to Cadiz with four Sail of the Line, a small
Frigate and the *THUNDER* bark on a partial clearance of
the fog, a sail or two was discovered to the Westward, and
on our standing towards them their number appeared to
be increasing, but still the fog for some time prevented our
making out what they were and we were disposed to think
them a convoy bound through the Straits, at last the Man at
the Mast Head pronounced one to be a Line of Battle Ship,
this did not alter the opinion, but, as the fog continued
to clear away, another Line of Battle Ship, another and
another, a Fleet!!! were the progressive proclamations from
aloft, and at last the Tricolour Flag was plainly discovered
floating in the wind, the wind was Southerly, and had they
when they first discovered [us] shaped their course for the
mouth of the Straits they must have reached there before
us, and cut us off from all retreat unless that of fighting
our way through. I suppose the Spectre of Nelson and his
fleet followed in their wake, and made their own safety
their first consideration. When doubt no longer existed
as to what they were, we tacked and stood in direct for the
Straits as the wind would allow, but it was very doubtful
whether we could fetch them. The headmost Ships of the
Enemy made Sail as if intending to follow and on a slight
change of wind taking place which would enable us to lay
our heads for the Straits, we brought to, to see whether
they would or not, but, they rejoined their main body and
stood for Cadiz, I think seven and twenty Sail of the Line.
The frigate and especially the old *THUNDER*, had a narrow
escape, several of them passing within half a gun shot of
her, but she having hoisted Danish colours, and being
Merchantman like in appearance, passed unsuspected.
The next morning saw us again at our old grounds, I
suppose I must not say Blockading but watching the united
squadrons of France and Spain.

Clarke's ship, the *ACHILLE*, and the *COLOSSUS* (74) were accompanying Collingwood who was flying his flag in the *DREADNOUGHT* (98). He captured the moment in a letter to his wife, as he pondered what he could do against such a formidable host and hoped for reinforcements 'suited to the occasion'.

> **I have very little time to write to you, but must tell you what a squeeze we had like to have got yesterday. While we were cruising off the town down came the combined fleet of 36 sail of men-of-war; we were only three poor things with a frigate and a bomb, and drew off towards the Straits, not very ambitious, as you may suppose, to try our strength against such odds. They followed us as we retired with 16 large ships, but on our approaching the Straits they left us, and joined their friends in Cadiz, where they are fitting and replenishing their provisions. We in our turn followed them back, and today have been looking in Cadiz, where their fleet is now as thick as a wood. I hope I shall have somebody come to me soon, and in the meantime I must take the best care of myself I can.**

On 30 August his hopes were fulfilled when Vice Admiral Sir Robert Calder arrived, bringing the blockading fleet to 26 sail of the line. Captain Edward Codrington of the *ORION* (74) remarked that had it not done so 'this immense force [the Combined Fleet] would probably by this time have been already in Toulon to co-operate with the French army in Italy'. He added, 'For Charity's sake send us Lord Nelson, ye men of Power.' Nelson was in England. He wrote in his diary, 'I hold myself ready to go forth whenever I am desired . . . God knows I want rest; but self is entirely out of the question.'

As the final chapter in Nelson's famous life was about to open, a 20-year-old ordinary seaman aboard *VICTORY*, anchored off Portsmouth, was writing on 30 August to his parents. The destinies of the two sailors were intertwined, and they would both draw their last breaths on 21 October.

Dear Father and Mother,
I had the pleasure of receiving your kind letter and glad to
hear that you was well I sent a letter when I was at Gibraltar
and not nowing where us was bound to told you to Direct to
Gibraltar or elsewhere have not had the pleasure of receiving
any letter from you Since but now I am Safe. Arrived at
Spithead and in good health not nowing how long us shall
Remain here should be very happy to hear from you before I
got out to sea I expect to go out Every Day I ham very sorry
to hear that my Aunt is Dead and likewise I should be very
happy to now how my Brother and Sister are and Mr Collett
and Mrs Collett and all friends I return you many thanks
for keeping of my cloths and giving of them to my brother
we have had the news that the French fleet is gon to their
destination and us are a'going after them and Expect to fall
in with them very soon. So no more
From your Loving Son
JOSEPH WARD

Nelson had at last rejoined his mistress Emma Lady Hamilton and their beloved daughter Horatia at Merton Place, near Wimbledon in Surrey, on 20 August. He did not know that he had only 25 days left with the woman he truly loved. It was the only time since the start of their relationship that they were alone together with their daughter Horatia, now four and a half years old. The *ménage a trois* with Emma's husband had ended when Sir William Hamilton died in April 1803, a few weeks before Nelson hoisted his flag in *VICTORY* for the first time. It was a happy time, but Nelson was keenly aware of the military situation and recognized that he was 'set up as a conjurer' to save England. He made frequent visits to the Secretary of State for War, the First Sea Lord at the Admiralty and other ministers with whom he discussed the strategic situation. His 14-year-old nephew, George Matcham, later wrote:

A few days before Nelson quitted England to take command
of the Trafalgar fleet, he seemed more than usually pensive.

I heard him say, 'They are mistaken, I will myself go and talk with Mr. Pitt.' Early next morning, Sunday, he went, and according to general orders, was admitted to the Minister's presence. On asking where he conceived the French Fleet was destined, 'Certainly,' Mr. Pitt replied, 'their destination is to the West Indies, does it not appear to you, my Lord?'

'No,' said Nelson, 'I may be wrong, but I have a different conception of their purpose.'

'What is it?'

'My idea is that they propose going to Cadiz and being joined by the Spanish ships lying there, then start for Toulon and assemble all their Fleet; they will then have collected sixty or seventy sail of the line and then there will be a difficulty in overcoming them.' Then he pointed out to Mr. Pitt what he imagined would be their course. After a long discussion, Mr. Pitt became a convert to Lord Nelson's opinion. After agreeing upon the number of ships that should be sent, 'Now,' said Mr. Pitt, 'who is to take command?'

'You cannot have a better man than the present one, Collingwood.'

'No,' said Mr. Pitt, 'that won't do, you must take the command.'

'Sir,' said Nelson, 'I wish it not. I have had enough of it, and I feel disposed to remain quiet the rest of my days.'

On returning to England in August 1805, Nelson had been concerned that his superiors and the public generally were going to be critical of him for not having brought the French and Spanish fleets to action during the last two years. The anxiety was sufficient to make him feel low. It was relieved by the support and adulation he encountered from both friends, the press and people in the street. One of his oldest friends, Thomas Fremantle, in command of the *NEPTUNE* (98) had tried to reassure him that on his arrival in England he would find everyone 'disposed to do you entire credit, and at no period according to my judgement did you ever stand higher in the estimation of the public, and indeed we are much in want of all the ability the country can find'. Admiral Sir Richard Keats also reassured Nelson of the public mood, telling him that 'all classes unite in one sentiment of admiration for your Lordship's judicious and persevering conduct'. In fact, the public worshipped him. He was their idol and redeemer, and the cause of crowds who just wanted to gaze upon him. Sir Gilbert Elliot, Lord Minto, one of Nelson's closest civilian friends, described their admiration and love as 'beyond anything represented in a play or a poem of fame'. Theophilus Lee walked with him down the Strand to Somerset House, home of the Navy Office, the administrative part of the Royal Navy. It built, maintained and equipped the ships, recruited and paid the men, purchased stores and food, provided medical care and controlled all the naval dockyards. Without it the Battle of Trafalgar could not have been fought.

> The crowd that waited outside . . . was very great. He . . .
> neither in look or dress betokened the naval hero, having
> on a pair of drab-green breeches, and high black gaiters,
> a yellow waistcoat, and a plain blue coat, with a cocked
> hat, quite square, a large green shade over the eye and gold
> headed stick in his hand, yet the crowd ran before him
> and said, as he looked down, that he was then thinking of
> burning a fleet &c. They gave his lordship repeated and
> hearty cheers; indeed the two pedestrians could hardly get to
> the Salter's shop, so dense was the crowd . . .

Nelson's attitude to the general public in England is an important one. He recognized the power and fickleness of public opinion and had shown himself to be a proficient self-publicist. He was also vain, as many great men are. On meeting strangers he seems to have deliberately 'pumped up his performance' in order to present to them the image he thought they expected of him. To some this made him appear superficial and belittled his strategic prowess. One such encounter took place on 12 September, the day before he left London to join *VICTORY*. He found himself in a government anteroom in the company of a soldier in his mid-thirties. The Royal Navy was a professional service, which meant that officers had to pass examinations to gain their commissions, whereas in the army commissions could be purchased. Skill and ability rarely came into it and there were many incompetent officers. This may have heightened Nelson's sense of display.

Lord Nelson was in different circumstances, two quite different men, as I myself can vouch, though I only saw him once in my life, and for, perhaps, an hour. It was soon after I returned from India. I went to the Colonial Office in Downing Street, and there I was shown into the little waiting-room on the right hand, where I found, also waiting to see the Secretary of State, a gentleman, who from his likeness to his pictures and the loss of an arm, I immediately recognised as Lord Nelson. He could not know who I was, but he entered at once into conversation with me, if I can call it conversation, for it was almost all on his side and all about himself, and in, really, a style so vain and so silly as to surprise and almost disgust me.

I suppose something that I happened to say may have made him guess that I was somebody, and he went out of the room for a moment, I have no doubt to ask the office keeper who I was, for when he came back he was altogether a different man, both in manner and matter. All that I had thought a charlatan style had vanished and he talked of the state of this country and of the aspect and probabilities of affairs on the Continent with a good sense, and a knowledge of subjects both at home and abroad, that surprised me equally and more agreeably than the first part of our interview had done; in fact he talked like an officer and a statesman.

Now, if the Secretary of State had been punctual, and admitted Lord Nelson in the first quarter of an hour, I should have had the same impression of a light and

trivial character that other people have had, but luckily
I saw enough to be satisfied that he really was a very
superior man; but certainly a more sudden and complete
metamorphosis I never saw. I don't know a conversation
that interested me more.

By a strange fluke the future heroes of Trafalgar and Waterloo had
been brought together. The soldier was General Sir Arthur Wellesley,
the victor of Assaye, just back from India: the future Duke of
Wellington. Posterity is indebted to the Duke's Irish-born friend John
Wilson Croker for recording the story. That Nelson could manage his
public personality is also evident from an account by Harriet, Lady
Bessborough, to her lover Lord Granville Leveson Gower, following a
dinner with Nelson and Emma three days before he left.

So far from appearing vain and full of himself, as one had
always heard, he was perfectly unassuming and natural.
Talking of Popular Applause and his having been Mobbed
and Huzzaed in the city, Lady Hamilton wanted him to give
an account of it, but he stopped her. 'Why', said she, 'you
like to be applauded – you cannot deny it.' 'I own it', he
answered; 'popular applause is very acceptable and grateful
to me, but no Man ought to be too much elated by it; it is
too precarious to be depended upon, and it may be my turn
to feel the tide set as strong against me as ever it did for
me.' Everybody joined in saying they did not believe that
could happen to him, but he seemed persuaded it might, but
added: 'Whilst I live I shall do what I think right and best;
the country has a right to that from me, but every Man is
liable to err in judgement.'

During the three weeks in England Nelson's self-assurance returned
and there can be little doubt that he was anxious to go back to sea
to claim the rewards that he felt were justly his. On 2 September
Captain Henry Blackwood of the frigate *EURYALUS* arrived early at the

Admiralty, with the intelligence that the Combined Fleets had put into Cadiz. An accomplished frigate captain with a dashing reputation, he had shadowed the Combined Fleet as it had made its way south after Calder's Action. At five o'clock on the same morning he made a brief call on Lord Nelson at Merton Place and found him already up and dressed. Immediately on seeing Blackwood, Nelson exclaimed, 'I am sure you bring me news of the French and Spanish Fleets, and I think I shall yet have to beat them. Depend on it, Blackwood, I shall yet give Mr Villeneuve a drubbing.'

He had a clear picture of how he was going to do it. Admiral Sir Richard Keats visited Merton and one morning walked with Nelson in the grounds. They discussed naval matters, and Keats prepared a memorandum of the conversation. It reveals the essence of Nelson's tactical thinking, which he discussed with his officers in advance of the battle:

> . . . he said to me, 'No day can be long enough to arrange
> a couple of Fleets, and fight a decisive Battle, according to
> the old system. When we meet them,' (I was to have been
> with him) 'for meet them we shall, I'll tell you how I shall
> fight them. I shall form the Fleet into three Divisions in
> three lines. One Division shall be composed of twelve or
> fourteen of the fastest two-decked Ships, which I shall
> keep always to windward, or in a situation of advantage;
> and I shall put them under an Officer who, I am sure, will
> employ them in the manner I wish, if possible. I consider
> it will always be in my power to throw them into Battle in
> any part I may choose; but if circumstances prevent their
> being carried against the Enemy where I desire, I shall feel
> certain he will employ them effectually, and, perhaps, in a
> more advantageous manner than if he could have followed
> my orders.' (He never mentioned, or gave any hint by
> which I could understand who it was he intended for this
> distinguished service). He continued – 'With the remaining
> part of the Fleet formed in two Lines I shall go at them

at once, if I can, about one-third of their line from their leading Ship.' He then said, 'What do you think of it?' Such a question I felt required consideration. I paused. Seeing it, he said, 'but I'll tell you what I think of it. I think it will surprise and confound the Enemy. They won't know what I am about. It will bring forward a pell-mell Battle, and that is what I want.'

Nelson was confident and decisive again, and Lord Barham, the First Lord of the Admiralty, had decided that he should rejoin the *VICTORY* at Portsmouth and resume the command of the fleet off Cadiz. Nelson wrote to Collingwood from the Admiralty on 7 September:

My Dear Coll.,
I shall be with you in a very few days, and I hope you will remain Second in Command. You will change the *DREADNOUGHT* for *ROYAL SOVEREIGN*, which I hope you will like. Ever, my dear Collingwood, most faithfully yours,
NELSON & BRONTE

Lord Barham is believed to have placed a List of the Navy in Nelson's hands, asking him to choose his own officers, to which Nelson replied, returning the list, 'Choose yourself, my Lord, the same spirit actuates the whole profession; you cannot choose wrong.' Nelson's confidence in his fellow officers was born of experience, reputation and friendship. On 11 September, after his interview, he came across Captain Charles Philip Durham. His ship, *DEFIANCE* (74), had been involved in Sir Robert Calder's action and had returned to England for repairs. Durham related how Nelson told him that he had just been appointed to command in the Mediterranean and was sailing immediately, adding, 'I'm sorry your ship is not ready, I should have been very glad to have you.' Durham said he could be ready and left for Portsmouth the next day. When he arrived at the George Inn he was greeted by two orders from Nelson. The commander in chief had wasted no time. One of the orders read as follows:

At the Admiralty Office, 11th September, 1805
You are hereby required and directed, the moment His
Majesty's Ship under your command is in all respects
ready for sea, to repair with her to St. Helen's, and join the
VICTORY, holding yourself in constant readiness to proceed
with her to sea. But should the VICTORY sail previous to
your joining her, as above, you are to apply to the Lords
Commissioners of the Admiralty, who will furnish you with
my Rendezvous, when I desire you will join me with the
utmost possible expedition.
NELSON & BRONTE

The second order was written to every captain now placed under
Nelson's command, including to his finest flag captain, Thomas
Masterman Hardy, commanding officer of VICTORY, who was also to
become his chief of staff. Hardy was nearly six inches taller than Nelson
and he told how they had walked the quarterdeck so many times
together that he had adopted the Admiral's gait. Their personalities
were very different, but Hardy was probably Nelson's closest friend.

At the Admiralty Office, 11th September, 1805
Pursuant to instructions from the Lords Commissioners of
the Admiralty, you are hereby required and directed to put
yourself under my command, and follow and obey all such
orders as you shall from time to time receive from me for
His Majesty's Service.
NELSON & BRONTE

The final days were hectic, but before he quitted London, Nelson
visited the hatters Lock & Co in St James' to order a new hat with a
special green eyeshade stitched like a peak over both eyes, and called
at Mr Peddieson's, his upholsterer in Brewer Street, Soho, where the
coffin presented him by Captain Hallowell after the Battle of the Nile
had been sent. Hitherto, he had always kept it in his cabin. 'With his
usual gaiety and good humour he desired him to get the attestation of

its identity engraved on the lid, "for," added his Lordship, "I think it highly probable that I may want it on my return".'

Lord Minto was probably the last visitor to Merton to say farewell to Nelson.

> I stayed till ten at night and I took final leave of him. Lady Hamilton was in tears all day yesterday, could not eat, and hardly drink, and near swooning, and all at table. It is a strange picture. She tells me nothing can be more pure and ardent than this flame. In her own words she was 'broken-hearted, as our dear Nelson is immediately going. It seems as though I have had a fortnight's dream and am awoke to all the misery of this cruel separation. But what can I do? His powerful arm is of so much consequence to the country.'

On the evening of Friday 13 September Nelson was ready to leave Merton Place, but just before he went out to the carriage waiting to take him to Portsmouth he ascended the stairs to Horatia's bedroom and knelt in prayer beside her as she lay sleeping. With a sentimental heart he climbed into the carriage and was gone. He wrote in his diary:

> At half-past ten drove from dear, dear Merton, where I left all which I hold dear in this world, to go to serve my king and country. May the great God whom I adore enable me to fulfil the expectations of my country and if it is His good pleasure that I should return, my thanks will never cease being offered up to the Throne of His mercy. If it is His good providence to cut short my days upon earth, I bow with greatest submission, relying that He will protect those dear to me, that I may leave behind. His will be done. Amen. Amen. Amen.

Nelson arrived at Portsmouth at six o'clock the following morning, arranged all his business and embarked at the bathing machines with George Rose and George Canning for the *VICTORY*, which was at anchor at St Helen's preparing for sea. He left from the bathing machines, rather than the usual sally port, in order to avoid the huge crowds, which had been gathering throughout the day in the hope of catching a glimpse of him. The attempt was futile. His last short walk in England involved jostling with so many people that the guards could not keep them back. He turned to Hardy, who was accompanying him, and marvelled that 'I had their huzzas before – I have their hearts now'.

He hoisted his flag at noon. Rose and Canning disembarked after lunch and at eight o'clock the following morning *VICTORY* weighed anchor and made sail before a light breeze to the south-south-east. She was accompanied by the *EURYALUS*, but Nelson had to leave the *ROYAL SOVEREIGN* (100), *DEFENCE* (74) and *AGAMEMNON* (64) to follow the moment they were ready for sea. After a short stop at Plymouth *VICTORY* sailed south.

Nelson was now safely aboard the ship that was so familiar to him. Before his brief and busy 25 days in England he had been at sea in *VICTORY* continuously for two years and two months, all but two days, since he had left England in May 1803. She was more like a home than a ship. His excitement must have been palpable. He was in high spirits and in his element. He knew clearly what he was going to do, and his sense of destiny was telling him that he was approaching his finest hour:

> My fate is fixed and I am gone, and beating down the
> Channel with a foul wind.

THE WATCH OFF CADIZ

Unaware that Nelson was already on his way from England, the long-suffering Collingwood, with his pet dog Bounce by his side, was again ventilating his grumbles. This time in a letter dated 21 September to John Blackett, Collingwood's rich father-in-law:

It would be a happy day that would relieve me from this
perpetual cruising, which is really wearing me to a lath. The
great difficulty I have is to keep up the health of the men.
We get good beef from the Moors; but to bring it requires a
number of ships, which I can ill spare. Two hundred bullocks
do not serve us a week, and a transport laden with wine but a
month. How we are to keep up our water I do not know.

How happy I should be, could I but hear from home, and
know how my dear girls are going on! Bounce is my only pet
now, and he is indeed a good fellow: he sleeps by the side of
my cot, whenever I lie in one, until near the time of tacking,
and then marches off, to be out of the hearing of the guns
for he is not reconciled to them yet. There is no end to my
business: I am at work from morning till even; but I daresay
Lord Nelson will be out next month.

Nelson's journey south had been held up by 'two nasty days', but by
perseverance he set off from Plymouth on 18 September, where he was
joined by *AJAX* (74) and *THUNDERER* (74), and tried hard to beat out
of the Channel so that 'the first northerly wind will carry me to Cape
St Vincent'. Two days later, at noon, he was able to communicate by
private signal with Rear Admiral Stirling, who passed within a few
miles of *VICTORY*, and later, south-west of the Scillies, spoke to Rear
Admiral Sir Richard Bickerton, his erstwhile second in command
returning to England, a sick man, in the frigate *DECADE*. In the Bay
of Biscay *VICTORY* encountered rough weather and adverse winds, but
Cape St Vincent was sighted on the 27th. Otherwise, the voyage south
was uneventful. There were eleven floggings (36 lashes apiece) for
drunkenness, and Able Seaman Robert Chandler was lost overboard,
even though *VICTORY* backed her main topsail and lowered a boat to
look for him.

One may imagine what thoughts went through Nelson's mind as he
sailed past Cape St Vincent, since it was in these waters on St Valentine's
Day 1797 that he had acted independently by wearing his ship out
of the line of battle in order to head off oncoming Spanish ships,

capturing two of them in the process. It was from this moment that he began to develop his personal style of leadership, promoting action in the spirit rather than the letter of orders, exploiting his ability to innovate and experiment, and devolving initiative to his captains.

On the 26th, Nelson had despatched the *EURYALUS* to advise Collingwood of his approach and to direct that there was to be no customary gun salute or hoist of colours, 'even if you are out of sight of land . . . for it is as well not to proclaim to the Enemy every ship which may join the Fleet'. He knew that Admiral Villeneuve was nervous and wanted to exploit this to his advantage. He even urged the Governor of Gibraltar, Lieutenant General Fox, to stop the *Gibraltar Gazette* announcing the strength of the fleet and the names of the ships. Consequently, on the eve of his 47th birthday he joined the fleet without fuss or panoply and brought its strength up to 23 ships of the line and two frigates. He recorded in his diary:

> Sunday, September 28th, 1805
> Fresh breezes at N.N.W. At daylight bore up, and made sail.
> At nine saw the *AETNA* [bomb vessel] cruising. At noon saw
> eighteen sail. Nearly calm. In the evening joined the fleet
> under Vice-Admiral Collingwood. Saw the Enemy's Fleet in
> Cadiz amounting to thirty-five or thirty-six Sail of the Line.

The city of Cadiz, the most elegant in Spain, displaying its attractive skyline of merchant watchtowers, *azoteas* or *miradores*, was about 15 miles away. The Combined Fleet at anchor was under the watchful eye of Admiral Thomas Louis, who commanded an inshore squadron of five ships. One of those in the blockading fleet was the *MARS* (74). Her Captain, George Duff, tried writing to 'his dearest wife and little ones' daily. He had last seen them on 24 April 1804. This letter is dated 23 September 1805:

> My dearest Sophia will readily believe how much I rejoiced
> on Saturday last to see our boy. He is very well, and has not
> been the least sick. All the rest are also well though they

have been sick during the passage. It was very fortunate my meeting with the *AURORA*, as I was ordered by the admiral to speak a frigate off the Gut, before I went to Tangier; and in doing so, I fell in with our boy, and got him out, otherwise it might have been some weeks before he had joined me. I have for the present taken him into the cabin to mess and sleep. He seems very well pleased with his choice of a profession, and I hope will continue to do so. I had the pleasure of receiving by the *AURORA*, yours of the 27th July, 2nd and 12th of August, but I was informed a week before of Norwich's coming. It is very odd, that on Sunday before he joined, our Captain of marines [Captain Thomas Norman, who died from a 'shattered skull' after the battle] who is a very pleasant fellow, told me when I went down to dine in the ward-room, that he seldom dreamt, but he could not resist telling me his dreams of last night, that my son had arrived, and that he was taking him all over the ship to show it to him. So when master Norwich made his appearance, the dream came into my head immediately.

He managed to write again on the day Nelson arrived:

I was called away yesterday, and now sit down again to write my ever dearest wife a few more lines, and to thank her for her picture; though I must own I am not at all pleased with it, as I don't think it does you any justice, nor do I think I should ever have taken it from you, if I had not been told it was intended for you. I think the one done by Smith was better.

On Saturday night we were joined by Lord Nelson with the *VICTORY, AJAX, THUNDERER*, and the *EURYALUS;* when I had the happiness of receiving yours, my dearest wife, of the 8th September, and the papers up to the 7th. Many, many thanks! I dined with his lordship yesterday, and had a very merry dinner; he certainly is the pleasantest Admiral I ever served under. I hope the Austrians and Russians will make

quick work with Buonaparte, and let us get to our homes
once more; when I expect to be an Admiral before I am
called upon again. (Dated 1 October).

Captain Edward Codrington exclaimed, 'Lord Nelson is arrived! A sort
of general joy has been the consequence and many good effects will
shortly arise from our change of system.' Nelson was equally pleased
and on 3 October wrote:

The reception I met with on joining the Fleet caused the
sweetest sensation of my life. The Officers who came on
board to welcome my return forgot my rank as Commander-
in-Chief in the enthusiasm with which they greeted me. As
soon as these emotions were past, I laid before them the
Plan I had previously arranged for attacking the Enemy; and
it was not only my pleasure to find it generally approved,
but clearly perceived and understood. The enemy are still in
Port, but something must be immediately done to provoke
or lure them to Battle. My duty to my Country demands it,
and the hopes centred in me, I hope in God, will be realized.
In less than a fortnight expect to hear from me, or of me, for
who can forsee [sic] the fate of Battle? Put up your prayers
for my success, and may God protect all my friends!

Nelson, many of whose letters use or paraphrase lines from Shakespeare,
famously referred to his captains at the Battle of the Nile as a 'band
of brothers', taken from the rousing Agincourt speech in *King Henry
V*. The phrase described perfectly the close bond and trust that
existed between them. Moreover, it is synonymous with his brand of
open-style leadership, which so markedly differentiated him from his
contemporaries. However, at Trafalgar only 12 of the captains had
served with him before, two of whom were frigate captains. Over two
consecutive days he invited all his captains to dinners in the Great
Cabin of *VICTORY*, starting with the senior officers like Thomas
Fremantle of *NEPTUNE* and Charles Tyler of *TONNANT* (80), followed

by the junior officers, like John Cooke of *BELLEROPHON* (74), and George Duff of the *MARS*. They were enjoyable affairs, not least the one celebrating his birthday, but they also had a deadly purpose. Nelson was welding his fleet into a fighting unit, and for him that entailed briefing all of his captains as quickly as possible.

Earl St Vincent is credited with describing Nelson as 'a natural born predator', concluding that his sole benefit was his animal courage. Captain William Gordon Rutherford of the *SWIFTSURE* (74), born in Williamstown, North Carolina, also recognized him as a 'fighting man', but after meeting him believed, 'If you do not know Lord Nelson, he is the most gentlemanlike, mild, pleasant creature that was ever seen.' Nelson had genuine charm as well as guts. He asked Thomas Fremantle whether he would have a girl or a boy. An anxious Fremantle replied the former, at which point Nelson handed him a letter that answered his wish. He told him to be satisfied. He liked delivering letters to his captains personally. Codrington recalled how 'He received me in an easy, polite manner, and on giving me your letter said that being entrusted with it by a lady, he made a point of delivering it himself.'

The effect of his arrival on morale was universal. Richard Anderson, the master of the *PRINCE* (98), wrote in his diary, 'This is a Great day all the Capts dine with Lord Nelson I get a letter & some clean shirts from my dear Mary – Hurra.' James Martin, a 28-year-old Able Seaman from Essex serving in the *NEPTUNE*, wrote that it was 'Imposeble to Discribe the Hearfelt Satisfaction upon the whole fleet on this Occasion and the Confidence of Success with wich we ware Inspired'. His sentiments were echoed by a 19-year-old Mancunian, Henry Walker, a midshipman in the *BELLEROPHON*, highlighting how Nelson had the rare ability to project his personality to the fleet as a whole:

> Though we had before no doubt of success in the event of an action, yet the presence of such a man could not but inspire every individual in the fleet with additional confidence. Every one felt himself more than a match for the enemy.

They believed in Nelson, responded to his unstuffy demeanour, admired his 'ordinariness' and felt that he genuinely cared for their well-being. Word about his kindness and consideration got around the fleet fast. One story involved the latest despatch of mail to England, which was widely regarded as being the last opportunity to write home before the battle. The ship was under full sail and already some distance away, when Nelson saw a midshipman come up and speak to Lieutenant John Pasco, the signal officer, who stamped his foot in annoyance. Nelson asked what was the matter, to which Pasco replied, 'Nothing that needs trouble your Lordship.' However, Nelson pressed him further, 'You are not the man to lose your temper for nothing. What was it?' Pasco answered, 'Well if you must know, my Lord, I will tell you. You see that coxswain, we have not a better man on board *VICTORY*, and the message which put me out was this. I was told that he was so busy receiving and getting off the mailbags, that he forgot to drop his own letter to his wife into one of them, and he has just discovered it in his pocket.' 'Hoist a signal to bring her back,' was Nelson's instant command, 'who knows that he may not fall in action tomorrow.'

The enthusiasm that greeted Nelson indicates the powerful force of his reputation. It preceded him like a great bow wave and it makes it easier for us to understand the fear he struck into his enemies, particularly Admiral Villeneuve.

During these first few days Nelson was attending to a wide range of administrative matters as well. On his birthday he ordered prompt and decisive measures to prevent the enemy from receiving any supplies by sea. He knew there was a serious shortage of food and believed that starvation was the most effective way to force the Combined Fleet to sea. *The Times* for 11 October reported the seriousness of the situation:

> The scarcity occasioned by the arrival of the Combined
> Fleet continues to be severely felt; recourse has been made
> to Seville, and a supply of corn, wine, etc., demanded;
> even the fountains of Puerta Santa Maria have been put
> in requisition for the use of the fleets.

Nelson stationed ships off the Capes St Vincent, St Mary and Trafalgar; and the frigates *EURYALUS* and *HYDRA* (38) were ordered to keep off the entrance to Cadiz and to cover the smaller ports around Cadiz. These were being used by Danish neutrals to transfer cargoes to smaller Spanish vessels, which then sailed close in to shore to Cadiz, out of harm's way of the English ships.

Nelson could not foresee when the enemy might make their move and had to ensure that his blockading ships were kept well supplied with water and victuals. This required him to reduce his force 'so low as 23 Sail of the Line but if I did not begin the whole fleet in three weeks must have gone inside the Mediterranean. Half of the two-decked ships are now under 90 tons of water.' He detached some of his best ships from the main fleet, including a 98, two 80s and two 74s. On 2 October the *CANOPUS* (80), *QUEEN* (98), *SPENCER* (74), *TIGRE* (80), *ENDYMION* (50) and *ZEALOUS* (74) left for Gibraltar under the command of Rear Admiral Thomas Louis. Knowing that Louis would be disappointed, Nelson encouraged him with the following words: 'The enemy will come out, and we shall fight them; but there will be time to get back first. I look upon *CANOPUS* as my right hand; and I send you first to insure you being there to help beat them.' He recognized that Gibraltar was not the only source of supplies, and a letter to the Dey of Algiers reveals again the breadth of his considerations and diplomatic abilities:

> I think your Highness will be glad to hear of my return to
> the command of His Majesty's Fleets in the Mediterranean:
> and I rely that nothing will ever be permitted to happen
> which can interrupt the most perfect harmony and good
> understanding which exists between your Highness and the
> Regency, and the British Nation. I am confident that your
> Highness will give orders for the most friendly reception
> of British Ships in all the Ports in your Dominions, and
> that they shall be furnished, for their money, with every
> article they may want to purchase. I shall be very anxious
> for the return of the Frigate, that I may know the state of

your Highness's health; and beg that your Highness will be assured of the most highest esteem of
NELSON & BRONTE

When Rear Admiral Louis quitted the fleet for Gibraltar, Nelson appointed Captain Duff to command the inshore squadron, consisting of four sail of the line. He gave him detailed instructions:

> As the Enemy's Fleets may be hourly expected to put to
> sea from Cadiz, I have to desire that you will keep, with
> the *MARS, DEFENCE*, and *COLOSSUS*, from three to four
> leagues between the Fleet and Cadiz, in order that I may get
> the information from the Frigates stationed off that port,
> as expeditiously as possible. Distant signals to be used,
> when Flags, from the state of the weather, may not readily
> be distinguished in their colours. If the Enemy be out, or
> coming out, fire guns by day or night, in order to draw my
> attention. In thick weather, the ships are to close within
> signal of the *VICTORY*: one of the ships to be placed to
> windward, or rather to eastward of the other two, to extend
> the distance of seeing; and I have desired captain Blackwood
> to throw a frigate to Westward of Cadiz, for the purpose of
> easy and early communication.

Duff was proud of his new responsibilities:

> My dearest Sophia,
> I have but just time to tell you that Norwich and all of us are
> well. The Admiral has for some days past detached me with
> three sail of the line under my command, as the advance
> squadron; and just called me in to give me some wine, when
> I found the *BITTERN* sloop of war was going to Lisbon,
> and I do not like to lose the opportunity. I will begin you
> another letter to-morrow, but since I am Commodore, I have
> not much time during the day, and am ready for my nap as

soon as I can in the evening. I hope our dear little ones are
well, and that our mother and sisters, &c. are so likewise.
With every good wish and love to you and them, I ever am,
my dearest Sophia, your own
GEORGE DUFF

However, in a subsequent letter written on 8 October he fretted about
missing the looming battle:

I wrote my dearest Sophia a few lines yesterday by the
BITTERN; but as I left the fleet immediately, I do not know
whether the *DEFIANCE* brought us any letters or not. We
are detached only three or four leagues from the fleet, and
always in sight of it. At present our squadron consists of the
MARS, DEFENCE, COLOSSUS, and *AJAX*. I suppose as soon
as Admiral Louis returns from Gibraltar, where he is now
gone to water &c., he will take the command of the advance
squadron, and deprive me of my honours.

Two days later he appeared more relaxed:

I am just returned from dining with Browne, of the *AJAX*,
one of my squadron. He is a very old acquaintance of
mine, ever since 1780, when we were in the West Indies
together, and have met frequently since on service. I am
sorry the rain has begun tonight as it will spoil my fine
work, having been employed for this week past to paint
the Ship à la Nelson, which most of the fleet are doing. He
is so good and pleasant a man that we all wish to do what
he likes, without any kind of orders. I have been myself
very lucky with most of my Admirals; but I really think
the present the pleasantest I have met with: even this little
Detachment is a kind thing to me, there being so many
senior officers to me in the Fleet, as it shows his attention
and wish to bring me forward; but I believe I have to thank

my old friend Collingwood for it, as he was on board the *VICTORY*, when I was sent for.

Nelson had now retired with the rest of the fleet to about 50 miles north-westwards of Cadiz, well over the horizon from its watchtowers, and kept in constant communication with the frigates inshore, by means of the four battleships under Duff's command. This tactic ensured that the French and Spanish would be kept in the dark about the size of his fleet and avoided the necessity of running his ships through the Straits of Gibraltar when westerly gales prevailed, which would give the Combined Fleet the opportunity to escape from Cadiz, or at the very least obtain supplies.

Nelson gave Captain Henry Blackwood in the frigate *EURYALUS* a central part in the relay of these communications. As ever, his instructions were clear and thorough:

> *MARS, COLOSSUS* and *DEFENCE* will be stationed four
> leagues East from the Fleet, and one of them advanced
> to the east towards Cadiz, and as near as possible in the
> latitude. The fleet will be from sixteen to eighteen leagues
> West of Cadiz; therefore if you throw a frigate west from
> you, most probably, in fine weather, we shall communicate
> daily. In fresh breezes, Easterly, I shall work up for Cadiz,
> never getting to the Northward of it; and in the event of
> hearing they are standing out of Cadiz, I shall carry a press
> of sail to the Southward towards Cape Spartel and Arrache,
> so that you will always know where to find me.

Throughout his career in the Mediterranean, Nelson had bemoaned the lack of frigates, the 'eyes of the fleet' as he called them. Things were no different now. He was 'dying with anxiety for frigates'. On about 5 October he dispatched short but to-the-point letters to Marsden:

> I am ever sorry to trouble their lordships with anything
> like a complaint of a want of Frigates and Sloops; but if the

different services require them, and I have them not, those
services must be neglected to be performed. I am taking all
Frigates about me I possibly can; for if I were an Angel, and
attending to all other points of my Command, let the enemy
escape for want of the eyes of the fleet, I should consider
myself as most highly reprehensible.

And to Viscount Castlereagh:

I have only two Frigates to watch them, and not one with
the Fleet. I am most exceedingly anxious for more eyes, and
hope the Admiralty are hastening them to me. The last Fleet
was lost to me for want of Frigates; God forbid this should.
I am, etc. NELSON & BRONTE

He used every opportunity to make his point, being careful in letters
to Admiral Gambier and the politician George Rose to stress that he
was not complaining! To Rose he wrote:

I think not for myself, but the Country, therefore I hope the
Admiralty will send the first force as soon as possible, and
Frigates and Sloops of War, for I am very destitute, I do not
mean this as any complaint, quite the contrary; I believe
they are doing all they can, if interest does not interfere;
therefore, if Mr. Pitt would hint to Lord Barham, that he
shall be anxious until I get the force proposed, and plenty
of Frigates and Sloops in order to watch them closely, it
may be advantageous to the Country: you are at liberty
to mention this to Mr. Pitt, but I should not wish it to go
farther. I am ever, my dear Rose,
Your most obliged and faithful friend,
NELSON & BRONTE

Fortunately for Nelson, Barham had already acted. Between 7 and
13 October the frigates *JUNO, NAIAD, NIGER, PHOEBE* and *SIRIUS*

arrived and he was also reinforced by a further six ships of the line: the *BELLEISLE* (74), *AFRICA* (64) and *DEFIANCE*, the *LEVIATHAN* (74) from Gibraltar, the *ROYAL SOVEREIGN* fresh from refit, and his first battleship command and self-confessed favourite, the 64-gun *AGAMEMNON*. She was under the command of Captain Sir Edward Berry, one of Nelson's 'band of brothers' and his flag captain at the Nile. Nelson exclaimed to one of his officers, 'Here comes Berry! Now we shall have a battle.'

Charles Newbolt, a Midshipman in *L'AIMABLE* (32), bound for the Mediterranean, saw the *AGAMEMNON*. The letter to his mother, dated 15 October, highlights how dangerous the waters off France and Spain were for British ships:

Dear Mother,
I hope you are all well at home and I am sure will be very
glad to hear from me, but you were very nearly losing me
the 10th of this month, for we were chaced [sic] by the
French Squadron and were very near being come up with,
but we cut away two of our boats and one anchor and hove
two or three hundred shot overboard. There were nine in
number, we saw them about nine o'clock in the morning,
and we tacked ship and after them, but we soon found them
out to be the wrong sort. H.M. Ship *AGAMEMNON* was
chaced the day before from four o'clock, and was within
pistol shot of them, she discovered six line of battle ships
and one three decked ship. We thought her to be a French
ship, she was so far to windward that had she been a French
ship we could not have escaped her. She began to fire a
great number of guns when we first saw the squadron, to
alarm us and our convoy. We made signal to our convoy
that an Enemy was in sight. They all bore up for our convoy
but one 74 which chaced us and came up with us very fast.
We were so deep we could not sail until we stoved 9 butts of
water and pumped it out, and cut the boats adrift. Besides
all, there was a very heavy squall came, and we had all sails

set were very near going down. She laid down on her beam ends for several minutes. We are all jolly and hearty thank God, but I believe the convoy are taken, though we saved ourselves. We was obliged to run for it. We depended on our sailing, she is a famous ship for sailing, not many ships come up with her . . .

We joined Lord Nelson on 13th, and we are now going to Malta with 150 casks of Dollars each containing 5000. That is a good sum for the Soldiers at Malta; another frigate is going with us with as many Dollars on board. It is beautiful to see Lord Nelson's Fleet. I hope I shall be able to give you more account of them when I have been longer with them. How are the rabbits and Ponto and Scug? . . .

I am able to stand a sailor's life, and I hope to conduct myself as an Officer in the British Navy. Do not fret about me, for if you cared no more for the French than I, you would care very little about them. Give my love to my Father Brothers and Sisters. Success to William and his rabbits.

Dear Mother I remain
Your ever affectionate Son
CHARLES NEWBOLT

It was at about this time that Nelson wrote to his wealthy friend and prize agent, Alexander Davison, forecasting his last battle. They had first met in Canada in 1782, when Nelson was appointed to the North American Squadron. Thereafter they remained in regular correspondence. At his own expense Davison struck medals for all the officers and men who had served at the Battle of the Nile and loaned Nelson sufficient money for him to buy Merton Place. He also acted as confidant and family go-between during the disintegration of Nelson's marriage to Fanny Nelson.

Day by day, my dear friend, I am expecting the Fleet to put to sea – every day, hour and moment; and you may rely that if it is the power of man to get at them, that it shall be done; and I am sure all my bretheren [sic] look to that day as the finish of our laborious cruise. The event no man can say exactly; but I must think, or render great injustice to those under me, that, let the Battle be when it may, it will never have been surpassed. My shattered frame, if I survive that day, will require rest, and that is all I shall ask for. If I fall on such a glorious occasion, it shall be my pride to take care that my friends shall not blush for me. These things are in the hands of wise and just Providence, and His will be done! I have got some trifle, thank God, to leave to those I hold most dear, and I have taken care not to neglect it. Do not think I am low-spirited on this account, or fancy anything is to happen to me; quite the contrary – my mind is calm, and I have only to think of destroying our inveterate foe. I have two frigates gone for more information, and we all hope for meeting the Enemy. Nothing can be finer than the Fleet under my command.

THE NELSON TOUCH

For Nelson, the sole purpose of all this preparation and activity was to execute his plan to bring the Combined Fleet to battle and destruction. As he told Rose:

I verily believe the Country will soon be put to some expense for my account, either a Monument, or a new Pension and Honours; for I have not the smallest doubt but that in a very few days, almost hours, will put us in Battle . . . it is as Mr Pitt knows, annihilation that the country wants. And not merely a splendid Victory of twenty three to thirty six, honourable to the parties concerned, but absolutely useless in the extended scale to bring Buonaparte to his marrow bones: numbers only can annihilate.

Nelson's tactics for the attack were the culmination of his naval experience. The basic concept was to secure the weather gauge and then to attack the enemy centre and rear with two divisions (he did not have enough ships for three), thus overwhelming them with superior numbers while leaving their vanguard untouched. He believed that by the time the van had turned around to help, the battle would have been decided. The various elements of the plan had evolved gradually in his mind. Individually they were probably not revolutionary, but united under his particular style of leadership they might as well have been. The key elements were that the order of sailing would be the order of battle, complete control would be given to his second in command – a remarkable sign of trust – and a fail-safe instruction that no captain would be failing in his duty if he came alongside an enemy ship. Attributes included efficient ship handling, close mutual support and good gunnery. This would bring about his fast and furious 'pell-mell' battle, where the superior speed of British gunnery would make its mark.

Crucially, these tactics were tailored explicitly to his enemy. He had calculated the specific risks. For instance, ramming his fleet into the enemy line seriously exposed his lead ships to multiple broadsides, which they would be unable to return. At long range both ships and guns would outnumber them. However, as they got closer the firepower would reduce since the enemy could not swivel their guns enough to hold their targets. Moreover, Nelson knew that their gunnery was poor and that they would aim at the sails and rigging rather than fire at the hulls; they had poor communications and their commander in chief was demoralized. All this would help to even the odds but he also knew he had to inspire confidence in his captains. He outlined these ideas during the Great Cabin meetings with his captains, and on 1 October described the reaction to Lady Hamilton:

> When I came to explain to them the 'Nelson touch', it was like an electric shock. Some shed tears, all approved; 'it was new – it was singular – it was simple!'; and, from Admirals downwards, it was repeated – 'It must succeed if ever they

will let us get at them! You are my Lord surrounded by
friends whom you inspire with confidence.'

On 9 October, and resigned to the inferior numbers of his fleet,
Nelson distilled his thoughts into written instructions, which he
addressed to all his captains. They foreshadowed the actual events
quite closely, apart from the number of ships available to him, which
ruled out forming the third division, which he described as the
Advance Squadron.

(Secret.)   VICTORY, off Cadiz, 9th October, 1805.
Memorandum.
Thinking it almost impossible to bring a Fleet of forty
Sail of the Line into a Line of Battle in variable winds,
thick weather, and other circumstances which must occur;
without such loss of time, that the opportunity would
probably be lost of bringing the Enemy to Battle in such a
manner as to make the business decisive, I have therefore
made up my mind to keep the Fleet in that position of
sailing (with the exception of the First and Second in
Command), that the Order of Sailing is to be the Order of
Battle; placing the Fleet in two lines of sixteen Ships each,
with an Advanced Squadron of eight of the fastest sailing
Two-decked Ships, whichever line the Commander in Chief
may direct.

The Second in Command will, after my intentions are
made known to him, have the entire direction of his line to
make the attack upon the Enemy, and to follow up the blow
until they are captured or destroyed.

If the Enemy's Fleet should be seen to windward in Line of
Battle, and that the two Lines and the Advanced Squadron
could fetch them; they will probably be so extended, that
their Van could not succour their Rear.

I should therefore probably make the Second in
Command's signal to lead through, about their twelfth Ship

from the Rear, (or wherever he could fetch, if not able to get so far advanced): my Line would lead through about their Centre, and the Advanced Squadron to cut two or three or four Ships a-head of their Centre, to ensure getting at their Commander in Chief; on whom every effort must be made to capture.

The whole impression of the British Fleet must be to overpower from two or three Ships a-head of their Commander in Chief, supposed to be in the Centre, to the Rear of their Fleet. I will suppose twenty Sail of the Enemy's Line to be untouched, it must be some time before they could perform a manoeuvre to bring their force compact, to attack any part of the British Fleet engaged, or to succour their own Ships, which indeed would be impossible without mixing with the Ships engaged.

Something must be left to chance; nothing is sure in a Sea Fight beyond all others. Shot will carry away the masts and yards of friends as well as foes; but I look with confidence to a Victory before the Van of the Enemy could succour the Rear, and then that the British Fleet would most of them be ready to receive their Twenty Sail of the Line, or to pursue them, should they endeavour to make off.

If the Van of the Enemy tacks, the Captured Ships must run to leeward of the British Fleet; if the Enemy wears, the British must place themselves between the Enemy and the Captured and disabled British Ships; and should the Enemy close, I have no fears as to the result.

The Second in Command will in all possible things direct the movements of his Line, by keeping them as compact as the nature of circumstances will admit. Captains are to look to their particular Line, as their rallying point. But in case Signals cannot be neither seen or perfectly understood, no Captain can do very wrong, if he places his Ship alongside that of an Enemy.

Of the intended attack from the windward, the Enemy in Line of Battle ready to receive an attack,

Sail 8	_____	Advanced Squadron	
Sail 16	_____	Weather Line	} British
Sail 16	_____	Lee Line	

_____ Enemy _____ 43 sail

The divisions of the British Fleet will be brought nearly within gun shot of the Enemy's Centre. The signal will most probably then be made for the Lee Line to bear up together, to set all their sails, even their steering sails, in order to get as quickly as possible to the Enemy's Line, and to cut through, beginning at the 12 Ship from the Enemy's Rear. Some Ships may not get through their exact place, but they will always be at hand to assist friends; and if they are thrown round the Rear of the Enemy, they will effectually complete the business of twelve Sail of the Enemy.

Should the Enemy wear together, or bear up and sail large, still the twelve Ships composing, in the first position, the Enemy's rear, are to be the object of attack of the Lee Line; unless otherwise directed from the Commander in Chief, which is scarcely to be expected, as the entire management of the Lee Line, after the intentions of the Commander in Chief is [are] signified, is intended to be left to the Admiral commanding that Line.

The remainder of the Enemy's Fleet, 34 Sail, are to be left to the management of the Commander in Chief, who will endeavour to take care that the movements of the Second in Command are as little interrupted as possible.
NELSON & BRONTE

Nelson was giving his second in command, Collingwood, considerable responsibility and freedom of action. Such delegation was unusual, but distinguished Nelson from his peers. It was inspired. Collingwood would not feel he had been pushed aside while Nelson took all the glory. In fact he considered that he and Nelson had made the plan 'together', which not only gave him a feeling of ownership but also committed him to it fully. Collingwood was expected to discuss the plan with his captains, which he did. This exemplifies Nelson's leadership skills, underpinned by his understanding of human psychology. His covering letter to Collingwood portrays his acumen brilliantly:

> My dear Coll,
> I send you my Plan of Attack so far as a man dare venture
> to guess at the very uncertain position the enemy may be
> found in. But, my dear friend, it is to place you perfectly
> at ease respecting my intentions, and to give full scope
> to your judgement for carrying them into effect. We can,
> my dear Coll, have no little jealousies. We have only one
> great object in view, that of annihilating our enemies, and
> getting a glorious Peace for our Country. No man has more
> confidence in another than I have in you; and no man will
> render your services more justice than your very old friend,
> NELSON & BRONTE

On 10 October Collingwood shifted his flag from the slow-sailing *DREADNOUGHT* to the newly refitted and faster *ROYAL SOVEREIGN*. 'I am sure you will admire her as a far better Ship than the *VICTORY*,' wrote Nelson, 'You need not hurry yourself, but change at your leisure'.

'RELY ON YOUR COURAGE!'

In Cadiz, Admiral Villeneuve was contemplating the nature of the Nelson Touch, although he did not know of the phrase. He had begun his final preparations on 1 October with the intelligence, provided by Admiral Gravina, that Nelson had joined the British fleet with four sail of the line and that he was considering an incendiary attack to destroy the Combined Fleet at anchor. This was remarkably accurate, except that Nelson, having considered the use of Congreve rockets, favoured starving the enemy to force them out to sea where he could be certain of annihilating them. Villeneuve believed this too. Moreover, with extraordinary prescience he informed his captains that:

> The British Fleet will not be formed in a line of battle parallel with the Combined Fleet, according to the usage of former days, engaging us in an artillery duel. Nelson will seek to break our line, envelop our rear, and overpower with groups of his ships as many of ours as he can isolate or cut off.

Surprisingly this is as far as he went. He proposed no method of countering the British tactics. He contented himself, 'for reasons of prudence,' as he put it to Decrès, with an order of battle, according to the drill book, which everyone would understand. Therefore if the Combined Fleet was too leeward of the British it would form in close line ahead, await the attack, and do its best to beat it off. Once the battle opened, every captain would have to look out for himself, and trust to his own efforts. 'All your efforts,' Villeneuve insisted,

> must be to assist one another, and, as far as possible, follow the movements of your admiral. You must be careful not to waste ammunition by long-range firing; wait and fight only at close quarters. At the same time you must, each captain, rely rather on your own courage and ardour for glory than on the admiral's signals. In the smoke and turmoil of battle an admiral can see very little himself; often he cannot make any signals at all.

These words were lifted directly from his *Ordre pour l'Armée* issued when he took command of the fleet at Toulon. Captain Jean Lucas of the *Redoubtable* (74) remarked sarcastically, 'Thus far in advance, it would seem, did the admiral foresee the manner in which we were actually attacked in the battle.' An unidentified Spanish admiral, reputed to be an officer of high professional eminence and character, was moved to highlight how the allies' adherence to regulations stifled initiative:

An Englishman enters a naval action with a firm conviction that it is his duty to hurt his enemies, and help his friends and allies, without looking out for directions in the midst of the fight; and while he thus clears his mind of all subsidiary distractions, he rests in confidence of the certainty that his comrades, actuated by the same principles as himself, will be bound by the sacred and priceless law of mutual support. Accordingly, both he and all his fellows fix their minds on acting with zeal and judgement upon the spur of the moment, and with the certainty that they will not be deserted.

Experience shows, on the contrary, that a Frenchman or Spaniard, working under a system which leans to formality and strict order being maintained in battle, has no feeling for mutual support, and goes into action with hesitation, preoccupied with the anxiety of seeing or hearing the commander-in-chief's signals for such and such manoeuvres. Thus they can never make up their minds to seize any favourable opportunity that may present itself. They are fettered by the strict rule to keep station, which is enforced upon them in both navies; and the usual result is that in one place ten of their ships may be firing upon four, while in another four of their comrades may be receiving the fire of ten of the enemy. Worst of all, they are denied the confidence inspired by mutual support, which is as surely maintained by the English as it is neglected by us.

There were other problems. Villeneuve wanted to put to sea at the first opportunity. However, strong westerly winds made it virtually impossible. Nevertheless, he was determined to do so the moment the wind changed, even though his allies, who understood the weather conditions on the Andalusian coast, advised him against it. Unable to move, Villeneuve decided to call a Council of War on his flagship *Bucentaure*. It did not go well. His decision to put to sea at the very first opportunity perturbed the Spanish. They knew that the falling barometer at this time of year heralded the approach of the October gales. The French responded with sarcasm: Admiral Magon used words that could only offend the honour of the Spanish officers, and Commodore Galiano laid his hand on his sword. A challenge to a duel was narrowly avoided, but tempers did not remain cool for long. The courtly, even-tempered Admiral Gravina was riled by Villeneuve's words and implied that only a woman would think of sailing at this time, adding, 'Do you not see sir, that the barometer is falling?' 'It is not the glass,' interrupted Villeneuve, 'but the courage of certain persons that is falling.' Gravina let forth. 'Admiral', he said, 'whenever the Spanish fleet has gone into action, side by side with allies, as has often happened, it has ever borne its part valiantly and led the way, the foremost under fire. This sir, as you yourself must admit, we fully proved to you at the recent battle of Finisterre.' Commodore Churruca stood up, and in an angry raised voice, added, 'Have we not all seen in the recent battle, the French fleet standing by, as passive spectators of the capture of our *San Rafael* and *Firme*, doing nothing, and making no serious attempt at rescue?' Eventually things calmed down and a compromise was reached. The Combined Fleet would move down to the mouth of the harbour and be ready to sail when the bad weather was over, and they placed on record that 'the vessels of both nations were for the most part badly equipped, that a portion of the crews had never been trained at sea, and that, in short, the fleet was not in a state to perform the services appointed to it'.

The Times correspondent in Cadiz was well informed. On 11 October the report from Cadiz stated that:

> **Admiral Gravina loudly accuses Villeneuve of treachery in**
> **the late action, and has solicited leave to resign. Between**

the sailors animosities have arisen to the highest pitch, and
scarce a night passes but the dead bodies of assassinated
Frenchmen are found in the streets.

While the French and Spanish sought to settle their differences and
waited for the gales, which blew from 10 October for seven days, to
abate, Captain Frances Austen was writing to his betrothed from the
CANOPUS at sea, off Gibraltar.

My dearest Mary,
Having now got over the hurry and bustle which
unavoidably attends every ship while in the act of
compleating provisions, water and stores, I think it
high time to devote some part of my attention to your
amusement, and to be in a state of preparation for any
opportunity which may offer of dispatching letters to
England. But in order to make myself understood I must
endeavour to be methodical, and therefore shall commence
the account I have now to send you from the date of my
last, which was finished and forwarded by the *NIMBLE* brig
on the 2nd of this month. We had then just joined the fleet
from the in-shore squadron, and, I believe I mentioned,
were about to quit it again for Gibraltar and Tetuan. We
sailed that evening with four other ships of the line, a
frigate, and five merchant vessels under convoy, and on the
following morning fell in with the *EURYALUS*, which we
had left off Cadiz to watch the enemy. Captain Blackwood
informed us by signal that he had received information by a
Swedish ship from Cadiz that the troops had all embarked
on board the men-of-war, and it was reported they were to
sail with the first easterly wind. Though much confidence
could not be placed on the accuracy and authenticity of
this intelligence, it was, however, of such a nature as to
induce Admiral Louis to return with four of the ships to
Lord Nelson, leaving the *ZEALOUS* and *ENDYMION* (both

of them crippled ships) to proceed with the convoy to Gibraltar. We rejoined the Commander-in-Chief on the morning of the 5th, and were again dispatched in the course of the day.

The wind being directly against us, and blowing very strong, we were not able to reach Gibraltar until the 9th, when every exertion was made to get on board such supplies of stores and provisions as we were in want of, and the Rock could supply. This was effected in three days, at which time the wind changed to the westward and became favourable for our watering at Tetuan, where we anchored on the evening of the 12th. We sailed again last night to return to the fleet, having got on board in the course of two days, with our own boats alone, 300 tons of water, and every other ship had got a proportionate quantity. You will judge from this that we have not been idle. We are now expecting a wind to take us out of the Mediterranean again, and hope to accomplish it in the course of the next twenty-four hours; at present it is nearly calm, but appearances indicate an easterly wind. We are, of course, very anxious to get back to the fleet for fear the enemy should be moving, for the idea of their doing so while we are absent is by no means pleasant. Having borne our share in a tedious chace and anxious blockade, it would be mortifying indeed to find ourselves at last thrown out of any share of credit or emolument which would result from an action. Such, I hope, will not be our lot, though, if they do venture out at all, it must happen to some one, as a part of the fleet will be constantly sent in to compleat as fast as the others arrive from having performed that duty . . .

He continued:

The hopes with which I had flattered myself of getting out of the Straits two days ago have not been realised, and, from the circumstances which have since occurred, it is very uncertain when we shall get to the fleet again. The wind on the evening of the 15th came to the westward and forced us back to Tetuan, where we remained till yesterday evening, at which time a frigate came over with orders for Admiral Louis to give protection to a convoy then collected at Gibraltar for Malta, as far as Cartagena, after which he is to return to the Commander-in-Chief. We accordingly came over to the Rock this morning, and are now proceeding fast as possible with the trade to the eastward. Our force consists of five sail of the line and three frigates, which last we shall leave in charge of the convoy as soon as we have seen them safe past the Carthagena squadron. I can't say I much like the prospect. I do not expect to derive any advantage from it, and it puts us completely out of the way in case the enemy should make an attempt to get to sea, which is by no means improbable, if he knows Lord Nelson's force is weakened by the detachment of so many ships.

Friday 18 October was a crucial day for Villeneuve. He heard rumours that his intended replacement, Vice Admiral François Etienne Rosily, had reached Madrid. He had written to Decrès:

> I shall be happy to yield the first place to Rosily, if I am allowed to have the second; but it will be too hard to have to give up all hope of being vouchsafed the opportunity of proving that I am worthy of a better fate.

In the hope of redeeming his reputation by following Napoleon's instructions before Rosily arrived, Villeneuve ordered the fleet to sail the next day. He tried to get out of harbour by sunset, but once more at the last moment the wind failed him. It dropped and died away to an almost dead calm. Commander Bazin of the *Fougueux* (74) reported to Decrès:

On 26 Vendémiaire, Year XIV [18 October] at 5 o'clock in the evening, Admiral Villeneuve, commanding the Combined Fleet, gave the signal to cast off and to successively hoist the boats, prepare to make sail, and to send an officer for orders. The wind at the time was from the west. The *Fougueux* was moored between the forts of Puerto Real and Puntalés and was therefore too far up the bay to make sail easily.

Rear Admiral Don Antonio Escano, Chief of Staff to Admiral Gravina and captain of the *Principe de Asturias* (112), also reported the occasion:

> I know that by the last mail General Gravina sent an account, dated October 18, in which he informed your Excellency that Admiral Villeneuve had made it clear that he had decided to sail the next day and that he had wished to know if the Spanish fleet was able to fulfil its role. Your Excellency is not unaware of the General's reply which, in short, was that his squadron was ready, assembled, and would follow the movements of the French, this being in accordance with the successive orders your Excellency had communicated. With this understanding the French Admiral went back to his ship and then signalled to weigh anchor and haul in boats. These signals were immediately acknowledged by the ship and were followed by the issue of most strict and urgent orders to recall pickets and to embark those artillerymen and sailors who for various reasons were on shore.

The sense of immediacy was frustrated by light airs, and it was not until the early hours of the following morning that the French and Spanish ships began to make their way out of the harbour into Cadiz Bay.

'THE ENEMY ARE COMING OUT!'

Nelson relied upon Captain Henry Blackwood and his little squadron of frigates to keep vigil over the stretch of five miles between Cadiz and Cape San Sebastian and to let him know every movement so that he would not 'miss getting hold of them'. He was going to 'give them such a shaking as they have never yet experienced'. At dawn on Saturday 19 October 1805 the chain of British frigates that stretched westward from Cadiz, 'masthead to masthead', announced to Nelson's fleet 50 miles away that the Combined Fleet was getting under sail. Captain Sir Home Riggs Popham's new telegraphic signal flags (see page 137) repeated the message.

William Wilkinson, the sailing master of the *SIRIUS* (36), recorded in his log:

> Observed the Enemy in Cadiz with their topsail yards up, preparing for sea. Made the signal for do. by telegraph.

From *SIRIUS*:

6.40 a.m.	Signal 249:	Enemy
	Signal 354:	have
	Signal 864:	their
	Signal 875:	top
	Signal 756:	sail
	Signal 986:	yards
	Signal 1374:	hoisted

> 7.00 a.m. Signal No 370: Enemy's ships are coming out of port.

Frederick Ruckert, Master of the *EURYALUS*, recorded in his log:

> At daylight observed the enemy's ships in Cadiz with topgallant yards across, and eight ships having their topsails

hoisted to the mastheads. At 7, saw the northernmost ships under way. At 7.20 dispatched the *PHOEBE* to repeat signals between us and the English fleet. At 8, saw 19 of the enemy under way.

From *EURYALUS*:

7.10 a.m. Signal No 108: Close nearer the Admiral.

EURYALUS to *PHOEBE* (36):

7.20 a.m. Signal No 370: Enemy are coming out of port.

PHOEBE to *MARS*:

Signal No 370: Enemy are coming out of port.

MARS to *VICTORY*:

Signal No 370: Enemy are coming out of port.

VICTORY to Fleet:

9.30 a.m. General chase, south east.

Nelson was directing his fleet towards the Gut, as the Strait of Gibraltar was known, to prevent the Combined Fleet from sailing into the Mediterranean.

Eighteen-year-old Midshipman Hercules Robinson from Dublin was aboard the *EURYALUS* and captured the flurry of signalling and general elation in his journal. Fellow Midshipman William Henry Bruce was two years younger than Robinson and eventually reached Admiral. Isaac Soper, aged 28, was listed as the Coxswain and came from Exeter:

The morning of the 19th October saw us and our inshore
squadron so close to Cadiz as to see the ripple on the beach
and catch the morning fragrance which came off the land;
and then as the sun rose over the Trocadero with what joy
we saw the fleet inside let fall and hoist their topsails, and
one after another slowly emerge from the harbour's mouth!
Blackwood threw out his frigates – *HYDRA, NAIAD, PHOEBE*
and *SIRIUS* – between our ship and our fleet twenty leagues
to the westward, and for two days there was not a movement
we did not communicate, until I thought that Blackwood,
who gave the orders, and Bruce, our signal Mid., and Soper,
our signalman who executed them, must have died of it.

Blackwood also ordered Bruce to signal the brig-sloop *WEAZLE*
to come within hail so he could order her to run immediately to
warn Rear Admiral Louis, who he hoped was on his way back from
escorting the Malta convoy, but was in fact still sailing eastwards
with it. As the *WEAZLE* parted company Soper hauled up signal
122: 'Make all possible sail with safety to masts'. This was followed
by signal 87: 'Let one reef out of topsails', to emphasize the need for
speed. Another officer aboard the *BELLEROPHON* was thinking of
Louis's ships as reinforcements when he described the excitement
that the news stirred:

We were not long kept in that state of anxiety and suspense,
which you will naturally suppose everyone in our situation
must have felt, for about nine o'clock in the morning of
the 19th October, the *MARS* was observed firing guns and
making signals for the enemy's fleet being getting under
weigh. The Admiral immediately made signal for the
general chase, and to clear for action, which was obeyed
with the greatest alacrity, and in ten minutes the whole fleet
was under sail, steering for the Straits, which was supposed
to be the enemy's destination, for the purpose of forming a
junction with the Carthagena and Toulon squadrons.

The general air of expectancy was for a battle the following day and the thoughts of many turned to their loved ones, getting home and the prospect of prize money. Blackwood, who had still to keep a close watch on the direction of the Combined Fleet, found time to write an optimistic letter to his wife Harriet:

> What think you my own dearest love? At this moment the Enemy are coming out, and as if determined to have a fair fight; all night they had been making signals, and the morning showed them to us getting under sail. They have thirty-four sail of the line, and five Frigates. Lord Nelson I'm sorry to say has but twenty-seven Sail of the Line with him; the rest are at Gibraltar, getting water. Not that he has not enough to bring them to close Action; but I want him to have so many as to make this the most decisive battle that was ever fought, and which will bring us a lasting Peace, I hope, and some prize-money.
>
> Within two hours, though our Fleet was sixteen leagues off, I have let Lord N. know of their coming out, and have been enabled to send a vessel to Gibraltar, which will bring Admiral Louis and the ships there.
>
> At this moment (happy sight) we are within four miles of the Enemy, and talking to Lord Nelson by means of Sir H. Popham's signals, though so distant, but repeated along by the rest of the Frigates of this Squadron.
>
> You see also, my Harriet, I have time to write to you, and to assure you that to the last moment of my breath, I shall be as much attached to you as man can be, which I am sure you will credit. It is very odd how I have been dreaming all night of my carrying home despatches. God send me such good luck! The day is fine, and the sight magnificently beautiful. I expect, before this hour tomorrow, to have carried General Decrès on board *VICTORY* in my barge, which I have just painted nicely for him. God bless you. No more at present.

A posthumous portrait of Nelson by Arthur William Devis (1805) used for Edward Scriven's engraving and frontispiece to Dr William Beatty's Authentic Narrative of the Death of Nelson. *Nelson is wearing his undress 'Trafalgar coat'.*

Lieutenant John Richard Lapenotiere (1770–1834), captain of the PICKLE, *which brought back the official news of the battle and the death of Nelson. He was later rewarded with £500, a Lloyd's Patriotic Fund sword and promotion to Commander.*

'The Right Hon. Lord Barham' was appointed by Prime Minister William Pitt in April 1805 as First Lord of the Admiralty. It was an inspired choice. He chose Nelson to lead the Mediterranean fleet and was in many ways the architect of Trafalgar.

Vice Admiral Pierre Comte de Villeneuve (1763–1805) joined the French navy when he was 15. He was friends with Napoleon's Minister of Marine, Decrès, and had seen Nelson in action before at the Battle of the Nile. He had an uncanny prescience of Nelson's tactics at Trafalgar.

BELOW British seamen were masters of their trade. 'Reefing Topsails' shows seamen on a yard shortening sail in a gale. The studding sail boom is lashed to the shrouds to keep it out of the way. Sail handling was fast – shifting topsails could be done in less than ten minutes.

REEFING TOPSAILS.

Captain George Duff (1764–1805) was Captain of the MARS. He was decapitated at Trafalgar by a broadside from the French Fougueux. This Scotsman met Nelson for the first time in September 1805 and was so impressed that he said that he would gladly follow him even without orders. His memorial is close to Nelson's tomb in St Paul's Cathedral.

Vice Admiral Cuthbert Lord Collingwood (1748–1810). Dispatched in 1805 to blockade Spanish ships at Cadiz he found himself under Nelson's command a few weeks before the battle, and succeeded him as Commander-in-Chief. Here he wears full dress uniform and his medals for the Battles of the Glorious First of June and Cape St Vincent.

Captain Sir Edward Berry (1768–1831). Nelson's flag captain in the VANGUARD at the Battle of the Nile, he commanded Nelson's favourite ship – the AGAMEMNON – at Trafalgar. He had been in more fleet actions than any captain in the service and had a lucky reputation, hence Nelson's gleeful remark, 'Here comes Berry! Now we shall have a battle.'

Captain Henry Blackwood (1770–1832) of the EURYALUS commanded the frigate squadron that kept watch over the Combined Fleet in Cadiz prior to the battle of Trafalgar. Among his accomplishments are taking his frigate into the thick of the battle, bringing Villeneuve back to England and being train-bearer to the chief mourner at Nelson's funeral.

'Lord Viscount Nelson, Duke of Bronte' in the undress uniform he wore when shot. Contrary to popular belief, Nelson did not wear an eye patch, instead using his hat to shade his good eye from the sun's glare. William Davis, painted the picture from which this engraving is taken, after his visit to VICTORY in December 1805, when he was shown Nelson's body.

Surgeon William Beatty, seen here wearing the Physician's Full Dress Uniform, published the most famous account of the death of Nelson in 1806. He carried out the autopsy, retrieved the fatal ball that had killed Nelson, and left one of the most lucid early descriptions of traumatic paraplegia. He was knighted in 1831.

Captain Jean-Jacques Lucas (1764–1819), captain of the Redoubtable, was a diminutive man with great determination. He was made an officer after the Revolution and was presented to the Emperor in April 1806. He used his time at Cadiz wisely, training his crew in both small arms and boarding tactics.

Captain John Cooke (1763–1805) was killed by musket balls during the battle. A successful and hardened frigate captain he commanded the BELLEROPHON with independent thought and initiative. By coincidence he was an old and close friend of George Duff, the only other captain to be killed at Trafalgar.

HORACIO NELSON
Barab. de Nilo Visconde de Nelson Duque de Bronte Vice Almirante.

Nelson was famous enough in Spain for pictures to be produced of him, as is shown by this contemporary engraving of 'Horacio Nelson'. He had visited Cadiz before Spain allied herself with France and was respected by his Spanish adversaries.

In March 1806 artist Robert Dodd published four coloured aquatints of the battle. They were taken from his two panorama paintings; joined the aquatints recreate the panoramas. This one illustrates 'the attack'. It is a little after noon and the British fleet, which is viewed from the rear, is bearing down on the Combined Fleet to the north-east. The weather column is to the left. The white ensign is being worn by both columns as Nelson ordered. The earlier picture published by Dodd shows Collingwood's ships wearing the blue ensign according to his rank. The second panorama illustrates 'the victory'.

BELOW This early engraving of the battle shows the Achille *on fire, the great four-deck* Santissima Trinidad *alongside* VICTORY, *and the* PICKLE *in the centre picking up survivors. The* Santissima Trinidad *was not alongside* VICTORY *at the end of the battle, but the artist believed that Nelson had chosen to engage her because she was the most prominent enemy ship.*

LEFT This oil painting depicts VICTORY, Redoubtable, TÉMÉRAIRE *and* Fougueux *locked in a lethal embrace on a crest of the Atlantic swell. Nelson's last signal, 'Engage the enemy more closely', still flies from* VICTORY'*s mainmast. It is about 2.30pm and to the right the* ROYAL SOVEREIGN *and* Santa Ana *are still battering each other.*

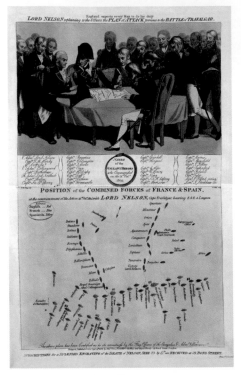

'England expects every man to do his duty: Lord Nelson explaining to the officers the Plan of Attack previous to the Battle of Trafalgar' and 'Position of the Combined Forces of France and Spain at the Commencement of the Action'. This engraving by James Godby was published by Edward Orme on the day of Nelson's funeral. It shows all the Trafalgar captains and the plan was certified as accurate by 'the Flag Officers of the EURYALUS and Vice Admiral Villeneuve'.

A watercolour from the journal of William Pringle Green, a Master's Mate in the CONQUEROR, showing the 'forest of masts' of the Combined Fleet blockaded in Cadiz harbour a short while before the battle.

Edward Codrington had to wait until the evening to write to his wife and was feeling tired. There was little privacy, since the *ORION* had cleared for action, the bulkheads had been removed and his cabin was opened up to the rest of the ship.

> How would your heart beat for me, dearest Jane, did you but know that we are now under every stitch of sail we can set, steering for the enemy. We have now a nice air, which fills our flying kites and drives us along four knots an hour.
>
> I trust by the morning we shall be united and in sight of the enemy. As to my coming out of the battle alive or dead, that is the affair of chance and the little cherub: but that I shall come out with dishonour is my affair; and yet I have but little apprehension about the matter, so great is my confidence in my ship, and our excellent Admiral.
>
> It is not my dear Jane, that I am insensible to the value of life with such a domestic circle as I belong to: no, my heart was never more alive to the sacrifice than at this very moment. But life in such a situation as this, even with the delightful prospect of returning to pass years in the society of a wife and children whom I love with a religious reverence, is really but a secondary consideration.
>
> I feel a little tired; and as now have nothing to do but keep the ship's head the right way, and take care that the sails are well trimmed, in readiness for the morning, I shall even make that over to the officer of the watch and go to my cot; nor do I think I shall sleep the worse for my cabin being only divided from the quarter-deck by a boat's sail. And so, dear, I shall wish thee once more a good night, and that thy husband's conduct in the hour of battle may prove worthy of thee and my children.

About noon Lord Nelson sat down to write to his daughter, Horatia. For the last few years he had addressed her as his 'goddaughter', but in his last letter to her he dropped the pretence.

My Dearest Angel.
I was made happy by the pleasure of receiving your letter
of September 19th, and I rejoice to hear that you are so very
good a girl, and love my dear Lady Hamilton, who most
dearly loves you. Give her a kiss for me. The Combined
Fleets of the Enemy are now reported to be coming out
of Cadiz; and therefore I answer your letter, my dearest
Horatia, to mark to you that you are ever uppermost in
my thoughts. I shall be sure of your prayers for my safety,
conquest, and speedy return to dear Merton, and our
dearest good Lady Hamilton. Be a good girl; mind what
Miss Connor says to you. Receive, my dearest Horatia, the
affectionate parental blessing of your Father,
NELSON & BRONTE

Although Horatia accepted that Nelson was her father for the rest of
her life (she died in 1881), she denied that she was Emma's daughter.
Even her gravestone in Pinner originally carried the inscription 'the
adopted Daughter of Vice Admiral Lord Nelson'. Nelson would have
wished otherwise but the thought was not on his mind when, 16
leagues from Cadiz, he wrote to:

My dearest beloved Emma, the dear friend of my bosom,
The signal has been made that the enemy's Combined Fleet
are coming out of Port. We have very little wind, so that I
have no hopes of seeing them before tomorrow. May the
God of Battles crown my endeavours with success: at all
events, I will take care that my name shall ever be most dear
to you and Horatia, both of whom I love as much as my own
life. And as my last writing before the battle will be to you,
so I hope in God that I shall live to finish my letter after the
battle. May heaven bless you, prays your
NELSON & BRONTE

On 20 October he added a postscript:

In the morning, we were close to the Mouth of the Straits, but the wind had not come far enough to the Westward to allow the Combined Fleets to weather the Shoals of Trafalgar; but they were counted as far as forty Sail of Ships of War, which I suppose to be thirty-four of the Line, and six Frigates. A group of them was seen off the Lighthouse of Cadiz this morning, but it blows so very fresh and thick weather, that I rather believe, they will go into the Harbour before night. May God Almighty give us success over these fellows, and enable us to get back to a Peace.

This letter was found open on his desk, and was brought to Lady Hamilton by Captain Hardy, on his return to England. Nelson was in good spirits as the closing words in his last letter to Vice Admiral Collingwood indicate: 'What a beautiful day! Will you be tempted out of your ship? If you will, hoist the Assent and *VICTORY*'s pendants. Ever, my dear Coll.' Whether Collingwood was tempted or not is unknown, but he did not join his old friend. Before retiring to his cot to sleep Nelson described the disposition of his fleet in his private diary:

Fine weather, wind Easterly. At half past nine, the *MARS*, being one of the look-out ships, repeated the Signal, 'that the Enemy were coming out of Port' – made signal for a 'General Chase S.E.'; wind at south Cadiz bearing E.N.E. by compass, distant sixteen leagues. At three the *COLOSSUS*, made the Signal, 'that the Enemy's Fleet was at sea.' In the evening directed the Fleet to observe my motions during the night, and for *BRITANNIA*, *PRINCE* and *DREADNOUGHT*, they being heavy sailers, to take their stations as convenient; and for *MARS*, *ORION*, *BELLEISLE*, *LEVIATHAN*, *BELLEROPHON*, and *POLYPHEMUS*, to go ahead during the night, and to carry a light, standing for the Strait's Mouth.

As 19 October passed by, frustrations mounted as it became clear that the weather was changing for the worse, with rough seas, strong winds and heavy rain. Codrington in the *ORION* put his own anxiety on paper in another letter to Jane, his wife:

> All our gay hopes are fled; and instead of being under
> all possible sail in a very light breeze and fine weather,
> expecting to bring the enemy to battle, we are now
> under close-reefed topsails in a very strong wind with
> this rainy weather, and the dastardly French we find
> returned to Cadiz.

In fact they had not cleared Cadiz yet, apart from Rear Admiral Magon with 12 Spanish and French ships. The rest were unable to do this because the wind had backed to the south-west. Nelson was under a similar impression and remarked, 'I rather believe, they will go into the harbour before night.' In such stormy conditions his own fleet could not stay so close to the lee shore in readiness to intercept the Combined Fleet on its way to the Straits, so he changed course by 180 degrees and took his ships to the north-west. Coincidentally, he received signals that confirmed the enemy were to the north anyway or still in Cadiz, including Villeneuve. He had arrived off Cape Trafalgar a day too early!

At daylight on Sunday 20 October the remainder of the Combined Fleet weighed anchor. The walls of Cadiz and the hundreds of merchant observation towers that adorned the city skyline were packed with people watching the stately procession of ships. Many others thronged the city's churches. Most were in tears, worried for their loved ones embarking for battle. At the Iglesia del Carmen, the old mariners' church of Cadiz, the numbers were so great that people had to be allowed inside in relays. Once inside they would have seen Archbishop Utrera, on his knees before the High Altar of Oratorio de San Felipe Neri, repeatedly pleading with Heaven for the safety of the crews. It was noon before they were all at sea. Villeneuve ordered his ships to form three sailing columns. This took another four hours.

In that formation they sailed as best they could in the shifting winds and drizzling rain for the Gut. Captain Jean Lucas, in command of the *Redoubtable,* takes up the story:

> On the 28th Vendémiaire An XIV [20 October 1805] the Combined fleet got under sail to leave Cadiz Bay. The wind was southerly; light at first, afterwards fresh. The fleet comprised thirty-three sail of the Line, of which eighteen were French, fifteen Spanish; with five frigates and two brigs French. We were hardly outside when the wind shifted to the south west and came on to blow strong. The admiral then ordered the fleet to reef sail, which was done, though some Spanish ships were so slow over it that they fell considerably to leeward. Some time was lost by that, but at length all worked back again, and then the fleet stood on, in no regular formation, heading to the west-north-west. The *Redoubtable* was next astern to the *Bucentaure,* and a short distance off, when towards noon, the flagship suddenly signalled 'Man overboard!' I brought to at once, lowered a boat, picked the man up, and regained my station.
>
> An hour after midday the wind shifted to the west, and the fleet went about all together. As soon as that was done, the *Bucentaure* signalled for the battle-squadron to form in three columns on the starboard tack, flagships in the centre of their divisions. In this order of sailing the *Redoubtable,* as leader of the first division, should have been at the head of her column, and I manoeuvred the ship to take that post. All the afternoon, however, was spent without the fleet being able to get into the formation designated, although the admiral kept signalling repeatedly to ships to take station.

The Franco-Spanish fleet knew that at least 18 British sail were threateningly close and Villeneuve was in his cabin trying to justify his position in a letter to Decrès:

They have signalled to me that eighteen of the enemy
are in sight . . . In leaving port I have only consulted my
anxious desire to conform to the wishes of His Majesty,
and to do everything in my power to remove that feeling of
dissatisfaction with which he has regarded the events of my
previous cruise.

Villeneuve detached some of his faster sailers under Gravina to
drive off the British frigates, but it was becoming increasingly clear
to everyone that, weather permitting, there would be a battle the
following day. Dr William Beatty's *An Authentic Narrative of the Death of
Lord Nelson*, published in 1806, described how:

In the afternoon the wind increased, and blew fresh from
the south-west; which excited much apprehension on board
the *VICTORY*, lest the Enemy might be forced to return to
port. The look-out ships, however, made several signals for
seeing them, and to report their force and bearings. His
Lordship was at this time on the poop; and turning round,
and observing a group of Midshipmen assembled together,
he said to them with a smile, 'This day or to-morrow will be
a fortunate one for you, young men,' alluding to their being
promoted in the event of a victory.

He made a similar comment to those who joined him at supper:

Tomorrow I will do that which will give you young
gentlemen something to talk and think about for the rest of
your lives, but I shall not live to know about it myself.

There was no foreboding. Nelson's only fear was that he might be
forced through the Straits by a strong westerly wind, and turned his
fleet south-west, so that for a few hours the two great fleets were
sailing away from each other. During the failing light of the afternoon
Beatty told how Nelson:

... ordered it to be signified to Captain Blackwood by signal, that 'he depends on the *EURYALUS* for keeping sight of the Enemy during the night.' The night signals were so clearly and distinctly arranged by his Lordship, and so well understood by the respective Captains, that the Enemy's motions continued to be made known to him with the greatest facility throughout the night: a certain number of guns, with false fires and blue lights, announced their altering their course, wearing, and shortening sail; and signals communicating such changes were repeated by the look-out ships, from the *EURYALUS* to the *VICTORY*.

Nelson backed up his signal with written orders explaining the meaning of these night signals. If the Enemy were to the south or close to the Straits, they were to burn two blue lights together, every hour, 'in order to make the greater blaze'. If the enemy were to the west they were to fire three guns, 'quick, every hour'. These signals were unknown to the Combined Fleet. Jean Lucas refers to them as if they were merely a firework entertainment: 'as the evening went on', the British 'made a great many signals showing for their purpose quite a remarkable display of coloured fires'. Sixteen-year-old Royal Marine Lieutenant Paul Nichols in the *BELLEISLE* was also probably unaware of the meaning of the various signals for 'during the night, the mind was kept in continual agitation by the firing of guns and rockets', but generally they were a comfort to the British, as the 20-year-old Midshipman William Stanhope Badcock (later Lovell) of the *NEPTUNE* related:

All hearts towards evening beat with joyful anxiety for the next day, which we hoped would crown our anxious blockade labours with successful battle. When night closed in, the rockets and blue lights, with signal guns, informed us that the inshore squadron still kept sight of our foes, and, like good and watchful dogs, our ships continued to send forth occasionally a growling cannon to

keep us alert and to cheer us with a hope of a glorious day on the morrow.

Nelson commended the effectiveness of the night signals in his diary: 'At 6 o'clock *NAIAD* made the signal for 31 Sail of the Enemy N.N.E. The Frigates and look out Ships kept sight of the Enemy most admirably all night and told me by signals which tack they were upon.'

A little after nine o'clock, there was urgent alarm in the Combined Fleet. Gravina had signalled what seemed impossible. The British fleet was 'less than two miles off'! Villeneuve, haunted by Nelson's night attack at Aboukir, was stunned. He immediately made the general signal for the whole fleet to form in line of battle without regard to the stations of the individual ships. An officer aboard Gravina's flagship, *Principe de Asturias,* reported:

> At nine o'clock the English squadron made signals by firing
> guns, and, from the interval which elapsed between the
> flash and report, they must have been about two miles from
> us. We informed the French Admiral by signal-lanterns that
> it was expedient to lose no time in forming line of battle
> on the leeward ships, on which an order to that effect was
> immediately given by the Commander-in-Chief.

The clocks on the French and Spanish ships appear to have been remarkably synchronized, for Captain Jean Lucas of the French *Redoubtable* recorded that:

> About nine o'clock at night the flagship made the general
> signal to the fleet to form in the order of battle at once. To
> carry out this evolution those ships most to leeward ought
> to have shown a light at each masthead, so as to mark their
> positions. Whether this was done I do not know: at any rate
> I was unable to see such lights. At that moment, indeed, we
> were all widely scattered. The ships of the battle squadron
> and those of the squadron of observation were all mixed up.

Another cause of confusion was this. Nearly all the ships had answered the admiral's signals with flares, which made it impossible to tell which was the flagship. All I could do was follow the motions of the other ships near me, which were closing on some to leeward.

Forming a line of sailing warships in the dark was never easy, but with raw sailors and tardy and unskilled captains the Combined Fleet did it poorly. The squadrons were mixed up in several adjacent lines and individual ships were sometimes as many as three abreast. Lucas continued:

Towards eleven I discovered myself close to Admiral Gravina, who with four or five ships, was beginning to form his own line of battle. I was challenged and our name demanded, whereupon the Spanish admiral ordered me to take post in his line. I asked leave to lead it and he assented, whereupon I stood into station. The wind was in direction and force as before, and we were all still on the starboard tack. The whole fleet was by this time cleared for action (*'Branle-bas-de-combat!'*), in accordance with orders signalled from the *Bucentaure* earlier in the night. In the *Redoubtable*, however, we had cleared for action immediately after leaving Cadiz, and everything had been kept since in readiness to go to quarters instantly. With the certainty of battle the next day, I kept few men on duty during the night. I sent the greater number of the officers and crew to lie down, sending most of the officers and men to rest, so that they might be as fresh as possible for the approaching fight.

Throughout all this manoeuvring the Combined Fleet's lights were 'like a well lit up street' six miles long and this allowed some of the British frigate squadron to get very close to the enemy, sailing at about half-gunshot distance for most of the time. An officer's account from the *DEFENCE* explained how the . . .

... absence of moon, and the cloudy state of the weather,
rendered it exceedingly dark so, that we came very near
the Combined Fleet without their being able to discern us.
While we concealed every light, they continued to exhibit
such profusions of theirs, and to make night signals in
such abundance, that we seemed at times in the jaws of a
mighty host ready to swallow us up. We, however, felt no
alarm, being confident that we could fight our way or fly,
as occasion required. The former was certainly congenial to
all our feelings; yet in the face of the enemy's whole fleet, we
did not regret that our ship was a fast sailer.

Aboard the *EURYALUS*, Midshipman Hercules Robinson observed:

... when we had brought the two fleets fairly together,
we took our place between the two lines of lights, as a
cab might in Regent Street, the watch was called, and
Blackwood turned in quietly to wait for the morning.

The Earl of Northesk, third in command, with Captain Bullen,
the commanding officer of *BRITANNIA* (100), Northesk's flagship,
and the officers aboard dined hurriedly before retiring as normal
behind 'hanging screens instead of cabins'. At ten o'clock, Lord
Northesk penned a few lines to the 'Countess of Northesk', before
closing his eyes.

My dearest wife,
We have every hope of bringing the enemy to action; if I
should not survive the glorious day; take care of yourself
and my dear children and I beg you may have one [crossed
out and 'two' written above it] thousand pounds after my
death for your own use and at your own disposal beside
what I left you by will – made in Scotland and at Battle
– Believe me ever to have been your affectionate husband,
Northesk

One man, if he had known what was happening, would have been very agitated. Captain Frances Austen, Rear Admiral Thomas Louis's flag-captain and brother of the novelist Jane, was in the squadron of five ships detached to get supplies from Gibraltar. He had earlier accompanied Louis at dinner in *VICTORY*'s Great Cabin and heard Nelson declare, 'The enemy will come out, and we shall fight them; but there will be time to get back first. I look upon the *CANOPUS* as my right hand, and I send you first to insure your being here to help beat them.' Writing to his sweetheart Mary Gibson on the day of the battle, Austen sensed that he was nevertheless about to miss out:

> We have just said adieu to the convoy, without attending
> them quite as far as was originally intended, having this day
> received intelligence, by vessel despatched in pursuit of us,
> that on Saturday, 19th, the enemy's fleet was actually under
> way, and coming out of Cadiz.
>
> Our situation is peculiarly unpleasant and distressing,
> for if they escape Lord Nelson's vigilance and get into the
> Mediterranean, which is not very likely, we shall be obliged,
> with our small force, to keep out of their way; and on the
> other hand, should an action take place, it must be decided
> long before we could possibly get down even were the wind
> fair, which at present it is not. As I have but no doubt that
> the event would be highly honourable to our arms, and at
> the same time be productive of good prizes, I shall have
> to lament our absence on such an occasion on a double
> account, the loss of pecuniary advantage as well as of
> professional credit. And after having been so many months
> in a state of constant and unremitting fag, to be at last cut
> out by a parcel of folk just come from their homes, where
> some of them were sitting at their ease the greater part of
> last year, and the whole of this, till just now, is particularly
> hard and annoying.

4

THE BATTLE: 'A BEAUTIFUL MORNING'

According to Hercules Robinson in the *EURYALUS* it was 'a beautiful misty sun-shiny morning' as the sun rose above the white cliffs of Cape Trafalgar on 21 October. The rain squalls had moved on and the sun's rays had banished the strange night of blue lights and false fires. There was just a gentle breeze from the west-north-west dappling the surface of the water, which resembled the surface of a millpond. The *VICTORY* was sailing south-east before the light airs but pitching and rolling in a long heavy Atlantic swell from the west, which gave notice of an approaching storm. As the sky brightened, the first signal flags of the day were run up the main mast of the *ACHILLE*. Her captain, Richard King, had 'discovered a strange fleet'. Thomas Atkinson, *VICTORY*'s sailing master, recorded in the ship's log, 'At 6 observed the enemy E by S distance 10 or 12 miles.' Midshipman Badcock in the *NEPTUNE* close by described his experience of the occasion:

> The sun rose, which, as it ascended from its bed of ocean, looked hazy and watery, as if it smiled in tears on many brave hearts which fate had decreed would never see it set. It was my morning watch; I was midshipman on the forecastle, and at the first dawn of day a forest of strange masts was seen to leeward. I ran aft and informed the officer of the watch. The captain was on deck in a moment, and ere it was well light, the signals were flying through the fleet to bear up and form the order of sailing in two columns.

The 'joyful acclamations of the watch on deck' and the commotion aboard the various ships aroused the crews not on watch and still swinging in unison in their hammocks, and one young sleeping marine officer in the *BELLEISLE*, Lieutenant Paul Nichols:

> As the day dawned the horizon appeared covered with ships.
> The whole force of the enemy was discovered standing to
> the southward distant, about nine miles, between us and the
> coast near Trafalgar. I was awakened by the cheers of the crew
> and by their rushing up the hatchways to get a glimpse of the
> hostile fleet. The delight manifested exceeded anything I ever
> witness, surpassing even those gratulations when our native
> cliffs are descried after a long period of distant service. There
> was a light air from the north-west with a heavy swell.

Able Seaman John Brown, a 25-year-old pressed man from Waterford, Ireland, aboard Nelson's flagship, captured the moment and morale in this sentence from a letter to 'Mr Thos Windever, at the sign of the blue bell new Albs Liverpool' postmarked Rochester Dec 30. 1805:

> At daylight the french and Spanish fleets were like a great
> wood on our lee bow which cheered the hearts of every
> British tar in the *VICTORY* like lions Anxious to be at it.

Any sailors who had managed to sleep through this hullabaloo would have been woken in next to no time by the bosun's mates doing the rounds of the decks piping their Spithead Nightingales (the shrill bosun's call or whistle still used in the Royal Navy today). As the sun continued to rise in the sky, casting its light to the eastern horizon, the lookouts in the Combined Fleet began to see their adversary. The French frigate *Hermione* (40) signalled 'The enemy in sight to windward number twenty-seven sail of the line'. It is reported that the sight of the British ships had an intoxicating effect on everyone, clearing away their dull feelings of doubt and gloom and replacing them with an eager sense of purpose and excitement. As the drums struck up the

Générale, and the captains did their rounds of the ships, there were enthusiastic shouts of '*Vive l'Empereur*', '*Vive le Commandant*' and '*Vive l'Armée*' throughout the fleet. However, to Villeneuve's dismay the British fleet was stronger than he had expected, and they were to windward of him. They appeared to be scattered across the ocean and it was to take him more than an hour and a half to ascertain the British fleet's precise intentions. Fortunately, this worked in Nelson's favour, since he wished to disguise until the last moment exactly where he would attack.

Meanwhile, the gravity of the situation meant that virtually the same thoughts were dominating the minds of close to 47,000 men who were poised to take part in the drama of the battle. Few had any doubts about what was facing them. It was a time for reflection. Many made their wills. Eighteen-year-old Midshipman John Aikenhead from Portsea, aboard the *ROYAL SOVEREIGN*, expressed his feelings in a letter to his family written about four hours before the start of the action.

> We have just piped breakfast; thirty-five sail, besides smaller vessels, are now on their beam, about three miles off. Should I, dear parents, fall in defence of my King, let that thought console you. I feel not the least dread of my spirits. Accept, perhaps for the last time, your son's love; be assured I feel for my friends, should I die in this glorious action – glorious no doubt, it will be. Every British heart pants for glory. Our old Admiral [Collingwood] is quite young with the thoughts of it. If I survive, nothing will give me greater pleasure than embracing my dearest relations. Do not, in case I fall, grieve – it will be to no purpose. Many brave fellows will no doubt fall with me on both sides. Oh my parents, sisters, brothers, dear grandfather, grandmother, and aunt, believe me ever yours! Oh with what ardour I shall, if permitted by God's providence, come to England to embrace you all!

Aikenhead was killed before tea-time. Captain George Duff of the *MARS* had started a new letter to his wife, on 17 October, but the

Advance Squadron responsibilities Nelson had given him appear to have completely occupied his time. Usually he had added to his letters every day, but he now jumps to 'Monday morning, Oct 21st.' and uses a separate half sheet of paper, sealed. This was found after the battle in his writing box together with his unfinished letter. In it he mentions Norwich, his 13-year-old son, whom he had taken to sea with him along with three other boys. He stationed them all on the lower deck, where their schoolmaster said they behaved like 'young Nelsons'.

> My dearest Sophia,
> I have just time to tell you we are going into action with the Combined. I hope and trust in God that we shall all behave as becomes us, and that I may yet have the happiness of taking my beloved wife and children in my arms. Norwich is quite well and happy. I have however ordered him of [*sic*] the quarter-deck.
> Yours ever, and most truly,
> Geo. Duff

After the battle Norwich enclosed his father's letters with a moving one of his own breaking the news to his mother that she was a widow.

Having just been ordered to repair on board the *VICTORY*, Captain Henry Blackwood found a brief moment to write an addendum to the letter he had started to his wife, Harriet, on the 19th:

> The last 24 hours has been most anxious work for me; but we have kept sight of them, and at this moment bearing up to come into action. Lord N. 27 sail of the line. French 33 or 34. I wish the six we have at Gibraltar were here. My signal just made on board *VICTORY*; I hope to order me into a vacant Line-of-Battle Ship [*AJAX* and *THUNDERER* were under the command of their first lieutenants since their captains had been sent back with Calder]. Adieu my dearest wife, your Henry will not disgrace his name; and if he dies, his last breath will be devoted to the dearest best of wives.

Take care of my boy; make him a better man than his father.
Most affectionately and very [indecipherable] your husband.
H. Blackwood

Collingwood and Nelson were both out of their cots at dawn preparing
for the momentous day. It took time to put on the complicated clothes
of the era and servants usually assisted senior officers to dress. Mr
William Smith, Collingwood's 21-year-old London-born servant:

> . . . entered the Admiral's cabin about daylight, and found
> him up and already dressing. He asked me if I had seen the
> French fleet; and on my replying that I had not, he told me
> to look at them. I then observed a crowd of ships to leeward;
> but I could not help looking with still greater interest at the
> Admiral, who, during all this time, was shaving himself with
> a composure that quite astonished me.
>   Admiral Collingwood dressed himself that morning with
> peculiar care; and soon after, meeting Lieutenant Clavell,
> advised him to pull off his boots. 'You had better,' he said,
> 'put on silk stockings, as I have done: for if one should get
> shot in the leg, they would be so much more manageable for
> the surgeon.'

Nelson was up and dressed early enough to catch the *ACHILLE*'s signal
about 'a strange fleet' and, once dressed, walked from his day cabin
up to the quarterdeck. Dr William Beatty was already there and gave
a vivid account of Nelson's supreme confidence. Nelson was always in
his element just before a battle, and 21 October was also a special day
for him because, on the same date, during the Seven Years' War (1756–
63) his uncle Captain Maurice Suckling had attacked a squadron of
seven ships, under Commodore de Kersaint, with only three sail of the
line and put them all to flight.

> Soon after daylight Lord Nelson came upon deck: he was
> dressed as usual in his Admiral's frock coat, bearing on the

left breast four stars of different Orders which he always
wore with his common apparel. He did not wear his sword
in the Battle of Trafalgar; it had been taken from the place
where it hung up in his cabin, and was laid ready on his
table; but it is supposed he forgot to call for it. This was
the only Action in which he ever appeared without a sword.
He displayed excellent spirits, and, expressed his pleasure
at the prospect of giving a fatal blow to the Naval power of
France and Spain; and spoke with confidence of obtaining a
signal Victory notwithstanding the inferiority of the British
Fleet, declaring to Captain Hardy that 'he would not be
contented with capturing less than twenty sail of the line.'
He afterwards pleasantly observed that, 'the 21st October
was the happiest day of the year among his family', but did
not assign the reason for this. His Lordship had previously
entertained a strong presentiment that this would prove the
auspicious day, and had several times said to Captain Hardy
and Dr Scott [chaplain of the ship, and foreign secretary
to the commander in chief, whose intimate friendship he
enjoyed], 'The 21st October will be our day'.

The morning light showed how the British ships had also had
difficulty keeping good order in the night. They were in two loose
groups and neither was in regular order. Consequently, as soon as it
was light enough for flags to be distinguished, Nelson made his first
general signal of the day:

6.10 a.m. *VICTORY* to Fleet:
Form the order of sailing in two columns.

His captains recognized that he was dispensing with the Advance
Squadron, which up until the previous afternoon had been led by
Duff of the *MARS*, and were able to respond adroitly because they
already knew that 'the order of sailing is to be the order of battle'.
Three minutes later, after ascending to the poop deck to have a better

view of both lines of the British Fleet, Nelson signalled, 'Bear up and sail large on course ENE.' Simultaneously he was heading his ships at the enemy, 'with their heads to southward', in order to cut them off from Cadiz, and placing himself at the head of the Weather Column. As he watched his fleet respond to his signals it became clear that a slight course adjustment to starboard would be necessary if they were to come up on the centre and rear of the enemy as he had planned, and so at 6.46 a.m. he ordered Signal 76: 'Bear up and steer East.'

The British Fleet had set all possible sail. The Lee Line, consisting of 13 ships, was led by Admiral Collingwood in the *ROYAL SOVEREIGN*; and the Weather Line, composed of 14 ships, by Nelson in the *VICTORY*. The ships at the head of the lines got roughly into their proper positions, but Nelson could see that his slower ships, such as *DREADNOUGHT, PRINCE* and *BRITANNIA,* were struggling to gain their stations and he reminded them that they were to 'take station as convenient without regard to the established order of sailing'. Nelson had briefed his captains so well that, remarkably, the fleet as a whole sailed for the next five and a quarter hours without further manoeuvring signals. He turned to Blackwood, who had now come aboard *VICTORY*:

> . . . and had the satisfaction to find the Admiral in good, but very calm spirits. After receiving my congratulations at the approach of the moment he so often and so long had wished for, he replied, 'I mean to bleed the Captains of the Frigates, as I shall keep you on board until the very last minute.' His mind seemed entirely directed to the strength and formation of the Enemy's Line, as well as the effects which his novel mode of attack was likely to produce.

Although Blackwood had served with Nelson on only two brief occasions his bearing and reputation had won the Admiral's confidence, and he was now a member of his closest circle of friends. At last, at 6.40 a.m. (7.00 a.m. in *EURYALUS*'s log) Nelson ordered the signal that everyone had been waiting for: Signal 13: 'Prepare for battle.'

Dr Beatty related that Nelson then quitted the poop, and retired to his cabin for 'a few minutes', but not before giving:

> . . . particular directions for taking down from his cabin the different fixtures, and for being very careful in removing the portrait of Lady Hamilton: 'Take care of my Guardian Angel,' said he, addressing himself to the persons to be employed in this business.

There was now plenty of time for everyone to reflect as the ships prepared for action. William Robinson, better known as 'Jack Nastyface', a 20-year-old volunteer from Farnham in Surrey serving in the *REVENGE*, the eighth ship in Collingwood's division, was one of them:

> During this time each ship was making the usual preparations, such as breaking the captain's and officers' cabins, and sending all lumber below. The doctors, parson, purser and loblolly men were also busy, getting the medicine chest and bandages out, and sails prepared for the wounded to be placed on, that they might be dressed in rotation as they were taken down to the after cockpit. In such a bustling, and it may be said trying as well as serious time, it was curious to notice the different dispositions of the British sailor. Some would be offering a guinea for a glass of grog, whilst others were making a sort of mutual verbal will, such as, 'If one of Johnnie Crapeau's shots knocks my head off, you will take all my effects; and if you are killed and I am not, why, I will have yours; and this was generally agreed to'.
> During this momentous preparation the human mind had ample time for meditation and conjecture, for it was evident the fate of England rested on this battle.

'Prepare for battle' was one of a number of levels of readiness in a warship of the sailing era, and crews were trained and rehearsed to a high state of discipline and efficiency. Every crew member would have a specific job to carry out. First came 'Clear for action', a process that could take several hours. It put the ship into a high state of readiness so that the Captain had then only to 'Beat to quarters' to summon his whole ship to battle stations.

Clearing for action meant what it said. The first stage involved putting out the galley fire and clearing the gun decks of all obstacles to allow free movement. This meant everything superfluous to battle had to go: cabin furniture, personal possessions, livestock, wooden ladders not needed in action, mess tables, forms, and the bulkheads that gave privacy to the officers. If any of these items could not be stowed away in the hold in time they would be thrown overboard. Stephen Trounce, the Cornish Master of the *BRITANNIA*, recorded in the log how, in clearing for action, they hove overboard '2 wine-pipes, 4 butts, 4 puncheons, 12 hogsheads, 12 barrels, and 64 half hogsheads'. Often the officers' possessions were placed in a cutter or jolly boat that would be towed astern. These boats had to be secure anyway and this was the safest method, because if hit they could shower lethal splinters. Splinter netting was rigged above the upper deck and quarterdeck to protect the crew from falling masts, yards and tackle, and thick wreaths of rope oakum were bound around the masts beneath the trusses of the yards on the fore and main masts to stop them falling if the halyards were hit. The yards themselves were secured with chain preventer slings. Fire hoses were laid along the decks. Hammocks were stowed along the rails to give protection from small arms fire. Jack Nastyface Robinson described the effectiveness of hammocks used in this way after the battle:

... in preparing to engage the enemy closely, and protect ourselves as much as possible, the seamen's hammocks with the bedding and blankets were lashed to the shrouds, which served much to save our rigging, as was very evident from examination on the second night after the battle; for when our men got their hammocks down, many were found to have received a great deal of damage, being very much cut with the large shot, and some were found to have had grape or canister shot lodged in them.

Concurrently attention would be given to the fighting aspects of the ship, the raison d'être of any warship, in particular the guns and gunpowder. Considerable attention was given to the design of a ship of the line to prevent accidental ignition and a resulting explosion. The planking of the gun decks was sanded and wetted, to deactivate loose powder, and the thick woollen cloth screens around the magazine, the passageway leading to it, and the ammunition paths were soaked with water to reduce the risk of fire. Fire was the great fear in a wooden warship and in action it was all too easy for loose grains of gunpowder to fall on to the decks and be ignited by a spark.

Sanding the gun decks had a dual purpose. On board the largest warship in the world at that time, the four-deck, 140-gun *Santissima Trinidad*, a member of her 1,048 crew who had not been in battle before was confused by the preparations:

> Early in the morning the decks were cleared for action, and when all was ready for serving the guns and working the ship, I heard some one say: 'The sand – bring the sand.' A number of sailors were posted on the ladders from the hatchway to the hold, and in this way were hauling up sacks of sand. Each man handed one to the man next to him and so it was passed on. A great quantity of sacks were thus brought up from hand to hand, and they were emptied out on the upper decks, the poop and forecastle, the sand being spread about so as to cover all the planking. The same thing was done between decks. My curiosity prompted me to ask a lad who stood next me what this was for. 'For the blood,' he said very coolly. 'For the blood!' I exclaimed, unable to repress a shudder. I looked at the men who were busily employed on this task – and for a moment I felt I was a coward.

Ships of the line were fighting machines bristling with guns, each first-rate at Trafalgar concentrating more firepower than the artillery at Waterloo. In the British ships the guns came in three sizes: 12-pounder, 24-pounder and 32-pounder. For stability the heaviest guns were on the deck nearest the waterline. While the largest guns in the field at Waterloo were 12-pounders, and the majority 6-pounders, the largest pieces at Trafalgar were the 68-pounder carronades, known as 'smashers', lightweight short-range guns that fired heavy charges at low velocity, which on impact caused massive splintering and horrific wounds. Round shot, usually sufficient for at least three rounds, was kept in deck racks and rope 'shot garlands' around the hatchways. Canister, grape, bar and chain shot would be taken from the shot lockers in the hold and hoisted through the hatches to the decks as required, although the grape would be stored in crates behind the guns. Cylindrical wooden cases were used to carry the powder cartridges. They varied in size, were prepared separately and carried along different routes. On arrival at the guns they were placed in wooden saltboxes, two at a time.

The gun captains would cast loose the breeching (a stout rope attached to the cascabel of a gun to secure it to the ship's side in order to check recoil), remove the aprons and muzzle tompions, and check the gun tackles, which were used to pull the gun up to the gun port after loading, and all the items needed to fire their guns. Secured to the deck head were sponges made of sheepskin, which were kept wet and used to wash the bore after each firing to extinguish any burning embers – one was on a wooden stave, the other on a 9-foot stiff rope; the worm or wad hook – a metal spiral at the end of a wooden pole also for clearing the barrel of undischarged material which would tend to accumulate; and the flat-headed rammer, used for pushing home the flannel bag cartridge, wad and shot. Next to the gun was the gun-spike, used to lever the gun carriage when traversing the gun, a match tub for a length of loose-laid rope steeped in nitre with a smouldering end, which could be used if the flintlock failed, and a cask of water with swabs, which were at hand to dowse small fires and provide quick refreshment for the gun crew.

The master-at-arms prepared the small firearms: 24-bore sea service pistols issued in pairs, sharpened cutlasses, pikes, tomahawks, bayonets and muskets. There were 142 in a first-rate ship like VICTORY. In addition the Royal Marines had their own muskets. Grenades, pungent smoke bombs known as 'stink pots', and swivel guns were all readied.

Below the waterline, the gunner and his mates, wearing soft leather or felt slippers to avoid kicking up sparks, would check the lanterns in the light rooms before entering the hanging magazine, the most protected part of a ship, to check the hundreds of cartridges which would soon be carefully handed out to the powder monkeys, who would carry them in covered wooden containers to the guns.

The carpenter and his mates would be preparing shot-plugs, sheets of lead, oakum and salted hides to bung up holes torn into the hull by enemy shot. Wooden hulls were extraordinarily resistant to gunshot, so although the superstructure and superficial parts such as the bulwarks, stern galleries and figurehead were easily splintered and shattered, the fundamental structure was resilient, unless the magazine exploded. At Trafalgar the VICTORY sustained 80 shot holes 'between wind and water', but all of them were plugged by her carpenters during and immediately after the battle and although her sailing capability was seriously impaired by the battle her integrity as a gun platform remained unquestionable. The carpenter would also prepare the emergency steering gear in case the wheel or tiller was shot away. This happened to VICTORY as she approached the *Bucentaure*, after which she was steered from down below in the gunroom.

In the cockpit on the orlop deck, the surgeon and his assistants converted the midshipmen's berth into an operating theatre. The wounded would be brought down to this dark and cheerless place to take their turn in the queue to go under the surgeon's knife. Amputations were the most common form of first aid and were undertaken quickly and usually without anaesthetic. Tubs were placed ready alongside the makeshift operating table for the blood, 'wings and limbs'.

During 'clear for action', officers would put on clean clothes to avoid infections getting into wounds, write letters home, exchange wills and, if there was time, enjoy a last meal. When possible the crew would follow suit. They would then await the fast hammering sound of a Marine's drum beating to quarters. Each and every man had their place and this was the signal for them to go to it. The lieutenants would report their decks were ready and the midshipmen would stand by to run messages.

Once the preparations were complete there was a stillness, a stark contrast to what had gone before. Charles Reece Pemberton, a Welsh seaman who blockaded Cadiz in 1808, described this phenomenon on a gun deck, including mention of the animals on board:

> Everything was now in order, fires extinguished, fearnought screens round the hatchways for passing powder from the magazines; shot racks drawn from their peaceable coverings, and arranged ready for their work; guns cast loose, crowbars for pointing the guns lying at hand on the deck; tompions out all ready for thunder . . . my friend the goat sent down to the cable tier – the captain's ducks and geese left in the coops, to cackle and quake and take their chance – the doctor's saws and knives and probes and bandages and tourniquets, all laid in order in the cockpit; and I devoutly hoping, as tempted by curiosity I looked at them, that I might be blown away all together, rather than that he should exercise his skill on my limbs or carcass. And every man and boy was mute as he stood at his station. Here and there might be seen one drawing the knot of his handkerchief, girt round his loins, or that of his head bandages; all grim in lip and glistening eye . . . But don't you imagine, reader, that I was not frightened in all this. Faith, there was something in the orderly stillness of lying there for half an hour with all this preparation for destruction and death that made me think there might be worse places than the counting house after all. There was no noise, no laugh, no show of hilarity: yet was there some interjectorial jesting bandied about which called upon grim smiles, but no laugh. Men shirtless, with handkerchiefs bandaged tightly around their loins and heads, stood with naked brawny arms folded on their hairy and heaving chests, looking pale and stern, but still hushed; or glancing with a hot eye through ports. I felt

a difficulty in swallowing. Now if we had gone at it at once, without this chilling prelude, why I dare say I should have known very little about the thing which we call fear. 'Stand to your guns!' At last came in a peal through the stillness from the captain's speaking trumpet; it swept fore and aft with such clear force, as though it had been spoken within a foot of the ear, and seemed to dash down into the holds, and penetrate to the very keel. The instant change this produced was magical. 'Take good aim! Ready the first platoon!' Ready? Aye, everyone was ready; stern, fixed, rigid in soul – pliant elastic body. 'Captains of the guns, watch the falling of the first shot, and point accordingly.' Not a word was replied; even the everlasting 'ay, ay, sir,' was refused now.

'YOU CAN SAY THAT I AM DEAD'

Villeneuve's first act that morning was to get his disorganized fleet into some semblance of order, and at 6.20 a.m. he had made the signal to form a line of battle on the starboard tack, which altered the course of the fleet from south to south-west-by-south. He knew he was in a difficult position. The British with the benefit of the weather gage looked as if they were 'standing in a body for my rear, with the double intention of attacking it advantageously and cutting off the retreat of the Combined fleet on Cadiz'. This refuge lay astern to the north and every moment he procrastinated meant he was drawing further away from it. Twelve miles to his east lay the dangerous shoals of Cape Trafalgar – a lee shore – and ahead of him there were six other ships of the line capable of blocking his way through the Straits. At last he made up his mind: he would turn his 33 ships about and steer for Cadiz some 20 miles away, his 'sole object being to protect the rear from the projected attack of the entire enemy force'. It was a fateful and disastrous decision. The manoeuvre took two hours to accomplish and meant that all his ships were heading northwards. They had not been in perfect order to begin with; they remained a higgledy-piggledy mess, a tribute to naval ineptitude. Some were bunched too close together, large gaps of many ships' lengths opened up between others. Much of the column was two and even three ships deep. His fleet was in a state of confusion. Lieutenant William Pryce Cumby aboard the *BELLEROPHON* had a more generous view of the situation:

> They were in the meantime employed in forming a close and well-imagined, though, till now, unexampled order of battle; but which, had their plan of defence been as well executed as it was contrived, would have rendered our victory much more dearly bought than it has been: they were formed in a double line, thus –
>
>
>
> 1   2   3
>
> 4   5   6
>
>
>
> French and Spaniards alternatively, and it was their intention on our breaking the line (which manoeuvre they expected we should as usual put in execution) astern of No. 4, for No. 2 to make sail, that the British ship in hauling up should fall on board of her, while No. 5 should bear up and rake her, and No. 1 would bring her broadside to bear on her starboard bow. – Luckily, this manoeuvre only succeeded with the *TONNANT* and *BELLEROPHON*, which were among the ships that suffered most.

Blackwood remarked that Nelson:

> . . . seemed very much to regret, and with reason that the enemy had tacked to Northward, and formed their line on the larboard instead of the starboard tack which later line of bearing would have kept the Straits' Mouth open; instead of which, by forming to the Northward, they brought the shoals of Trafalgar and St Pedro under our lee; and also with the existing wind, kept open the Port of Cadiz, which was of infinite consequence to them. This movement was in a great degree the cause of Lord Nelson making the signal to

'Prepare to Anchor', the necessity of which was impressed on his mind to the last moment of his life; and so much did he think of the possibility of the Enemy's escape into Cadiz, that he desired me to employ the frigates, as much as I could to complete the destruction of the Enemy, whether at anchor or not: and not to think of saving Ships or men, for annihilation to both was his first object, and capture but a secondary one.

The slowly advancing British watched the two hours of allied manoeuvring closely. Lieutenant Nicholas on board the *BELLEISLE* described the approach:

At eight the enemy wore to northward, and owing to the light wind, which prevailed during the day, they were prevented from forming with any precision, and presented the appearance of a double line convexing to leeward. At nine we were about six miles from them, with studdingsails set on both sides; and as our progress never exceeded a mile and a half an hour, we continued all canvas we could spread until we gained our position alongside our opponent.

At about the same time a fellow Marine aboard the *AJAX*, Second Lieutenant Samuel Burdon Ellis, three years older than Nicholas and destined to become a KCB and a Lieutenant General, was:

. . . sent below with orders and was much struck with the preparations made by the bluejackets, the majority of whom were stripped to the waist; a handkerchief was tightly bound round their heads and over the ears, to deaden the noise of the guns, many men being deaf for days after an action. The men were variously occupied; some were sharpening their cutlasses, others polishing the guns, as though an inspection was about to take place instead of a mortal combat, whilst three or four, as if in mere bravado, were dancing a hornpipe; but all seemed deeply anxious to come to close quarters with the enemy. Occasionally they would look out of the ports and speculate as the various ships of the enemy, many of which on former occasions had been engaged by our vessels.

As the bands played aboard the *BELLEROPHON* one of the midshipmen remarked that 'One would have thought that the people were preparing for a festival rather than combat, and no dissatisfaction was expressed except at the state of the weather which prevented our quickly nearing the enemy.' All the known accounts of the battle portray the eagerness and confident enthusiasm of the British seamen and their officers. There is no evidence of doubt or gloom, as is found in the Combined Fleet. This contrast in morale was an essential factor of Nelson's plan. Commodore Don Cosmé Churruca, commanding the *San Juan Nepomuceno* (74), one of Spain's finest naval captains, a tough-minded officer and devotee of his craft, had a deep sense of duty and honour and a great pride in his nation. Like Nelson, he was a humanitarian and matched Nelson's best captains in professionalism and style. He had a lifelong disdain for the French as seamen and naval allies, though French sailors considered him a model officer. But this morning his heart was heavy with foreboding and lack of confidence in his French commander in chief. He told his nephew, Don José Ruiz de Apodoca, who was serving in his ship as a volunteer, that he should write to his friends that he was:

> . . . going into a battle that will be desperate and bloody. Tell them also that they can be certain of this – that I, for my part, will meet my death there. Let them know that rather than surrender my ship I shall sink her. It is the last duty that an officer owes to his king and country.

Later that morning he wrote to a close friend, 'If you hear that my ship has been taken, you can say that I am dead.' (In the battle he was terribly mangled and died, leaving behind a bride of only five months.) This mood transferred itself to those around him and is even evident in his rallying speech to his ship's company:

> My sons, in the name of the God of Battles I promise eternal
> happiness to all those who today fall doing their duty. On
> the other hand, if I see any man shirking I will have him
> shot on the spot. If the scoundrel escapes my eye, or that
> of the gallant officers I have the honour to command, rest
> assured of this, that bitter remorse will dog the wretch for
> the rest of his days, for so long as he crawls through what
> may remain of his miserable and dishonoured existence.

He then called for three cheers for the King, *'Viva el Rey!'* The drums
and fifes struck up and the crew reportedly went to their stations full
of eagerness and excitement but not, one surmises, with the same
spring in their step as the crew of the MINOTAUR (74) following
Captain Charles Mansfield's speech. He encouraged, was concise and
gave his men a rousing flourish. He was promptly cheered.

> Men, we are now in sight of the enemy whom there is every
> probability of engaging, and I trust that this day will prove
> the most glorious our country ever saw. I shall say nothing
> to you of courage. Our country never produced a coward.
> For my own part I pledge myself to the officers and ship's
> company not to quit the ship I may get alongside of till
> either she strikes or sinks – or I sink.
>   I have only to recommend silence, and a strict attention to
> the orders of your officers. Be careful to take good aim, for it
> is to no purpose to throw shot away. You will now, every man,
> repair to your respective stations, and depend, I will bring the
> ship into action as soon as possible. God save the King!

Re-emerging from his cabin, Nelson went over the different decks of
the VICTORY with Captain Hardy and spoke to the different classes
of seamen, 'encouraging them with his usual affability, and was
much pleased at the manner in which the seamen had barricaded the

hawse holes of the ship'. The mood below decks was jubilant at the expectation of another great victory. He came across a young Irishman carving a notch on his gun carriage. The seaman explained to Nelson that he was adding the notch to the others he had cut for previous victories, in case he should fall in battle. Nelson laughed, saying, 'You'll make notches enough in the enemy's ships.'

All good captains in both fleets encouraged their crews. As Collingwood was going around the decks of the *ROYAL SOVEREIGN* he came upon a group of fellow Tynesiders. 'Today, my lads,' he said, 'we must show those fellows what the "Tars of the Tyne" can do!' Addressing a group of his officers he said, 'Now, gentlemen, let us do something today which the world may talk of hereafter.' Six miles away the intrepid but diminutive Captain Jean Lucas was making his rounds in the *Redoubtable*:

> Preceded by the drums and fifes that I had on board, I paraded at the head of my officers round all the decks; everywhere I found gallant lads burning with impatience to begin the fray; many of them saying to me, 'Captain, don't forget to board!'

Flag Captain Jean Magendie, accompanied by Admiral Villeneuve, Major General Contamine, who commanded the troops, and the rest of *Bucentaure*'s officers on a similar tour of the decks, also encountered excitement:

> It is impossible to display greater enthusiasm and eagerness for the fray than was shown and evinced by all the officers, sailors and soldiers of the *Bucentaure*, each one of us putting our hands between the Admiral's and renewing our oath upon the eagle entrusted to us by the Emperor, to fight to the last gasp; and shouts of *'Vive l'Empereur, vive L'Amiral Villeneuve'* were raised once more. We returned to the upper decks and each of us resumed our post; the Eagle was displayed at the foot of the mainmast.

Villeneuve wrote later, 'I did not observe a single man daunted at the sight of the formidable enemy column, headed by four three-deckers which bore down on the *Bucentaure*.' Yet, that same morning he confessed that he could in no way prevent such a novel mode of attack and called the officers of his ship around him, pointing out the manner in which the first and second in command of the British fleet were each leading their columns, and exclaiming, 'Nothing but victory can attend such gallant conduct.' As Nelson himself remarked, in spite of their many disadvantages, 'They put a good face upon it.' The underlying factor of morale remained vital, but when it came to the fight the French and Spanish displayed bravery and courage that was more than a match for their British opponents.

THE VIRTUE OF FORTITUDE

Remorselessly, but at little more than a walking pace, the British columns bore down on the disorganized Combined Fleet. All preparations complete, there was even time for them to eat. One of *VICTORY*'s midshipmen, 20-year-old Richard Francis Roberts from Burton Bradstock in Dorset, wrote in his Remark Book, 'At 11 – Dinner and grog.' Able Seaman John Brown, also in the flagship, recalled, 'We piped to dinner and ate a bit of raw pork and a half pint of Wine.' Captain Edward Codrington had just ordered lunch for his crew in the *ORION* and was pleased that his steward had anticipated the occasion and brought him a leg of cold turkey. Nicholas recalled how something as ordinary as sitting down to a meal could be tinged with pathos:

> The officers now met at breakfast; and though each seemed
> to exult in the hope of a glorious termination to the contest
> so near at hand, a fearful presage was experienced that
> all would not again unite at that festive board. One was
> particularly impressed with a persuasion that he should
> not survive the day, nor could he divest himself of this

presentiment, but made the necessary disposal of his property in the event of his death. The sound of the drum, however, soon put an end to our meditations, and after a hasty, and alas, a final farewell to some, we repaired to our respective posts. Our ship's station was far astern of our leader, but her superior sailing caused an interchange of places with the TONNANT. On our passing that ship the captains greeted each other on the honourable prospect in view. Captain Tyler exclaimed: 'A glorious day for old England! We shall have one apiece before night!'

Volunteer Able Seaman John Cash, aged 20, was in the TONNANT:

> Our good captain called all hands and said, 'My lads, this will be a glorious day for us and the groundwork of a speedy return to our homes.' He then ordered bread and cheese and butter and beer for every man at the guns. I was one of them, and, believe me, we ate and drank, and were as cheerful as ever we had been over a pot of beer.

While Nelson had been in his cabin 'for a few minutes' Senior Lieutenant John Pasco interrupted him to make a report and also to air a personal grievance. He had been appointed to the junior role of VICTORY's signal officer. It appears Nelson favoured Pasco for this vital role, but without regard to its consequences for his career. As the ship's first lieutenant, the highest on the list, Pasco could look forward to promotion to Post Captain after a battle. But Nelson had delegated the first lieutenant's post to John Quilliam, a pressed Manxman, who was fifth in seniority. Pasco had a legitimate grievance. However, approaching Nelson:

> . . . I discovered his Lordship on his knees writing. He was then penning that beautiful prayer. I waited until he rose and communicated what I had to report, but could not at such a moment disturb his mind with any grievances of mine.

Nelson was a religious man who prayed to God every day of his life. He had what can probably be best described as a private relationship with his Maker, and his instincts and strong belief in Providence quashed the conventions of public morality. At the climax of his career he managed to compose a few lines that are regarded as amongst the finest written by any soldier or sailor about to go into battle. The prose is unfussy and mellifluous, and Beatty described it as a 'devout and fervent ejaculation, which must be universally admired as truly characteristic of the Christian hero'. The prayer is written in his personal pocket book and, as ever thinking of posterity, he made a copy of it.

> Monday, Octr 21st, 1805 at day Light saw the Enemys
> Combined fleet from East to E.S.E. bore away made the
> Signal for Order of Sailing, and to prepare for Battle the
> Enemy with their heads to the Southward, at seven the
> Enemy wearing in succession.
>
> May the Great God whom I worship grant to my Country
> and for the benefit of Europe in General a great and
> Glorious Victory; and may no misconduct in anyone tarnish
> it, and may humanity after Victory be the predominant
> feature in the British Fleet. For myself individually I commit
> my life to Him who made me, and may His blessing light
> upon my endeavours for serving My Country faithfully. To
> Him I resign myself and the Just cause which is entrusted to
> me to Defend. Amen. Amen. Amen.

Nelson also penned a codicil to his will, in which he highlighted the unrewarded services of 'Emma Lady Hamilton' to her country while at Naples, leaving her as:

> . . . a legacy to my King and Country, that they will give her
> an ample provision to maintain her rank in life.
>
> I also leave to the beneficence of my Country my adopted
> Daughter, Horatia Nelson Thompson; and desire she will
> use in future the name Nelson only.

These are the only favours I ask of my King and Country, at this moment when I am going to fight their battle. May God bless my King and Country, and all those I hold dear! My relations it is needless to mention: they will of course be amply provided for.

The codicil was witnessed by 'Henry Blackwood' and 'T. M. Hardy'. His mind now clear and composed, Nelson rejoined them on deck and made his tour of the ship.

In Collingwood's Lee Column, Captain John Cooke of the *BELLEROPHON* was careful to ensure that his 'Reflections on Fortitude', written a few weeks earlier, were safely in his pocket.

The Virtue of Fortitude tends greatly to the happiness of the individual, by giving composure and presence of mind; and keeping the other passions in due subordination. Nothing so effectively inspires it, as rational piety; the fear of God, is the best security against every other fear. A true estimate of human life; its shortness and uncertainty; the numberless evils and temptations to which by a long continuance in this world we must unavoidably be exposed; ought by no means to discourage, or to throw any gloom on our future prospects; they should teach us: that many things are more formidable than Death; and that nothing is lost, but much gained, when by the appointment of providence, a well spent life is brought to a conclusion. Let it be considered too, that pusillanimity, and fearfulness, can never avail us anything. On the contrary, they debase our nature, poison all our comforts, and make us despicable in the eyes of others; they darken our reason, disconcert our schemes, enfeeble our efforts, extinguish our hopes, and add tenfold poignancy to all the evils of life. In battle, the Brave is in less danger than the Coward; in less danger of even death and wounds, because better prepared to defend himself; in far less danger of infelicity; and has before him the

animating hope of victory and honour. So in life the man
of true fortitude is in less danger of disappointment than
others are, because his understanding is clear and his mind
disencumbered; he is prepared to meet calamity without
the fear of sinking under it; and he has before him the near
prospect of another life, in which they who piously bear the
evils of this, will obtain a glorious reward.

After his visit to every deck of the VICTORY, Nelson returned to
the poop at about ten o'clock and asked Blackwood what he would
consider a victory, notwithstanding that there might be a difficulty
preserving the prizes.

> My answer was that, 'considering the handsome way in
> which battle was offered by the enemy, their apparent
> determination for a fair trial of strength, and the proximity
> of the land, I thought, if fourteen ships were captured, it
> would be a glorious result'; to which he replied: 'I shall not
> be satisfied with anything short of twenty.'

At about the same time, the NEPTUNE got close to the VICTORY and
Captain Thomas Fremantle, one of Nelson's 'band of brothers', clearly
intended to pass. Midshipman William Badcock said that 'Nelson
himself hailed us' and shouted: 'NEPTUNE, take in your stuns'ls
and drop astern. I shall break the line myself.' He then signalled
the TÉMÉRAIRE (98) to 'take station between us and the VICTORY'.
Blackwood observed that:

> Lord Nelson's anxiety to close with the Enemy became very
> apparent; he frequently remarked that they put a good face
> upon it; but always quickly added: 'I'll give them such a
> dressing as they never had before', regretting at the same
> time the vicinity of the land. At that critical moment I
> ventured to represent to his Lordship, the value of such
> a life as his, and particularly in the present battle; and I

proposed hoisting his Flag in the *EURYALUS*, whence he could better see what was going on, as well as what to order in case of necessity. But he would not hear of it, and gave as his reason the force of example, and probably he was right. My next object, therefore, was to endeavour to induce his Lordship to allow the *TÉMÉRAIRE*, *NEPTUNE*, and *LEVIATHAN* to lead the Action before the *VICTORY*, which was then the headmost. After much conversation, in which I ventured to give it as the joint opinion of Captain Hardy and myself, how advantageous it would be to the Fleet for his Lordship to keep as long as possible out of the Battle, he at length consented to allow the *TÉMÉRAIRE*, which was then hailing abreast of the *VICTORY*, to go-ahead, and hailed Captain Harvey to say such were his intentions, if the *TÉMÉRAIRE* could pass the *VICTORY*. Captain Harvey being rather out of hail, his Lordship sent me to communicate his wishes, which I did; when on returning to the *VICTORY*, I found him doing all he could to increase rather than diminish sail, so that the *TÉMÉRAIRE* could not pass the *VICTORY*.

Nevertheless, Captain Eliab Harvey continued to push ahead and ranged up on the *VICTORY*'s quarter until close enough for Nelson to hail. 'I'll thank you, Captain Harvey, to keep in your proper station, which is astern of the *VICTORY*!' Nelson had always led from the front and he had no intention of changing now, so this rebuke, given his high spirits and the luxury of time, was more than likely a gesture to amuse. Nelson is said to have been smiling significantly at Captain Hardy when he agreed the *TÉMÉRAIRE* could pass the *VICTORY*, implying he meant if she could. It was a challenge. 'As regards it being safer and easier for him to direct the course of the battle if he shifted his flag to a frigate, Nelson had a ready answer for what he took to be a caring gesture, rather than a tactical consideration. He pointed out how Admiral Rodney had found he could hardly control affairs if he was not part of the main battle group. We know from his own words to Henry Blackwood that he realized that once the battle had started there was nothing else he could do anyway!

Some two hours later those around him would again try to minimize his personal danger by suggesting that he should change his admiral's undress uniform with its four embroidered stars for a plain coat. John Scott, his secretary, warned Beatty, 'Take care, doctor, what you are about. I would not be the man to mention such a matter to him.' In the end it was Hardy who raised the matter, to which Nelson replied that 'he was aware it might be seen but it was now too late to be shifting a coat!' Popular imagination has Nelson wearing a full dress coat conspicuous for the amount of gold braid on it and, in Nelson's case, the set of sparkling decorations on his left breast. In fact he was wearing his 'undress coat' – a threadbare frock coat that he had worn daily for two years. The gold epaulettes were tarnished by the salt air, as were the embroidered decorations.

ENGLAND CONFIDES

The morning wore on and the fleets gradually grew closer. They were nevertheless spread out over more than two square miles of ocean, their respective manoeuvrings hindered by the lack of wind. It was painfully slow for everyone. Villeneuve's disordered ships, sailing northwards, were virtually drifting. The speed of his slowest sailers was as little as one knot. Villeneuve gave us this account:

> The enemy continued to steer for us under all sail, and
> at nine o'clock I was able to make out that their fleet was
> formed in two columns, of which one was heading directly
> for my flagship and the other towards the rear of the
> Combined Fleet. The wind was very light, the sea with a
> swell on, owing to which our formation in line was rendered
> very difficult to effect; but in the circumstances, considering
> the nature of the attack that I foresaw the enemy were
> about to make, the irregularity of our order did not seem a

disadvantage, if each ship could have continued to keep to the wind, and close upon the ship next ahead . . . The enemy meanwhile came steadily on, though the wind was very light. They had their most powerful ships at the head of the columns. That to the north had four three-deckers.

Captain Lucas in the *Redoubtable* was trying to get closer to the *Bucentaure*:

They were under all sail – they even had studding sails out – and heading directly for our fleet . . . in [our] new order the *Redoubtable*'s place was third ship astern of the flagship *Bucentaure*. I at once made every effort to take station in the wake of the flagship, leaving between her and myself the space necessary for my two immediate leaders. One of them was not very far of its station, but the other showed no signs of trying to take post.

Meanwhile, Admiral Gravina had, it seems, acted independently and chosen to move to the rear, lengthening the line, rather than covering the centre as his orders required, and according to Villeneuve's Flag Captain, Captain Prigny, ignored a signal 'to keep its luff, in order to be able to proceed to reinforce the centre of the line against the attack of the enemy who was bearing down on it in two columns.' Throughout the morning Villeneuve and Gravina signalled incessantly to get the various ships into station, but by the time the battle commenced the line was far from being regularly formed and there was still a gap wide enough for five ships between the flagship and the *Santa Ana* (112).

Collingwood was experiencing similar difficulties with his column and, as the log shows, was regularly calling for more sail:

9.00 a.m. *ROYAL SOVEREIGN* to the Lee Division:
Make more sail.
9.30 a.m. *ROYAL SOVEREIGN* to *BELLEISLE*:
Make more sail.

9.40 a.m. *ROYAL SOVEREIGN* to *REVENGE*:
Make more sail.

Lieutenant Frederick Hoffman in the *TONNANT*, who was to be wounded at the battle, thought:

> . . . we answered with alacrity the signal to make all sail
> for the enemy, preserving our order of sailing. The sails
> appeared to know their places and were spread like magic.
> The wind was very light, and it was nearly noon before we
> closed with the enemy.

Nelson had long recognized that 'No day can be long enough to arrange a couple of fleets, and fight a decisive battle according to the old system'. The wisdom of his strategy was now becoming clear. His ships were moving more slowly through the water than possibly even he had envisaged. It was clearly not a time to adhere to the letter of his written instructions, which required the faster ships to slow down so that the stragglers could catch up to form two properly parallel lines. This is why he told Blackwood 'to tell all the captains of the line of battleships that he depended on their exertions and that if by the mode of attack prescribed they found it impossible to get into action immediately, they might adopt whatever they thought best, provided it led them quickly and closely alongside an enemy.' Consequently, Nelson's Weather Column went into battle in line ahead, while Collingwood's Lee Column was more like three lines ahead. Captain Robert Moorsom of the *REVENGE* described the battle in a number of letters to his father. Writing from Spithead in December he explained the order of battle as effectively as anyone present:

> I have seen several plans of the action but none to answer
> my idea of it – indeed scarce any plan can be given; it was
> irregular and the ships got down as fast as they could
> and into any space where they found the enemy without
> attending to their place in the line – A regular plan was laid

down by Lord Nelson some time before the Action, but not acted upon; his great anxiety seemed to be to get to leeward of them, lest they should make off for Cadiz before he could get near.

At 11.25 a.m., according to the account of Captain Blackwood, Nelson turned again to his busy signal lieutenant, John Pasco, and said:

> 'I'll now amuse the Fleet with a signal;' and he asked me, 'if I did not think there was one yet wanting?' I answered that I thought the whole Fleet seemed very clearly to understand what they were about, and to vie with each other who should first get nearest to the *VICTORY* or *ROYAL SOVEREIGN*. These words were scarcely uttered, when his last well-known Signal was made . . .

Pasco picks up the story:

> His Lordship came to me on the poop, and after ordering certain signals to be made, about a quarter to noon he said, 'Mr Pasco, I wish to say to the Fleet. ENGLAND CONFIDES THAT EVERY MAN WILL DO HIS DUTY;' and he added, 'you must be quick, for I have one more to make, which is for Close Action.' I replied, 'If your Lordship will permit me to substitute *expects* for *confides*, the signal will sooner be completed, because the word *expects* is in the vocabulary [the Signal Book], and *confides* must be spelt.' His Lordship replied in haste, and with seeming satisfaction, 'That will do, Pasco: make it directly.'

There is some evidence that Hardy, who accompanied Blackwood and Nelson on the poop, also influenced the wording of the original signal. Apparently, Nelson's first musings were to telegraph 'Nelson confides . . .' but the officer he was then addressing, believed to be Hardy, suggested whether it might not be better to substitute

'England confides . . .' and Nelson is said to have rapturously exclaimed, 'Certainly, certainly!' Therefore it seems that the first two words may have been changed. The original words 'Nelson confides' are much more typical of Nelson's personality and leadership style. He knew how important he was to the morale of the British fleet and he genuinely had *confidence* that everyone would do their duty.

The signal was hoisted at the *VICTORY*'s mainmast using 12 successive numeral flag groups from a new signal book devised by ever-ingenious Captain Sir Home Riggs Popham: *Telegraphic Signals or Marine Vocabulary* (published in 1800). The crucial advantage of the system was that it was possible to send messages not covered in Lord Howe's *Fighting Instructions for His Majesty's Fleet*. Nelson immediately recognized how this would improve communications and issued Popham's signal code to all his ships. He was the first to use its versatility to convey an emotional message, a signal never before seen in the annals of the Royal Navy, to thousands of men.

All the words of the signal except 'duty' had a flag group consisting of three flags. 'Duty' was not in the signal book and therefore was spelt with a separate flag for each of the four letters. 'Confides' would have required 15 more hoists, more than the whole signal! Each flag group was hoisted separately, and not all at once as is done today on Trafalgar Day, which explains why Pasco was keen to substitute 'expects'. In speaking to Pasco, Nelson would have almost certainly used the word 'that', but there is evidence to suggest that the flag hoist omitted this word. Moreover, both Blackwood and Beatty recorded ENGLAND EXPECTS EVERY MAN WILL DO HIS DUTY.

Curiously, the words 'England expects every man to do his duty' had appeared eleven years earlier on an attractive panel commemorating the Battle of the Glorious First of June 1794. It is possible that Nelson may have seen this and that it was in his subconscious. Whatever, as the flags fluttered up the halyards the telescopes of the fleet were trained upon them and the signal was logged by seven ships; '. . . it was received throughout the fleet with a shout of answering acclamation, made sublime by the spirit which it breathed and feeling which it expressed', according to Captain Blackwood. Dr Beatty wrote:

About half an hour before the enemy opened their fire, the
memorable telegraphic signal was made, that 'ENGLAND
EXPECTS EVERY MAN WILL DO HIS DUTY.' Which
was spread and received with enthusiasm. It is impossible
adequately to describe by any language, the lively emotions
excited in the crew of the VICTORY when this propitious
communication was made known to them: confidence and
resolution were strongly pourtrayed [sic] in the countenance
of all; and the sentiment generally expressed to each other
was, that they would prove to their Country that day, how
well British seamen could 'do their duty' when led to battle
by their revered Admiral.

Midshipman Badcock in the NEPTUNE, third in the line behind
VICTORY, saw 'Captain Fremantle inspect the different decks and make
known the signal, which was received with cheers'. Lieutenant Barclay
said that it was 'joyfully welcomed by the ship's company'. Second
Lieutenant Samuel Burdon Ellis in the AJAX, ninth in the line, said:

> I was desired to inform those on the main deck of
> the Admiral's signal. Upon acquainting one of the
> quartermasters of the order, he assembled the men with
> 'Avast there, lads, come and hear the Admiral's words!'
> When the men were mustered, I delivered with becoming
> dignity the sentence, rather anticipating that the effect
> on the men would be to awe them by its grandeur. Jack,
> however, did not appreciate it; for there were murmurs from
> some, whilst others, in an audible whisper, murmured, 'Do
> our duty! Of course we'll do our duty! I've always done mine,
> haven't you?' Still, the men cheered vociferously – more, I
> believe, from love and admiration of their admiral and leader
> than from a full appreciation of this well known signal.

Midshipman Hercules Robinson aboard the EURYALUS expressed
another cynical view, claiming Blackwood's words to be an 'historical

lie', adding, 'Why, it was noted in the signal-book and in the log, and that was all about it in our ship till we heard of our alleged transports on our return to England.' However, the majority of accounts from other ships suggest that the reaction of the crew of the *EURYALUS* was untypical. Lieutenant Paul Nicholas of the *BELLEISLE*, immediately astern of Collingwood's *ROYAL SOVEREIGN* at the head of the Lee Column, wrote:

> As this emphatic injunction was communicated through
> the decks, it was received with enthusiastic cheers,
> and each bosom glowed with ardour at this appeal to
> individual valour.

Acting Lieutenant John Barclay in the *BRITANNIA*, the fifth ship astern of *VICTORY,* said that the 'signal was joyfully welcomed by the ship's company' and Midshipman Henry Walker in the *BELLEROPHON* that it was 'received on board our ship with three cheers and a general shout of, No fear of that!' Captain John Cooke of the *BELLEROPHON*, fifth in line behind the *ROYAL SOVEREIGN*:

> . . . went below and exhorted his men on every deck, most
> earnestly entreating them to remember the words of their
> gallant Admiral just communicated by signal . . . He was
> cheered on his return upward by the whole ship's company
> who wrote on their guns in chalk: *BELLEROPHON!* Death
> or Glory!

Lieutenant Frederick Hoffman in the *TONNANT*, fourth in line astern of the *ROYAL SOVEREIGN,* believed the cheers 'must have shaken the nerve of the enemy', while aboard the *DEFIANCE*, near the rear of the Lee Column, Midshipman Colin Campbell recorded that:

> Lord Nelson made the expressive signal 'England expects
> every man to do his duty!' Captain Durham then turned
> the hands up and made a short, but very expressive speech

to the ship's company which was answered by three cheers. Everything being then ready – Matches lit – guns double shotted with grape and rounds and decks clear – we piped to dinner and had a good glass of grog.

Immediately after the battle the Reverend John Greenly in the *REVENGE*, which had been tenth in line after the *ROYAL SOVEREIGN*, wrote down his recollection of the signal, which is a good example of the many elaborations and misquotes that were to occur:

Lord Nelson's ship, which you may be sure, behaved as he always does. The last signal he made by telegraph, was: 'England expects everything from this day's action, and trusts every man will do his duty'. Our Captain told his men, he would act as Lord Nelson had always done, lay his ship alongside the largest he came near and would leave the rest to his men, they gave him three cheers, and they fought like lions.

On seeing the signal, the second in command, Admiral Collingwood, gave the impression that he was irritated by it, exclaiming, 'What *is* Nelson signalling about? We all know what we have to do', but once he grasped its psychological meaning 'he expressed great delight and admiration, and made it known to the officers and ship's company'.

Pasco relates that when 'England expects . . .' had 'been answered by a few Ships in the Van, he [Nelson] ordered me to make the signal for Close Action and to *keep it up*; accordingly I hoisted No. 16 at the top-gallant mast-head, and there it remained until shot away'.

'NOW I CAN DO NO MORE'

While Nelson may have been satisfied with the gentle roar that he heard from thousands of men around him, his mind was troubled by the ground swell coming in from the Atlantic. It was growing at an alarming rate. *VICTORY*'s stern was rising and falling, giving the impression that she was being levered forward towards the enemy. The bright sunshine of the early morning was being dimmed by cloud. It heralded any sailor's worst nightmare: a storm blowing on to a rocky lee shore with shoals, little sea room and possibly a disabled ship. Nelson ordered Signal 63: 'Prepare to anchor', followed by Signal 8: 'The above signal to take place immediately after the close of the day'. He needed to communicate his concern before the battle started because it was the last chance he could be sure of relaying a message to all his ships, before masts and yards were carried away. Some sources say this signal was hoisted before 'England expects . . .'

For over three hours the fleets had stood in view of each other. With every stitch of canvas set, they presented a spectacle of immense beauty. It was a sight that had never been seen before and would never be seen again. Captain Edward Codrington had called all his lieutenants to witness it, since 'I suppose no man ever before saw a sight of such beauty'. The Combined Fleet, with the sun shining on the freshly painted sides of its ships, was still sailing in a confused, overlapping line spread out over more than a mile of ocean and presenting itself as a vast concave arc. Now, at last, the fleets were almost within gunshot. Midshipman Badcock in the *NEPTUNE* gives an account of the splendour that also captures its deadly menace.

> At this period the enemy were forming their double line in
> the shape of a crescent. It was a beautiful sight when their
> line was completed: their broadsides turned towards us,
> showing their iron teeth, and now and then trying the range
> of a shot to ascertain the distance, that they might, the
> moment we came within point blank (about six hundred
> yards), open their fire upon our van ships, no doubt with
> the hope of dismasting some of our leading vessels before
> they could close and break their line.
>
> Some of the enemy's ships were painted like ourselves
> – with double yellow sides, some with a broad single red
> or yellow streak, others all black, and the noble *Santissima
> Trinidad* with four distinct lines of red, with a white ribbon

between them, made her seem to be a superb man-of-war, which, indeed, she was. Her appearance was imposing, her head splendidly ornamented with a colossal group of figures, painted white, representing the Holy Trinity from which she took her name. This magnificent ship was destined to be our opponent. She was lying-to under topsails, topgallant-sails, royals, jib and spanker; her courses were hauled up, and her lofty, towering sails looked beautiful, peering through the smoke, as she waited the onset.

The flags of France and Spain, both handsome, chequered the line, waving defiance to that of Britain. Then in our fleet, union jacks and ensigns were made fast to the fore and fore-topmast stays, as well as to the mizzen rigging, besides one at the peak, in order to show the enemy our determination to conquer . . .

Hoisting colours in four different places meant that if one were shot away others would be left flying. Villeneuve hoisted his flag in three places. Identifying friend from foe in the smoke of naval battle was vitally important. Nelson was a vice admiral of the White and at Trafalgar he decided that the whole fleet was to wear his flag, the White Ensign, because it was more easily distinguishable from the French tricolour. Normally, Collingwood's ships would have worn the Blue Ensign, since he was a vice admiral of the Blue. As soon as Nelson noticed that the iron hoops round the enemy's masts were painted black he ordered the British ships to paint theirs white so that even with ensigns shot away, friend could be distinguished from foe.

Nelson's last telegraphic message came at 11.40 a.m. It was sent to only one ship, ROYAL SOVEREIGN, just as she was coming under fire: 'I intend to push or go through the end of the enemy's line to prevent them from getting into Cadiz.' This took Collingwood by surprise since everyone was expecting Nelson to aim for the centre. However, to Nelson it was looking more and more as if the enemy were cruising for Cadiz rather than preparing for a battle. Not only had they failed to form a proper line but they had refused to hoist their colours. Nelson always wanted to attack his opposite number, who should have been in the centre, but he could not identify Villeneuve's ship. Then at 11.45 a.m. the Combined Fleet, all except the *Bucentaure*, hoisted their colours, opening fire as they did so. Hesitantly, Villeneuve's colours were run up as well and on seeing them Nelson reverted to his original plan.

At about this time Nelson turned to Blackwood and said:

> Now I can do no more. We must trust the great Disposer
> of events, and the justice of our cause. I thank God for this
> great opportunity of doing my duty.

On the gun decks, all was 'perfect death-like silence', until just before the action began. The morning as a whole was brilliantly summarized by 34-year-old William Price Cumby, the First Lieutenant of the *BELLEROPHON*:

> About a quarter before six I was roused from my slumbers
> by my messmate Overton, the Master, who called out,
> 'Cumby, my boy, turn out; here they are all ready for you,
> thirty three sail of the line close under our lee, and evidently
> disposed to await our attack.' You may readily conclude
> I did not remain long in a recumbent position, but of my
> cot put up a short but fervent prayer to the great god of
> battles for a glorious day to springing out of bed, hurried
> on my clothes, and kneeling down by the side the arms of
> my Country, 'committing myself individually to His all-wise
> disposal, and begging His gracious protection and favour
> for my dear wife and children, and whatever His unerring
> wisdom might see fit to order for myself.' This was the
> substance and, as near as memory will serve me, the actual
> words of my petition.
> I was soon on deck, when the enemy's fleet was distinctly
> seen to leeward, standing to the southward under easy sail,
> and forming in line on the starboard tack; at six o'clock the

signal was made to form the order of sailing, and soon after to bear up and steer ENE. We made sail in our station, and at twenty minutes past six we answered the signal to prepare for battle, and soon afterwards to steer east; we then beat to quarters, and cleared ship for action.

After I had breakfasted as usual at eight o'clock with the Captain in his cabin, he begged me to wait a little as he had something to show me, when he produced, and requested me to peruse, lord Nelson's private memorandum, addressed to the captains, relative to the conduct of the ships in action, which having read he inquired whether I perfectly understood the Admiral's instructions. I replied that they were so distinct and explicit that it was quite impossible they could be misunderstood. He then expressed his satisfaction, and said he wished me to made acquainted with it, that in the event of his being 'bowl'd out' I might know how to conduct the ship agreeably to the Admiral's wishes. On this I observed that it was very possible that the same shot which disposed of him might have an equally tranquillising effect on me, and indeed that idea I submitted to him the expediency of the Master as being the only officer who in such case would remain on the quarterdeck being also apprised of the Admiral's instructions, that he might be enabled to communicate them to the next officer, whoever might be, that should succeed to the command of the ship. To this Captain Cooke immediately assented, and poor Overton, the Master, was desired to read the memorandum, which he did. And here I may be permitted to remark en passant that, of the three officers who carried the knowledge of this private memorandum into the action, I was the only one who brought it out.

On going round the decks to see everything in its place and all in perfect order, before I reported to the Captain the ship in readiness for action, the junior lieutenant who commanded the seven foremost guns at his quarters, where the zeal of the seamen had led them to chalk in large characters on their guns the words, 'Victory or Death' – a very gratifying mark of the spirit with which they were going to their work.

At eleven o'clock, finding we should not be in action for an hour or more, we piped to dinner, which we had ordered to be in readiness for the ship's company at that hour thinking that Englishmen would fight all the better for having a comfortable meal; and at the same time Captain Cooke joined us in partaking of some cold meat, etc on the rudder head, all our bulkheads, tables, etc, being necessarily taken down and carried below. May here observe that all the enemy's fleet had changed their former position, having wore together, and were now forming their line on the larboard tack. The wind having shifted a few points to the southward of west, their rear ships were thrown far to windward of their centre and van, and the wind being light, they were, many of them, unable to gain their proper stations before the battle began.

A quarter past eleven Lord Nelson made the telegraphic signal, 'England expects that every man will do his duty', which, you may believe, produced the most animating and inspiring effect on the whole fleet; and at noon he made the last signal observed from the BELLEROPHON before the action began which was to, 'Prepare to anchor after the close of the day.'

We were now rapidly closing with the enemy's line . . . with the signal for close action flying.

5

THE BATTLE: 'HERE BEGAN THE DIN OF WAR'

'SEE HOW THAT NOBLE FELLOW COLLINGWOOD TAKES HIS SHIP INTO ACTION!'

The ships of the Combined Fleet waited for Nelson's two columns to ram them. The beauty of 27 British warships bearing down with every stitch of canvas set may have been an awesome sight, but it also presented a wonderful target. As Lieutenant Frederick Hoffman in the *TONNANT* said, 'We were saved the trouble of taking in our studding sails, as our opponents had the civility to effect it by shot before we got into their line.'

Villeneuve made the general signal to commence the action, No 242: 'Open Fire!' As soon as the British were within range – about a thousand yards – the *Fougueux* fired the first shots of the battle at the *ROYAL SOVEREIGN*. It was twelve noon. One minute later the *Santa Ana*, immediately ahead of the *Fougueux*, also opened fire on the *ROYAL SOVEREIGN*. Commander Bazin, second in command of the *Fougueux*, noted that his captain 'had the colours and the French pendant hoisted and fired the whole broadside at the foremost ship'. 'Here began the din of war,' wrote Lieutenant Barclay in the *BRITANNIA*.

Round shot whistled through the still air, whipped through her canvas, holes appeared in her sails and the splashes of the enemy gunfire landed all around, yet *ROYAL SOVEREIGN* stood on, increasing her lead over her immediate supporters, the *BELLEISLE, MARS* and

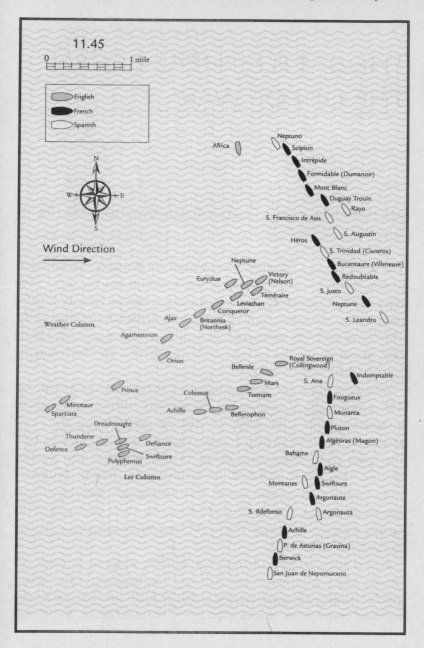

11.45

0 |———|———|———|———|———|———| 1 mile

English
French
Spanish

N
W ——— E
S

Wind Direction

Neptuno
Scipion
Intrépide
Formidable (Dumanoir)
Mont Blanc
Duguay Trouin
Rayo
S. Francisco de Asis
S. Augustin
Héros
S. Trinidad (Cisneros)
Bucentaure (Villeneuve)
Redoubtable
S. Justo
Neptune
S. Leandro

Africa

Neptune
Euryalus
Victory
(Nelson)
Téméraire
Leviathan
Conqueror
Ajax
Britannia
(Northesk)
Agamemnon

Weather Column

Orion

Belleisle
Royal Sovereign
(Collingwood)
Mars
S. Ana
Indomptable
Tonnant
Fougueux
Prince
Colossus
Monarca
Minotaur
Achille
Bellerophon
Pluton
Spartiate
Algésiras (Magon)
Dreadnought
Bahama
Thunderer
Defiance
Aigle
Defence
Swiftsure
Swiftsure
Polyphemus
Montanes
Argonaute
Lee Column
S. Ildefonso
Argonauta
Achille
P. de Asturias (Gravina)
Berwick
San Juan de Nepomuceno

TONNANT. Fresh out of a dockyard, and with a clean copper bottom, she was a fast sailer. During her approach Lieutenant Clavell, a favourite of Collingwood's, had seen the VICTORY setting her studding sails and pointed it out to the admiral, requesting his permission to do the same. 'The ships of our line,' replied Collingwood, 'are not yet sufficiently up for us to do so now; but you may be getting ready.' The studding sail and royal halyards were accordingly manned. Fewer than ten minutes passed before the admiral, observing Lieutenant Clavell's eyes fixed upon him with a look of expectation, gave the nod. The order was given to rig out and hoist away, and the massive three-decker under its crowd of sail, went rapidly ahead. Collingwood seemed determined to be the first to exchange fire with the enemy. He entered the fray as if in a single-ship fight. His supporters were more than 15 minutes behind. Captain Edward Rotherham, pacing the deck with Collingwood, relished the moment. 'What would Nelson give to be here?'

Nelson was indeed impressed. 'See how that noble fellow Collingwood takes his ship into action!' he exclaimed to Blackwood. A short while later Dr William Beatty overheard Lieutenant Pasco say while looking through his glass:

> 'There is a top-gallant-yard gone.' His lordship eagerly
> asked, 'Whose top-gallant-yard is that gone? Is it the ROYAL
> SOVEREIGN's?' and on being answered by Lieutenant Pasco
> in the negative, and that it was the Enemy's, he smiled, and
> said: 'Collingwood is doing well.'

Captain Charles Tyler of the TONNANT was so impressed by the ability with which the ROYAL SOVEREIGN engaged the enemy that he 'felt for a few moments as if' he 'had nothing to do but look on and admire'.

Nelson had proposed in his Memorandum that Collingwood should cut the line of the Combined Fleet at the 12th ship from the rear but he found himself heading for a gap between the 18th, the Santa Ana, flagship of Vice Admiral Don Ignacio María de Álava y Navarette, and 19th, the *Fougueux*, Captain L A Beaudouin. In the last moments before impact the *Fougueux* tried to forge ahead and the *Santa Ana* tried to slow down by filling the front of her topsails with wind, but it was too late and Collingwood ordered, 'Steer for the Frenchman and carry away her bowsprit.' At this point the weight of the *Santa Ana's* first full broadside made the *ROYAL SOVEREIGN* heel two strakes out of the water. Nevertheless, Collingwood broke the enemy's line at 12.20 a.m., firing double-shotted broadsides into the stern of the *Santa Ana* and raking the bows of the *Fougueux* as he went through. The killing had begun. Captain Servaux of the *Fougueux* relates the story:

The *Fougueux*, on board which I was master-at-arms, had for her immediate leader (*chef de file*) the Spanish man-of-war *Santa Ana*, of 110 guns. By bad handling that ship left a gap of at least a cable across, between herself and the next astern ourselves; thus offering the enemy an easy passage through. It was just on this point that Admiral Collingwood directed his attack, as he advanced to break the line. It necessarily resulted that he crossed right in front of our bows, and so our first antagonist was Admiral Collingwood.

At a quarter past twelve o'clock the *Fougueux*, a man-of-war of seventy-four guns, fired the first gun in the fleet. As she did so she hoisted her colours. She continued her cannonade, firing on the English flagship. Which was a greatly superior vessel in size, height, guns and the number of crew. Her main-deck and upper-deck guns, in fact, could fire right down on to our decks, and in that way all our upper-deck men employed in working the ship, and the infantry marksmen posted on the gangways, were without cover and entirely exposed. We had also, according to our bad habit in the French Navy, fired away over a hundred rounds from our big guns at long range before the English ship had practically snapped a gun lock. It was, indeed, not until we found ourselves side by side and yardarm to yardarm with the English flagship that she fired at all.

Then she gave us a broadside from five and fifty guns and carronades, hurtling forth a storm of cannonballs, big and small, and musket shot. I thought the *Fougueux* was shattered to pieces – pulverised. The storm of projectiles that hurled themselves against and through the hull on the port side made the ship heel to starboard. Most of the sails and rigging were cut to pieces, while the upper deck was swept clear of the greater number of the seamen working there, and of the soldier sharpshooters. Our gun-decks below had, however, suffered less severely. There not more than thirty men in all were put *hors de combat*.

This was to be a typical situation for ships on both sides during the battle. Casualties were distributed disproportionately throughout the ships, with those on the upper decks suffering the most, particularly the officers, whose job it was to stand tall without showing fear as hell was let loose around them. Generally, about a fifth of officers in the British fleet became casualties as a consequence of their exposed positions, and more than one third of sailing masters and boatswains, who were stationed on the quarterdecks and forecastles respectively, were killed or wounded.

The log of the *POLYPHEMUS* (64) observed the '*ROYAL SOVEREIGN* break the Enemy's line in the centre, and placed herself alongside a Spanish three-decker'. In passing the *Santa Ana* Collingwood's flagship had fired a devastating broadside into her stern, 'tearing it down', dismounting 14 of her guns and killing and wounding close to a hundred of her crew. Then with her helm hard a-starboard she had ranged up alongside the Spanish ship so closely that the lower yards of the two vessels became locked together, the muzzles of the two ships literally touching. According to Collingwood, the *Santa Ana* was a 'Spanish perfection. She towered over the *ROYAL SOVEREIGN* like a castle. No ship fired a shot at her but ourselves and you have no conception how completely she was ruined.'

Within 15 minutes of the start of the engagement, and before any other British ship had taken part in the action, an optimistic

Captain Rotherham came up to Collingwood and, shaking him by the hand, said, 'I congratulate you, sir: she is slackening her fire, and must soon strike.' However, the *Santa Ana* was not going to give up that easily. Three-deckers could take tremendous punishment and the battle between them, broadside to broadside, lasted another two hours. Worse, the ROYAL SOVEREIGN soon found that she had more than one opponent to contend with. The *Fougueux*, having bore up, raked her stern; and ahead of her, at the distance of about 400 yards, lay the *San Leandro* (64), who, wearing, raked her in that direction; while upon the ROYAL SOVEREIGN's starboard bow and quarter, within less than 300 yards, were the *San Justo* (74) and *Indomptable* (80). So incessant was the fire kept up by all these ships that men in the ROYAL SOVEREIGN frequently saw the shots come in contact with each other. It was Collingwood's flagship that was now at risk with five ships mauling him, four with raking fire. Captain Pierre Servaux continued:

> The preliminary greeting, rough and brutal as it was did not dishearten our men. A well-maintained fire showed the Englishman that we too had guns and could use them.
>
> The English ship having come up to us, made to break the line between us and the *Santa Ana*. The Spanish ship, in fact, during our action with the English leader, had not fired a single shot. She had stolidly kept on and continued her course without shortening sail, thus giving an easy passage through the enemy. After that, however, by the smart handling of our captain, we managed to come within our proper distance of her; as a fact, indeed, almost with our bowsprit over her poop. By this manoeuvre we had the enemy's ship on the port quarter in such a way that whilst we could only receive a few shots from their stern guns, they were exposed to our whole broadside, raking the enemy end-on, along all his decks. We soon saw the English vessel's mizzen-mast go by the board, and then her rudder and steering gear were damaged, making the ship unmanageable.

Her sails flapped loose in the wind, and her sheets and
running rigging were cut to pieces by our hail of shot. For
some time she ceased firing. We, for our part, now redoubled
our efforts and we next saw her main topmast come down.

Heavy showers of Spanish musketry swept the upper decks of the
ROYAL SOVEREIGN, and Collingwood directed Captain Joseph Vallack,
Royal Marines, who was to be wounded later in the battle, to take his
men off the poop so that they might not be unnecessarily exposed.
However, 'Old Cuddie', as he was known to his sailors, remained there
with Captain Rotherham 'amongst the dead, dying and wounded,
which strewed the deck' wearing 'his little triangular gold-laced cocked
hat, tight silk stockings, and buckles, musing over the progress of the
fight and munching an apple'. Collingwood knew how to keep his
cool. His servant, William Smith, was amazed:

> . . . the Admiral spoke to me about the middle of the
> action, and again for five minutes immediately after
> its close: and on neither occasion could I observe the
> slightest change from his ordinary manner. This . . .
> made an impression on me which will never be effaced . .
> . I wondered how a person whose mind was occupied by
> such a variety of most important concerns could, with
> the utmost ease and equanimity, inquire kindly after my
> welfare, and talk of common matters as if nothing of
> consequence was taking place.

Rotherham put on a fine show as well. He wore a remarkably large
gold-laced cocked hat and gold epaulettes. On being asked why
he exposed himself so much to the enemy's sharpshooters in such
conspicuous dress, he replied, 'I have always fought in a cocked hat,
and I always will.'
   Collingwood, admiral though he was, moved among his gunners
to encourage and direct their fire, looking along the guns himself
to see that they were properly pointed and commending the sailors,

particularly a black man, who was afterwards killed, but who stood firm and fired ten times directly into the porthole of the *Santa Ana*. Collingwood escaped with his life by a miracle, but was hit, oddly enough in the leg, as if a justification of his use of silk stockings. He wrote to his wife:

> Did I but tell you how my leg was hurt. It was by a splinter. It was a pretty severe blow. I had a great many thumps, one way or the other; one in the back, which I think was the wind of a great shot, for I never saw anything that did it.

One of *ROYAL SOVEREIGN*'s gunners wrote home a week later to his father in Odiham, Hampshire. It is possible to identify the author only as 'Sam'. It may be that some accounts of the battle, including this famous one, are bogus, or more likely that the muster list is innaccurate.

> Honoured Father,
> This comes to tell you I am alive and hearty except three
> fingers; but that's not much, it might have been my head.
> I told brother Tom I should like to see a great battle, and I
> have seen one, and we have peppered the Combined navy;
> and for matter of that, they fought us pretty tightish for
> French and Spanish. Three of our mess were killed, and
> four more of us winged. But to tell you the truth of it, when
> the game began, I wished myself at Warnborough with my
> plough again; but when they had given us one duster, and
> I found myself snug and tight, I bid fear kiss my bottom
> and set to in good earnest, and thought no more about
> being killed than if I were at Murrell Green Fair; and I was
> presently as busy and as black as a collier. How my fingers
> got knocked overboard I don't know; but off they are, and
> I never missed them till I wanted them. You see, by my
> writing, it was my left hand, so I can write to you, and fight
> for my King yet.

ROYAL SOVEREIGN's followers eventually came to her support, although she continued to engage with the *Santa Ana* almost single-handed. Collingwood was to remark that 'it seemed a very long time before he found his friends around him'. The *BELLEISLE, MARS, TONNANT* and *BELLEROPHON* were all about to give and take a heavy beating.

'GO ON BOARD WHICH YOU PLEASE'

It was not until between 40 and 50 minutes after Collingwood had broken through the line, at about 1.00 p.m., that Nelson, leading the Weather Column in single line ahead, got into action. *VICTORY* was under fire for the whole length of the time without being able to return it. Midshipman Badcock in the *NEPTUNE* described the column as it came within range.

> Lord Nelson's van was strong: three three-deckers
> [*VICTORY, TÉMÉRAIRE* and *NEPTUNE*] and four seventy-fours, their jibbooms nearly over the taffrails, the bands
> playing 'God Save the King', 'Rule Britannia', 'Britons
> Strike Home'; the crews stationed on the forecastles of the
> different ships, cheering the ship ahead of them when the
> enemy began to fire, sent those feelings to our hearts that
> insured victory.

Reluctantly aiming for the enemy van under the command of Rear Admiral Dumanoir Le Pelley, Nelson was relieved when the enemy simultaneously broke out their ensigns and commanders' flags and opened fire because he could now alter course and aim for Villeneuve in the *Bucentaure*, 11th from the van. *VICTORY* was under heavy fire for at least 40 minutes. Her speed, slow enough at first, decreased continually as the hail of shot riddled the sails, or stripped them from the yards, and about 500 yards from the Combined Fleet's line she lost her mizzen-topmast and had her wheel shot away, having from then on to be steered from down below in the gunroom. Captain Jean Lucas in the *Redoubtable* was particularly pleased with the way his ship ran up the colours:

> That of the *Redoubtable* was done in an imposing manner: the drums were beating and the musketry presented arms to the standard, it was saluted by the officers and crew with seven cheers, '*Vive l'Empereur!*'

His account described how:

> The enemy's column, which was directed against our centre, was at eleven o'clock on the port side, and the flagship *Bucentaure* began firing. I ordered a number of the captains of the guns to go up on the forecastle and observe why it was some of our ships fired so badly. They found that all their shots carried too low and fell short. I then gave orders to aim for dismasting and above all to aim straight. At a quarter to twelve the *Redoubtable* opened fire with a shot from the first gun division. It cut through the foretopsail yard of *VICTORY*, whereupon cheers and shouts resounded all over the ship. Our firing was well kept up, and in less than ten minutes the British flagship had lost her mizzen-mast, foretopsail, and main topgallant mast.

In spite of Captain Lucas's observation that the French and Spanish guns were being aimed too low, the general opinion was that the opposite was in fact true. The Combined Fleet tried to aim for the masts and rigging of the British ships. Some believe this reflected their tactical instinct to escape from an engagement with their foe being unable to follow, which can be traced back to the battles of the Seven Years' War. However, the British deliberately aimed their great guns low, which, combined with their more rapid rate of fire, brought devastation to the decks of the French and Spanish ships. This explains the hundreds of casualties in the enemy ships and why so many of them struck their colours. Lieutenant Pierre-Guillaume Gicquel des Touches recognized the problem:

> The audacity with which Admiral Nelson had attacked us, and which had so completely succeeded, arose from the complete scorn which, not without reason, he professed for the effects of our gunfire. At that time our principle was to aim at the masts and, in order to produce any real damage, we wasted masses of projectiles which, if they had been aimed at the hulls, would have felled a proportion of the crews. Thus our losses were always incomparably higher than those of the English, who fired horizontally and hit our wooden sides, letting fly splinters which were more murderous than the cannon ball itself. We were still using the linstock match to fire our guns, which dispatched the ball with an excruciating delay, so that if the ship was rolling, as it was on October 21, complete broadsides flew over the enemy's mastheads without causing the slightest damage. The English had flintlocks, rather than our crude linstocks.

The damage to the British ships might have been worse but for the heavy swell rolling the Franco-Spanish ships, which made firing very wild. Lucas continued his story:

> Meanwhile I always kept so close the *Bucentaure* [he had declared that he was fully resolved to sacrifice his ship in defence of Villeneuve's flag] that several times they called from their stern gallery that I should run them down; indeed, the bowsprit of the *Redoubtable* touched the crown of the flagship's taffrail; but I assured them that they had nothing to be anxious about.
>
> The damage done to *VICTORY* did not affect the daring manoeuvre of Admiral Nelson. He repeatedly persisted in trying to break the line in front of the *Redoubtable*, and

threatening to run us down if we opposed. But the proximity of the British flagship, though closely followed by the *TÉMÉRAIRE*, instead of intimidating my intrepid crew, only increased their ardour; and to show the English Admiral that we did not fear his fouling us, I had grappling irons made fast at all the yard-arms.

THE GAUNTLET OF OVERWHELMING FIRE

VICTORY was about a mile and a quarter distant when the enemy van opened fire on her. Captain Charles Bérenger in the *Scipion* (74) sailing astern of the *Neptuno* (80), the leading ship of the Combined Fleet, recorded that 'at 12.35 the *Formidable* (80) opened fire, and I did so immediately after her, at a three-decker at the head of the northern column which was steering for the centre of our van'. A minute or two of silence followed, and then in unison at least seven or eight of the weather-most ships opened fire upon the *VICTORY*, 'such a fire as had scarcely before been directed at a single ship'.

Captain Blackwood of the *EURYALUS*, who was then still chatting to Nelson and watching the exploits of the *ROYAL SOVEREIGN*, recalled that:

When Lord Nelson found the shot passing over the *VICTORY*, he desired Captain Prowse, of the *SIRIUS* and myself, to go on board our Ships, and in our way to tell all the Captains of the Line-of-Battle Ships, that he depended on their exertions; and that if, by the mode of attack prescribed, they found it impracticable to get into Action immediately, they might adopt whatever they thought best, provided it led them quickly and closely alongside an Enemy. He then again desired me to go away; and as we were standing on the front of the poop, I took his hand, and said, 'I trust, my Lord, that on my return to the *VICTORY*, which will be as soon as possible, I shall find your Lordship well, and in possession of twenty prizes.' On which he made his reply, 'God bless you, Blackwood; I shall never speak to you again.'

Blackwood got away just in time as this account by Dr Beatty confirms:

At fifty minutes past eleven the enemy [van] opened their fire on the Commander in Chief. They shewed [*sic*] great coolness in the commencement of the battle; for as the VICTORY approached their line, their ships lying immediately ahead of her and across her bows fired only one gun at a time, to ascertain whether she was yet within their range. This was frequently repeated by eight or nine of their ships, till at length a shot passed through the VICTORY's main top-gallant-sail; the hole in which being discovered by the Enemy, they immediately opened their broadsides, supporting an awful and tremendous fire. In a very short time afterwards, Mr Scott, Public Secretary to the Commander in Chief, was killed by a cannon-shot while in conversation with Captain Hardy. Lord Nelson being then near them, Captain Adair of the Marines, with the assistance of a Seaman, endeavoured to remove the body from His Lordship's sight: but he had already observed the fall of his Secretary; and now said with anxiety, 'Is that poor Scott that is gone?' and on being answered in the affirmative by Captain Adair, he replied, 'Poor fellow!'

Lord Nelson and Captain Hardy walked the quarter-deck in conversation for some time after this (after Scott was killed), while the Enemy kept up an incessant raking fire. A double-headed shot struck one of the parties of Marines drawn upon the poop, and killed eight of them; when his Lordship, perceiving this, ordered Captain Adair to disperse his men round the ship, that they might not

suffer so much from being together. In a few minutes
afterwards a shot struck the fore-brace-bits on the quarter-
deck, and passed between Lord Nelson and Captain Hardy;
a splinter from the bits bruising Captain Hardy's foot,
and tearing the buckle from his shoe. They both instantly
stopped; and were observed by the Officers on deck to
survey each other with enquiring looks, each supposing
the other to be wounded. His Lordship then smiled, and
said: 'This is too warm work, Hardy, to last long;' and
declared that 'through all the battles he had been in, he had
never witnessed more cool courage than was displayed by
VICTORY's crew on this occasion.'

The VICTORY by this time having approached close to
the Enemy's van, had suffered very severely without firing
a single gun; she had lost about twenty men killed, and
had about thirty wounded. Her mizzen-topmast, and all
her studding topsails and their booms, on both sides were
shot away; the Enemy's fire being chiefly directed at her
rigging, with a view to disable her before she could close
with them.

Beatty also noted that:

The Enemy's fire continued to be pointed so high
throughout the engagement, that the VICTORY did not lose
a man on her lower deck; and had only two wounded on that
deck, and these by musket-balls.

Having drawn Dumanoir's fire, and used his move as a feint on the
eight ships of the van, Nelson altered course to starboard and led his
column down the enemy line towards Villeneuve in the centre. As she
drew near, Hardy, scanning the hostile array, saw three ships crowded
together behind and beyond the *Bucentaure* and concluded that he
would not be able to pass through the line unless he ran on board one
of the enemy. According to Beatty:

> At four minutes past twelve o'clock she [the VICTORY]
> opened fire, from both sides of her decks upon the Enemy;
> when Captain Hardy represented to His Lordship that 'it
> appeared impracticable to pass through the Enemy's line
> without going on board some of their ships.' Lord Nelson
> answered, 'I cannot help it: it does not signify which
> we run on board of. Go on board which you please:
> take your choice.'

Given a free choice by Nelson, Hardy had decided to take the VICTORY under the stern of the *Redoubtable*. However, as he steered for this narrow gap in the opposing line, the *Neptune* (84) managed to close it. At the last moment Hardy had to push the VICTORY between the *Bucentaure* and *Redoubtable*, which brought him within range of the guns of the *Santissima Trinidad, San Justo* and *Neptune* as well. The VICTORY withheld her fire until 12.40 p.m. when, at a range of 500 yards, she opened fire with her starboard guns on the *Santissima Trinidad*.

VICTORY's log states, 'In attempting to pass through their line fell on board the tenth and eleventh ships when the action became general.' At about this time her wheel was shot away, leaving her out of control until her master, Thomas Atkinson, dashed to the gunroom and rigged the reserve gear to the tiller.

The *Santissima Trinidad* ('The Most Holy Trinity') was the most prominent ship at Trafalgar and the most attractive prize. Launched in Havana on 3 March 1769, four years after VICTORY, she was the seventh ship since the Spanish Armada to have born this name, and her four decks carrying 140 guns made her the largest warship in the world at the time. At Trafalgar she was the flagship of Rear Admiral Don Báltasar Hidalgo de Cisneros, who was famed for recapturing her from the British at the Battle of Cape St Vincent in 1797. On Monday 21 October VICTORY, which had also been at Cape St Vincent, was for a while heading for her old adversary. In fact some of the early reports claim that Nelson was shot from her tops rather than the *Redoubtable*'s. Cisneros wrote in his report:

Admiral Nelson's ship presently arrived within gun-shot, followed by two three-deckers which were making towards us; but when he drew nearer, recognising that his course was shaped so as to break the line astern of the *Trinidad* and ahead of the French Admiral, at 11.30, in order to frustrate him, I ordered the topsails to be laid aback, bringing myself as near as possible to the above-mentioned French ship, and at 12 o'clock opening a vigorous and well-sustained fire to the same end; in this manner I completely frustrated the English Admiral's intention.

Don Benito Pérez Galdós, in his account of the battle based on his interviews with Spanish survivors, described the opening moves from the point of view of the *Santissima Trinidad*:

The *VICTORY* fired first on the *Redoubtable*, and being repulsed she came to windward of the *Trinidad*. The moment had come for us. A hundred voices shouted 'Fire!' loudly re-echoing the word of command, and fifty round shot were hurled against the sides of the English man-of-war. For a minute I could see nothing of the enemy for the smoke, while they as if blinded by rage, came straight down on us before the wind. Just within pistol shot they put the *VICTORY* about and gave us a broadside. In the interval between our firing and theirs, our crew, who had taken note of the damage done to the enemy, became very enthusiastic. The guns were rapidly served, though not without some trouble, owing to want of experience in some gunners. It seemed as though the *VICTORY* must fall into our hands, for the *Trinidad*'s fire had cut her tackle to pieces, and we saw with pride that her mizzen-mast had gone by the board.

The *Trinidad* was doing the *VICTORY* immense damage, when the *TÉMÉRAIRE*, by a wonderfully clever manoeuvre, slipped in between the two vessels; thus sheltering her consort from our fire. She then passed through the line astern of the *Trinidad*, and as the *Bucentaure*, during the firing, had moved up so close alongside the *Trinidad* that their yardarms touched, there was a wide space beyond, into which the *TÉMÉRAIRE* settled herself, and then she came up on her lee side and delivered a broadside into us there. At the same time the *NEPTUNE*, another large English ship, placed herself where the *VICTORY* had previously been, while the *VICTORY* also wore round, so that, in a few minutes, the *Trinidad* was quite surrounded by the enemy and riddled by shot from all sides.

The line of the Combined Fleet was after that broken in several points, and the loose order in which they had been formed at the outset gave place to disastrous confusion. We were surrounded by the enemy, whose guns kept up a tornado of round shot and grape-shot on our ship, and on the *Bucentaure* as well. The *Agustin*, the *Héros*, and the *Leandro*, were also engaged at some distance from us, where they had rather more sea-room, while the *Trinidad*, and the Admiral's ship, cut off on all sides and held fast by the genius of the great Nelson, were fighting desperately.

Meanwhile, Captain Jean Lucas could see very clearly from the *Redoubtable* what was happening:

The *VICTORY* with the flag of Admiral Nelson came on; she seemed to be aiming to break the line between the *Santissima Trinidad* and the bows of the *Bucentaure*. I was all the time following the wake of the Commander-in-Chief; but there was still a wide gap between him and myself. I pressed on and closed the flagship so as, in effect, to keep the *Redoubtable*'s bowsprit almost touching the taffrail of the *Bucentaure*. I made up my mind to sacrifice my ship, if necessary, in defence of the flagship. This I told my officers and men, who answered me with shouts and cheers, repeated over and over again. *'Vive l'Empereur!' 'Vive l'Amiral!' 'Vive le Commandant!'*

At approximately 1 p.m. the VICTORY's bowsprit pushed through the line under the *Bucentaure*'s stern, and ahead of the *Redoubtable* whose port side she grazed. She passed so close to the *Bucentaure* that her yardarm caught the Frenchman's after rigging. VICTORY's 50 double- and even treble-shotted port-side guns fired into the French flagship's flimsy stern galleries, sweeping her open decks with a blunder of metal and shattered timber that dismounted 20 guns and killed and wounded hundreds of her crew. In addition to her great guns, Boatswain William Willmet yanked the firing lanyard of VICTORY's deadly port 68-pounder carronade mounted on the forecastle, containing its one round shot and a keg of 500 musket balls. Villeneuve sent below to inquire the number and was stunned at the high figures in such a short space of time. It was a terrible blow from which the *Bucentaure* never recovered, although she went on fighting gallantly for another hour. The VICTORY's crew were nearly suffocated with clouds of black smoke that entered her portholes. Nelson, Hardy and others walking the quarter deck had their clothes covered with dust from the crumbled woodwork of the *Bucentaure*'s stern. The wreck continued on a hapless northerly course.

Putting her helm hard a-starboard, VICTORY fell alongside the *Redoubtable* and did horrendous damage to her with her starboard broadsides. The concussion of the firing would probably have rebounded her from the *Redoubtable* had not her starboard fore-topmast studding-sail boom-iron hooked into the leach of the *Redoubtable*'s fore topsail. This held the ships together. Captain Jean Lucas relished the opportunity to be fighting the British commander in chief's flagship:

> In the end, the VICTORY not having succeeded in passing astern of the French Admiral, ran foul of us, dropping alongside and shearing off aft in such a way that our poop lay alongside her quarter-deck. From this position the

grappling irons were thrown on board her. Those at the stern parted, but those forward held on; and at the same time our broadside was discharged, resulting in a terrible slaughter. We continued to fire for some time, although there was some delay at the guns. We had to use rope rammers in several cases, and fire with the guns run in, being unable to bowse them, as the ports were masked by the sides of the *VICTORY*. At the same time, elsewhere, by means of muskets fired through the ports into those of the *VICTORY*, we prevented the enemy from loading their guns, and before long they stopped firing on us altogether. What a day of glory for the *Redoubtable* if she had had to fight only with the *VICTORY*!

The first part of Nelson's plan had been fulfilled. The enemy's line had been broken in two places and his foremost ships had managed to run the gauntlet of overwhelming enemy fire aimed against their sails, rigging and fragile bows. Two separate actions were underway, close to each other in the Combined Fleet's centre, involving small clusters of ships, initially focused on the leading ships of the two British columns. This was the most critical point of the battle since the British ships were outnumbered, out-gunned and suffering attack from all sides.

As the *VICTORY* and *Redoubtable* drifted off, locked in the lethal embrace that was to seal the battle in popular imagination, they left a gap through which the rest of Nelson's Weather Column streamed, splitting the Franco-Spanish fleet in two, achieving the second part of his plan. As the rear ships of the two columns made their way into the fight, the remainder of the battle was dominated by relatively small and isolated groups of ships slugging it out with each other with breathtaking ferocity and courage. These cluster actions were battles within a battle and created the confusing mêlée that Nelson had intended. Superior British gunnery took its inevitable deadly toll, and by early afternoon the enemy's ships had already begun to strike their colours, six doing so within a space of 20 minutes (*San Juan Nepomuceno, Bucentaure, Fougueux, Santa Ana, Algésiras* (74) and

Redoubtable). Most were captured by the Weather Squadron, which also drove off the belated attack by the enemy's van, under Rear Admiral Dumanoir, in support of the ships already engaged. The battle was not long. It took little more than four hours from start to finish. When it was over 17 French and Spanish ships had been captured and another had blown up.

6
THE BATTLE: THE LEE COLUMN

'THE VAULT OF MISERY'

Even though the first broadsides had killed hundreds, the ROYAL SOVEREIGN battled it out unrelentingly with the Santa Ana for some two hours. She had inflicted crippling damage on Álava's flagship, bringing down all of her three masts, leaving her upper decks a tangled mass of splinters and shredded canvas, her starboard side nearly beaten in; 'completely ruined' in Collingwood's words. One English midshipman described how:

> We led the van and ran right down among them. This
> ship was fifty-five minutes [an exaggeration] engaged before
> any other ship came to our assistance, and we were alongside
> a three-decker. I can assure you it was glorious work. I'm
> stationed at the heaviest guns in the ship, and I stuck to
> one gun and poured it into her; she was so close it was
> impossible to miss her. Crash went her masts, and then she
> was fairly sicken'd . . . I looked once out of our stern ports;
> but I saw nothing but French and Spaniards around, firing
> at us in all directions. It was shocking to see the many brave
> seamen mangled so; some with their heads half shot away,
> others with their entrails mashed, lying panting on the deck.
> Our main and mizzen masts went overboard soon after
> the Spaniard struck to us . . . We have got 200 prisoners on

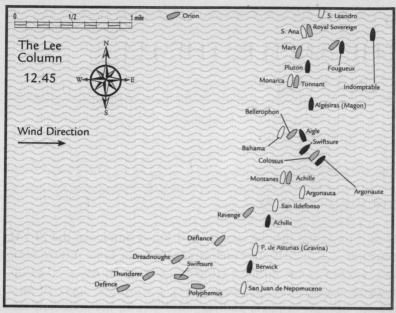

The Lee
Column

12.45

Wind Direction

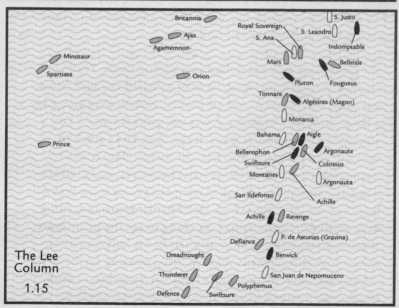

The Lee
Column

1.15

board – French and Spaniards . . . they say they took us for
the *VICTORY*, and were determined to sink us, but . . . found
it hard work to sink a British man-of-war. About the middle
of the action a lieutenant came and said Lord Nelson . . .
was afraid we should go down. Indeed, she rolled so much
after her masts were gone we could scarcely fight the lower
deck, the water was almost knee deep; however it served to
wash away the blood.

The *Santa Ana* struck her colours at about 2.15 p.m. The 'butcher's bill'
was 97 killed and 141 wounded including, among the latter, her gallant
captain, Don José Gardoquí and Vice Admiral Álava, who was 'on the
point of death'. The *ROYAL SOVEREIGN* was herself left with only a
tottering foremast, while Collingwood's cabin had been shattered. The
British casualties were lower with 47 killed and 94 wounded. Climbing
on to the *ROYAL SOVEREIGN*'s quarterdeck, Gardoquí asked a sailor the
name of the ship. When told he patted one of the guns and in broken
English remarked, 'I think she should be called the Royal Devil.'

The task of securing the position around the *ROYAL SOVEREIGN*
first fell to the *BELLEISLE*, under the command of Captain William
Hargood, which poured a heavy fire into the *Santa Ana*'s lee quarter
as she penetrated the line before bearing away to rake the stern of
the *Indomptable*. She was then blasted by the *Fougueux* with whom
she fought a fierce hour-long duel that reduced both ships to wrecks.
Lieutenant Paul Nicholas's description led through the attack and its
consequences, starting with Hargood announcing to his officers:

'Gentlemen, I have only to say that I shall pass close under
the stern of that ship [*Santa Ana*]; put in two round shot
and then a grape, and mind not to fire until each gun will
bear with effect.' With this laconic instruction the gallant
little man posted himself on the side of the foremost
carronade on the starboard of the quarterdeck.

The determined and resolute countenance of the weather
beaten sailor, here and there brightened by a smile of

exultation was well suited to the terrific appearance which they exhibited. Some were stripped to the waist; some had bared their necks and arms; others had tied a handkerchief round their heads; and all seemed eagerly to await the order to engage. My two brother officers and myself were stationed, with about thirty men at small arms, on the poop, on the front of which I was now standing. The shot began to pass over us and gave us an intimation of what we should in a few minutes undergo. An awful silence prevailed in the ship, only interrupted by the commanding voice of Captain Hargood, 'Steady! Starboard a little! steady so!' echoed by the master directing the quartermasters at the wheel. A shriek soon followed – a cry of agony was produced by the next shot – and the loss of the head of a poor recruit was the effect of the succeeding, and as we advanced, destruction rapidly increased. A severe contusion on the breast now prostrated our captain, but he soon resumed his station. Those only who have been in a similar situation to the one I am attempting to describe can have a correct idea of such a scene. My eyes were horror struck at the bloody corpses around me, and my ears rang with the shrieks of the wounded and the moans of the dying.

At this moment seeing that almost everyone was lying down, I was half disposed to follow the example, and several times stooped for the purpose, but – and I remember the impression well – a certain monitor seemed to whisper, 'Stand up and do not shrink from your duty.' Turning round, my much esteemed and gallant senior fixed my attention; the serenity of his countenance and the composure with which he paced the deck, drove more than half my terrors away; and joining him I became somewhat infused with his spirit, which cheered me on to act the part it became me. My experience is an instance of how much depends on the example of those in command when exposed to the fire of the enemy, more particularly in the trying situation in which we were placed for nearly thirty minutes from not having the power to retaliate.

It was just twelve o'clock when we reached their line. Our energies became roused and the mind diverted from its appalling condition, by the order of 'Stand to your guns!' which, as they successively came to bear were discharged into our opponents on either side; but as we passed close under the stern of the *Santa Ana*, of 112 guns, our attention was more strictly called to the ship. Although until that moment we had not fired a shot, our sails and rigging bore evident proofs of the manner in which we had been treated: our mizzentopmast was shot away and the ensign had been thrice rehoisted; numbers lay dead upon the decks, and eleven wounded were already in the surgeon's care. The firing was now tremendous, and at intervals the dispersion of the smoke gave us a sight of the colours of our adversaries.

At this critical period, while steering for the stern of *L'Indomptable* (our masts and yards and sails hanging in the utmost confusion over our heads), which continued a most galling raking fire upon us, the *Fougueux* being on our starboard quarter, and the Spanish *San Juste* on our larboard bow, the Master earnestly addressed the Captain. 'Shall we go through, sir?' 'Go through by . . .' was his energetic reply. 'There's your ship, sir, place me close alongside of her.' Our opponent defeated this manoeuvre by bearing away in a parallel course with us within pistol shot.

About one o'clock the *Fougueux* ran us on board the starboard side; and we continued thus engaging, until the latter dropped astern. Our mizzenmast soon went, and soon afterwards the maintopmast. A two-decked ship, the *Neptune* 80 [she had 84 guns], then took a position on our bow, and a 74, the *Achille*, on our quarter. At two o'clock the mainmast fell over the larboard side; I was at the time under the break of the poop aiding in running out a carronade, when a cry of 'stand clear there! here it comes!' made me look up, and at that instant the mainmast fell over the bulwarks just above me. This ponderous mass made the ship's whole frame shake, and had it taken a central direction it would have gone through the poop and added many to our list of sufferers. At half-past two our foremast was shot away close to the deck. In this unimaginable state we were but seldom capable of annoying our antagonists, while they had the power of choosing their distance, and every shot from them did considerable execution. We had suffered severely as must be supposed; and those on the poop were now ordered to assist at the quarter-deck guns, where we continued until the action ceased. Until half-past three we remained in this harrowing situation. The only means at all in our power of bringing our battery towards the enemy, was to use the sweeps out of the gunroom ports; to these we had recourse, but without effect, for even in ships under perfect command they prove almost useless, and we lay a mere hulk covered in wreck and rolling in the swell.

The scene below the *BELLEISLE*'s decks was recalled by one of her gunners:

At every moment the smoke accumulated more and more thickly, stagnating on board between decks at times so densely as to blur out the nearest objects and to blot out the men at the guns from those close at hand on each side. The guns had to be trained as it were mechanically by means of orders passed down from above, and on objects that the men fighting the guns hardly ever got a glimpse of . . . You frequently heard the order . . . to level the guns 'two points abaft the beam', 'point-blank', and so on. In fact, the men were as much in the dark as if they had been blindfolded, and the only comfort to be derived from this was that every man was isolated from his neighbour that he was not put in mind of his danger by seeing his messmates go down all round. All that he knew was that he heard the crash of the shot smashing through the rending timbers, and then followed at once the hoarse bellowings of the captains of the guns, as men were missed at their posts, calling out to the survivors, 'Close up there! close up!'

Captain Pierre Servaux in the *Fougueux* had been encouraged when the *ROYAL SOVEREIGN*'s main-topmast came down, but the fortunes of naval warfare change quickly and he was no longer an excited observer but part of the adventure as the *BELLEISLE* disabled his ship.

At that moment the English ship hoisted two signal flags at the foremast. It made us think that she was calling for help. And we were not wrong. After a very little time two fresh English men-of-war came up [one of them being the *BELLEISLE*, the other the *MARS*] and began to attack us; the one on the starboard-quarter, the other at the stern. Under their fire, we held out for more than an hour but they almost overpowered us with their terrible storm of round shot and a fusillade of bullets which carried death among our men.

Our mizzen-mast was now shot by the board, while our spars were shot from the masts and were lying in wreckage along the sides of the ship. Then, too, fire broke out in the stern walk of the poop. We tried our best, in spite of the hail of shot, to put the fire out, and with hatchets to cut adrift the mass of wreckage from the fallen masts, yards and cordage. It lay along the ship's sides by the gun-tiers and was endangering the ship and exposing her to the most imminent risk of destruction by fire. At this moment the captain ordered me to climb outboard and see if the wreckage of the mainsail was not in danger of being set on fire from the main-deck guns. I obeyed; but as I clambered from the gangway into the chains one of the enemy fired her whole starboard broadside. The din and concussion were fearful; so tremendous that I almost fell headlong into

the sea. Blood gushed from my nose and ears, but it did
not prevent my carrying out my duty. Then our mainmast
fell. Happily it was shot through some ten or twelve feet
above the deck and fell over to port. At once we cut away
the shrouds to starboard; but it was with great difficulty
that in the end we were able to clear ourselves. Our fire was
well maintained all this time: though the great superiority
of the heavy guns of the English ships, and their very
advantageous position, decimated our men in a fearful
manner. More than half the crew had by this time been
struck down, killed or wounded. Then, at length, our last
remaining mast went; falling forward on to the fore part
of the ship. It was the only thing left above the deck. All
the same, neither our brave captain, nor a single one of our
men, had a thought of lowering it.

The *Fougueux*'s fate was sealed when she came alongside the *TÉMÉRAIRE*
later in the afternoon. Meanwhile, the *BELLEISLE* was knocked about
by a succession of other ships, including the *Neptune,* and she became
the most damaged British ship in the battle. Totally dismasted, she was
unable to fire most of her guns for fear of igniting the wreckage. Her
colours were nailed to the mizzen stump. Lieutenant Nicholas conveyed
the apprehension as yet another ship emerged from the smoke:

. . . a two-decker ship was seen, apparently steering towards
us. It can easily be imagined with what anxiety every eye
turned towards this formidable object, which would either
relieve us from our unwelcome neighbours or render our
situation desperate. We had scarcely seen British colours
since one o'clock – it was now half past three – and it is
impossible to express our emotion as an alteration of the
stranger's course displayed the White ensign to our sight.
The *SWIFTSURE*, an English 74, came looming through
the smoke, and passed our stern. Everyone eagerly looked
toward our approaching friend, who came speedily on, and

then, when within hail, manned the rigging, cheered and boldly steered for . . . the French *Neptune* which had so long annoyed us.

A Lieutenant in the *SWIFTSURE* recalled the happy meeting:

> Though an immovable log, the *BELLISLE* still kept up a smart fire upon the enemy whenever it was possible to bring a gun to bear . . . When we came up with her the ship's company was crowded upon the poop . . . and every other part of the ship to cheer us . . . by giving loud 'Huzzas' which we were not dilatory in returning. Captain Hargood then requested our Captain [William Rutherford] to engage a ship [the *Aigle*] to windward of him that was firing into the *BELLISLE*, as it was impossible for him to return her fire.

During the action Captain Hargood had suffered 'a severe contusion on the breast'. He had been hit by a splinter, but refused to leave the deck. Another member of the crew saw what happened: 'The splinter-netting was cut away, and knocked Hargood down, and entangled him in the meshes. On getting clear, half stunned by the blow, he called out 'Let 'em come on; I'll be damned if I'll strike. No, never – to nobody whatever.' A survivor of the battle, Hargood could give his own account of the fight. He was struck by the misery of it all:

> Our First Lieutenant was severely wounded in the thigh, and underwent amputation . . . He expired before the action ceased. The Junior Lieutenant was also mortally wounded on the quarterdeck. These gallant fellows [Lieutenant Ebenezer Geale and Lieutenant John Woodin from Gosport] were lying beside each other in the gunroom preparatory to their being committed to the deep, and here many met to take a last look at their departed friends, whose remains were soon followed by the promiscuous multitude, without distinction of . . . rank or station, to their . . . ocean grave.

In the act of launching a poor sailor over the poop he was discovered to breathe. He was, of course, saved, and after being a week in hospital the ball, which had entered at his temple, came out of his mouth.

From our extensive loss, thirty-four killed, and ninety-six wounded, our cockpit exhibited a scene of suffering and carnage which rarely occurs . . . So many bodies in such a confined place and under such distressing circumstances would affect the most obdurate heart. Even the dangers of the battle did not seem more terrific . . . On a long table lay several, anxiously looking for their turn to receive the Surgeon's care, yet dreading the fate which he might pronounce. One subject was undergoing amputation and every part was heaped with sufferers; their piercing shrieks and expiring groans were echoed through the vault of misery. What a contrast to the hilarity and enthusiastic mirth which reigned in this spot on the preceding evening.

'MY GOD, WHAT SHALL WE DO?'

The *MARS*, under the command of the massive figure of Captain George Duff, was the third ship in Collingwood's column to engage. Worthy Duff, as he was called in the Navy, was above six feet in height, and 'had a manly, open, benevolent countenance. He lost no opportunity of improving himself in the theory as well as the practice of his profession, and acted the part of an instructor and father to the numerous young men who were under his command.' He had tried to race ahead of the flagship as the column descended on the enemy but had given up on his hope of leading when the *ROYAL SOVEREIGN* drew away. He had difficulty breaking the line. Aiming for a gap that had opened up between the *Fougueux* and the *Monarca* (74) he was foiled by Commodore Cosmao-Kerjulien in the 74-gun *Pluton*, which quickly set sail, passed the *Monarca* and headed off the *MARS* in anticipation of pouring a raking broadside into her. To prevent this Duff luffed up to windward. This put him parallel to the *Pluton*, which maintained a heavy fire on him, and on a collision course with the *Santa Ana*. To avoid her he brought his ship into the wind, exposing her stern to the *Monarca*'s raking fire. As the *MARS* came to a stop the *Pluton* poured in broadsides from off the *MARS*'s starboard quarter. Then the *Fougueux*, which had drifted clear of the *BELLEISLE*, raked the *MARS* as well. Duff was hemmed in and in serious trouble, but didn't show it. Midshipman James Robinson, a 20-year-old from Edinburgh, said:

> Captain Duff walked about with steady fortitude, and said: 'My God, what shall we do? Here is a Spanish three-decker raking us ahead, a French one under our stern!' In a few minutes our poop was totally cleared, the quarter-deck and foc'sle nearly the same, and only the Boatswain and myself and three men alive.'

Commodore Cosmao-Kerjulien of the *Pluton* wrote in his report:

> At noon the enemy being within range, firing commenced on both sides; our line was penetrated at different points. An 80-gun ship [*MARS*, although she had only 74 guns] attempting to break through ahead of me, I crowded on sail and came up to windward to close on the *Monarca*, my next ahead; this manoeuvre obliged the enemy to haul her wind and she then attempted to penetrate between the *Monarca* and the *Fougueux*. The distance was great between these two ships; I hastened to fill the gap and found myself alongside the same enemy ship; in this position I fought her for half an hour.

The wind had dropped and Duff and his Captain of Marines, Thomas Norman, struggled to see through the smoke whether the guns could be aimed at the *Fougueux*. Leaning over the side of the quarter rail for a better view Duff saw that they might if pointed further aft. He had just instructed 16-year-old Midshipman Dundas Arbuthnot to tell the gun crews to re-lay their pieces when the *Fougueux* fired a full broadside. Duff was decapitated and his body fell on the gangway. The same shot killed two seamen. In another letter, addressed this time to his father, Midshipman James Robinson wrote:

> In my letter to my mother I gave as especial an account as I could of the action and the result of it. I am proud to say it is a general remark the beautiful and steady manner Captain Duff brought the ship into the battle. He stood with his arms across with <u>undaunted fortitude</u> until his head and neck were entirely severed from his body.

Robinson added that 'they held his body up and gave three cheers to show they were not discouraged by it, and then returned to their guns', whereafter the body was covered with a spare colour until the end of the action. He said that 'The battle continued from twelve o'clock till three'. Nevertheless, the damage had all been done in less than an hour. *MARS*'s stern, including her rudder, and all her masts were badly shot up. The final casualty tally was 29 killed and 69 wounded. The log of the *MARS* recorded that:

> The poop and quarterdeck [were] almost left destitute, the carnage was so great; having everyone of our braces and running rigging shot away, which made the ship entirely ungovernable, and was frequently raked by different ships of the enemy.

Lieutenant William Hennah, 37, from St Austell in Cornwall was now in command of the helpless ship, whose stern was again blasted by the destructive guns of the *Pluton*. However, the Frenchman was far from unscathed. Duff had inflicted nearly 300 casualties and the ship was taking on water quickly. As Commodore Cosmao-Kerjulien records:

> My main deck was totally obstructed by splinters, nine guns were dismounted, several had their breeching tackle cut away and I had the few men that remained on the poop

and on the upper works sent below to clear the battery. The ship was making 2½ feet of water when on the larboard tack and could not be pumped out on the other tack; the masts, rigging and canvas were no longer holding; finally I had 280 men killed and wounded.

'SAUVEZ, SAUVEZ, L'HONNEUR DU PAVILLION!'

The *TONNANT*, captured by the British at the Battle of the Nile, had followed the *MARS* into the action, breaking the line between the stern of the *Monarca* and the bows of the 74-gun *Algésiras*, the flagship of Rear Admiral Charles Magon de Médine, the youngest of Villeneuve's admirals, with a reputation as a fire-eater. The gap was so narrow that according to Lieutenant Frederick Hoffman, 'a biscuit might have been thrown on either of them'.

The *TONNANT*'s guns were all double-shotted, so that being so close when the order to fire was given every shot crashed into the enemy hulls. Her third broadside was concentrated on the *Monarca*, which could only partially return the fire because she was already badly damaged. She gradually fell astern and hauled down her colours; only to re-hoist them when she thought she was safe. Meanwhile, Captain Charles Tyler brought the *TONNANT*, already with her foremast and main yard shot away, round to starboard to assist the *MARS*, which was suffering heavy broadsides from the *Pluton*. While he was pouring his port guns into her, Magon in the *Algésiras* saw his chance and forged ahead to get under the *TONNANT*'s stern in order to rake her. Tyler reacted quickly and brought his ship to starboard so that the *Algésiras* crashed into her amidships instead. Magon's plan had been reversed. The *TONNANT* could now rake the Frenchman from stem to stern. She unleashed her big guns, and carronades, loaded with musket balls, and in commander Laurent Le Tourneur's words, 'totally stripped us of our rigging'. George Sartorius, a 21-year-old midshipman from Bath serving in the *TONNANT*, attributed her success to the superior gunnery training of the British ship. The *TONNANT*:

. . . was one of the very few, perhaps one of the four or five, that had been constantly exercised at her guns. At the battle of Trafalgar a line-of-battle ship ran alongside us, her yard got entangled with our main rigging, and in the course of six-and-thirty minutes, from the extreme rapidity of our firing we managed to knock away all her masts, and to kill and wound 436 of her men [in fact 216]. Had we not been well exercised at our guns, I think the Frenchman would have got the advantage of us. We had actually our engine playing on her broadside to put out the fire caused by the flame of our guns.

A fellow officer described the start of the engagement:

A French ship of eighty guns with an admiral's flag came up, and poured a raking broadside into our stern which killed and wounded forty petty officers and men, nearly cut the rudder in two, and shattered the whole of the stern with the quarter galleries. She then, in the most gallant manner, locked her bowsprit in our starboard main shrouds and attempted to board us with the greater part of her officers and ship's company. She had riflemen in her tops, who did great execution. Our poop was soon cleared and our gallant captain shot through the left thigh and obliged to be carried below.

But the *Algésiras* was as good as a rat in a barrel. The only aggressive thing she could do was to attempt to board the *TONNANT*. Rear Admiral Magon took the initiative and, tomahawk in hand, led the boarders himself. Almost at once a musket ball took away his hat and wig, another hit his right arm and a third struck his shoulder. Undeterred, he shouted, 'The first man that boards that ship with me shall have the Cross!' No sooner had the words left his mouth than grape shot smashed into his stomach nearly severing him in two and he fell backwards on to the deck. He is said to have cried '*Sauvez,*

Sauvez, l'honneur du Pavillion!' ('Save the honour of the flag!') Captain le Tourneur was also hit and dangerously wounded in the shoulder. Similar fates befell the first and second lieutenants, M Verdreau and M Plassan, the *officier de manoeuvre*, and the command passed quickly to the young Lieutenant de la Bretonnière. With the battered ship now on fire below, from the blazing wads of the British guns, he hauled down her colours and surrendered. Captain Tourneur described the fight:

> . . . she [the *TONNANT*] then fired a whole volley of grape which totally stripped us of our rigging; but our well sustained fire soon reduced her to the same state as ourselves. General Magon gave orders to board and all those told off for this service advanced most gallantly; we have to lament Lieutenant Verdreau who commanded the boarders as well as the greater part of the brave lads who followed him. We had at this moment four ships engaging us at pistol shot, which poured in such musketry fire that our upper works were cleared in a quarter of an hour. We were then so engaged with the enemy, who surrounded us at all points that it was no longer possible for us to distinguish the movements of our Fleet or the signals that might be made. The General feeling our position to be critical went about everywhere encouraging us by his presence and displaying the most heroic coolness and courage.

The *TONNANT*'s account continued:

> We were not idle. We gave it to her most gloriously with the starboard and main deckers, and turned the forecastle gun, loaded with grape, on the gentleman who wished to give us a fraternal hug. The marines kept up a warm destructive fire on the boarders. Only one man made good his footing on our quarter-deck, when he was pinned through the calf of his right leg by one of the crew with his half-pike, whilst another was going to cut him down, which I prevented,

and desired him to be taken to the cockpit . . . Our severe
contest with the French Admiral lasted more than half an
hour, our sides grinding so much that we were obliged to
fire the lower-deck guns without running them out.

In fact the desperate struggle lasted for more than an hour. Both ships
were badly knocked about and Captain Charles Tyler had been severely
wounded. The firing at point-blank range had set both ships ablaze
and they were only saved by the *TONNANT*'s fire-engine spraying its
water on both hulls. George Sartorius concludes the engagement:

At length both ships caught fire before the chess trees and
our firemen, with all the coolness and courage so inherent
in the British seamen, got the engine and played on both
ships, and finally extinguished the flames, although two of
them were severely wounded in doing so. At length we had
the satisfaction of seeing her three lower masts go by the
board, ripping the partners up in their fall, as they had been
shot through below deck, and carrying with them all their
sharpshooters to look sharper in the next world; for as all our
boats were shot through we could not save one of them in
this. The crew were then ordered with the second lieutenant
to board her. They cheered, and in as short time carried
her. They found the gallant French Admiral Magon killed
at the foot of the poop ladder, and the captain dangerously
wounded. Out of eight lieutenants, five were killed with three
hundred petty officers and seamen and about one hundred
wounded. We left the second lieutenant and sixty men in
charge of her and took some of the prisoners on board when
she swung clear of us. We had pummelled her so handsomely
that fourteen of her lower deck guns were dismounted and
her larboard bow exhibited a mass of splinters.

By now the focus of the battle for Collingwood's ships was shifting to
the *BELLEROPHON*, *TONNANT*'s follower.

THE ROYAL NAVY SURROUNDED!

Within the first half hour of the battle the five leading ships in Collingwood's Lee Column were engaged. They had broken the line between different enemy ships and found themselves out-gunned and often involved in individual ship-to-ship duels. While it was the 'pell-mell battle' that Nelson had envisaged, for first the few hours it was the Royal Navy that was tactically outnumbered rather than the other way round. The *ROYAL SOVEREIGN*, *BELLEISLE* and *MARS*, and the *VICTORY* to the north, were all suffering attack from all sides. The *BELLEROPHON* was about to join them.

The veteran *BELLEROPHON*, the fifth ship of Collingwood's division, succeeded in breaking the line astern of the *Monarca* just as the Spanish ship was re-hoisting her colours. The wind was so light that she had time to fire two port broadsides and to use her carronades three times. This was sufficient to blow up the *Monarca*'s hanging magazine, which meant she was effectively beaten, although her colours were still flying. Hauling to the wind to fire again *BELLEROPHON* suddenly saw looming over the smoke close on her starboard bow the topgallant sails of another ship. To avoid a collision she was forced to haul back by turning head to wind, so as to spill the wind from her sails. It was too late. She smashed into her new opponent, the French *Aigle* (74) (Captain Pierre Paul Gourrège) and their masts became entangled. *BELLEROPHON*'s log records the incident:

> 12.35 P.M. fell on board the French two-deck Ship *l'Aigle* whilst hauling to the wind, our fore-yard locking with her main yard, kept up a brisk fire both on her, on our starboard bow, and a Spanish two-decker [*Monarca*] on the larboard bow, at the same time receiving and returning fire with a Spanish two-decker [*Bahama*] on the larboard quarter, and receiving the fire of a Spanish two-decker [*St Juan Nepomuceno*] athwart our stern, and a French two-decker (*la Swift-sure!*) on the starboard quarter: the action soon after became general.

BELLEROPHON, affectionately known to sailors as 'Billy Ruffian', was in the thick of it and earning her soubriquet. The opposing gun crews were fighting hand-to-hand through the ports, battering each other with rammers and slashing out with their cutlasses. The French were tossing grenades through the ports. Both sides were using muskets. Of the *Aigle*'s 750 crew, 150 were soldiers, enough to pack the tops and rigging with marksmen and grenadiers, where they were as deadly as Lucas's trained musketeers in the *Redoubtable*.

> At about 1 P.M. the *BELLEROPHON*'s main and mizzen top-masts fell over on the starboard side, and the main topsail and topgallantsail immediately caught fire with the flash of the guns, assisted by the hand-grenades which the *Aigle*'s people kept throwing from her tops.

Meanwhile, her dare-devil 43-year-old captain John Cooke was discharging his pistols very frequently at the enemy, killing a French officer on his own quarterdeck. He now directed First Lieutenant William Pryce Cumby to the *BELLEROPHON*'s gun decks. He was to order the gun captains to keep the starboard guns firing at all costs. As the 34-year-old Cumby returned, choking from the thick acrid smoke that stifled the gun-decks, he met two sailors carrying Mr Edward Overton, the master, with a horribly shattered leg. He did not survive. Overton had been standing next to Captain Cooke. Even before Cumby got back to the quarterdeck he was met by James Barker, the quartermaster, who had come to inform him that Cooke was very badly wounded, shot twice in the chest by musket balls while reloading his pistols. When Cumby reached the quarterdeck Cooke was dead. His last words were, '. . . let me lie quietly one minute. Tell Lieutenant Cumby never to strike!'

All of a sudden, his senses reeling from the din and amidst the fiercest of fights, Cumby found himself in command. In retrospect he would learn that *BELLEROPHON*'s situation was at that very moment far graver than that to be suffered by any other British ship during the whole of the battle.

I went immediately on the quarterdeck and assumed the command of the ship – this would be about quarter past one o'clock – when I found we were still engaged with the *Aigle*, on whom we kept up a brisk fire, and also on our old opponent on our larboard bow, the *Monarca*, who by this time was nearly silenced, though her colours were still flying; at the same time we were receiving the fire of two other of the enemy's ships, one nearly astern of the other on the larboard quarter. Our quarterdeck, poop and forecastle were at this time almost cleared by musketry from troops onboard the *Aigle* . . . I ordered all the remaining men down from the poop, and, calling boarders, had them mustered . . . and held . . . in readiness to repel any attempt that might be made by the enemy to board us; their position rendering it quite impracticable for us to board them in the face of such musketry . . .

Slowly but surely the upper parts of the *BELLEROPHON* were being slashed and pulverized into wreckage and swept clear by the deadly hail of musket balls and grenades. Shouts of '*A l'abordage*!' could be heard. '*L'Aigle* twice attempted to board us,' wrote Cumby. Groups of Frenchmen mustered to clamber across, grabbing a handhold wherever they could.

John Franklin, the signal midshipman of the *BELLEROPHON*, afterwards Sir John Franklin, the doomed Arctic explorer who became famous as 'the man who ate his shoes', wrote to his brother-in-law:

In the attempt their hands received some severe blows from whatever the English could lay their hands on. In this way hundreds of Frenchmen fell between the ships and were drowned.

Five climbed along the spritsail yardarm but were thrown into the sea when a sharp-witted member of the crew, named Peter Macfarlane from Fifeshire, ran to the starboard side of the forecastle and let go of the spritsail-brace supporting the end of the yard. Most of the others were stopped by fire that 'was so hot, that we soon drove them from the lower deck'. Cumby continued:

> But whatever advantage they had over us on these upper decks was greatly overbalanced by the superiority of our fire on the lower and main decks, the *Aigle* soon ceasing . . . to fire on us from her lower deck . . . whilst the fire from ours was vigorously maintained . . . While thus closely engaged and rubbing sides with the *Aigle*, she threw many hand grenades on board us, both on our forecastle and gangway and in at the ports. Some of these exploded and dreadfully scorched several of our men; one of them I took up myself from the gangway where the fuse was burning, and threw it overboard . . .

This was a classic example of bravery. Grenades caused great destruction on the main deck, igniting loose powder spilt near the guns. One alone accounted for 25 of *BELLEROPHON*'s crew. Another:

> . . . had been thrown in at a lower deck port and in its explosion had blown off the scuttle of the gunner's storeroom setting fire to the storeroom, and forcing open the door into the magazine passage. Most providentially the same blast that blew open the storeroom door shut-to the door of the magazine; otherwise we must all in both ships inevitably have been blown up together. The Gunner [John Stevenson], who was in the storeroom at this time, went quietly up to Lieutenant [George] Saunders on the lower deck, and acquainting him that the storeroom was on fire, requested a few hands with water to extinguish it; these being instantly granted, he returned with them and put the fire out without its having been known to any person on board, except to those employed in its extinction.

The *BELLEROPHON* had had a very lucky escape. A fire in the magazine was a potential catastrophe, since it was the only way a man-of-war could be utterly destroyed. Heroism and chivalry went hand-in-hand that afternoon. John Franklin described how the veteran sailor:

> . . . Christopher Beatty, yeoman of signals, seeing the ensign shot away a third time, mounted the mizzen-rigging with the largest Union Jack he could lay his hands upon, deliberately stopped the four corners of it with as much spread as possible to the shrouds, and regained the deck unhurt. The French riflemen in the tops and on the poop of the *l'Aigle*, seeing what he was about, seemingly in admiration of such daring conduct, suspended their fire for the few seconds that he remained aloft. This forbearance of the enemy was the more noble, as they had previously picked off every man that appeared before *BELLEROPHON*'s mizzen mast.

The French sharpshooters resumed their deadly business. Midshipman John Simmons from Totnes in Devon, a great friend of Franklin, was shot dead by one, conspicuous by his accurate shooting and cocked hat! Another of his musket balls tore into the heart of a wounded black seaman whom Franklin and a Marine sergeant were trying to get to safety. 'He'll have you next!' exclaimed Franklin. 'Indeed he will not!' declared the Marine. Franklin would have been able to see the whites of the sharpshooter's eyes as he found himself the Frenchman's next target but, in the words of his biographer, 'with an elasticity very common in his family, [he] bounded behind a mast' and the ball hit the deck just behind him. That was when Franklin saw 'features he vowed he would never forget so long as he lived as the sharpshooter' fell 'over foremast into the sea'. The Marine had killed him with his seventh shot.

Aigle's rate of fire eased off. She was nearly beaten. The *BELLEROPHON*'s fast and efficient gunnery had saved the British ship. The gun crews had been fighting in an unimaginable hell, but when the enemy's fire slackened they took the opportunity to elevate their guns to shoot through the *Aigle*'s decks. As Franklin observed:

. . . our people took the quoins out and elevated their guns,
so as to tear her decks and sides to pieces: when she got
clear of us, she did not return a single shot whilst we raked
her, her starboard quarter was entirely beaten in, and, as we
afterwards learnt, four hundred men *hors de combat*, so that
she was an easy conquest for the *DEFIANCE*, a fresh ship: we
were well matched, she being the best manned ship in the
Combined, and we in the British fleet. I have no doubt she
would have struck had we been able to follow and engage
her for a quarter of an hour longer.

Lieutenant Asmus Classen, who took command of the *Aigle* after
the very first broadside had mortally wounded her captain, Pierre
Gourrège, was laconic with his account that the two ships 'engaged
with the utmost fury'. But the killing was not over yet.

At forty minutes past one the *Aigle* hoisted her jib and
dropped clear of us, under a tremendous raking fire from us
she paid off: our ship at this time was totally unmanageable,
the main and mizzen topmasts hanging over the side, the
jib-boom, spanker boom and gaff shot away, and not a
brace or bowline serviceable. We observed that the *Aigle* was
engaged by the *DEFIANCE* . . .

Captain Philip Durham in the 74-gun *DEFIANCE* chose to run
alongside the *Aigle*, lashing his ship to her at the place just vacated by
BELLEROPHON. He thought the Frenchman had struck and started
to board. A master's mate, 29-year old James Spratt, an Irishman and
a veteran of the Battle of Copenhagen 1801, led the way:

Mr Spratt, who had been selected to lead the men in [this]
desperate service . . . volunteered, as all the boats had been
disabled, to [do so] by swimming. His offer being accepted,
he instantly, with his sword in his teeth and his battleaxe
in his belt, dashed into the sea, calling upon the others to

follow the order, however, in the general din was not heard
. . . Though alone, Spratt, on reaching the French ship,
contrived . . . to enter the stern gunroom port, and thence
to fight his way through all the decks until he reached the
poop. Here he was charged by three grenadiers with fixed
bayonets but, springing . . . past them . . . before they could
repeat the operation, disabled two of them. Seizing the third
one, he threw him from the poop onto the quarterdeck,
where he fell and broke his neck . . .

By this time the boarding party from the *DEFIANCE* . . .
were . . . making a successful attempt to carry the enemy's
ship. Midshipman Spratt joined in the desperate hand-to-
hand conflict . . . when a French grenadier [tried] to run
him through with his bayonet. The thrust was parried,
whereupon the Frenchman presented his musket at Spratt's
breast and fired . . . The Midshipman succeeded in striking
the muzzle down with his cutlass [so that] the charge passed
through his right leg a little below the knee, shattering
both bones. Spratt immediately backed between two of the
quarterdeck guns to prevent being cut off from behind, in
which position he continued to defend himself.

Eventually, Spratt dragged himself to the side of the ship, and putting
his bleeding limb over the side, called out, 'Captain, poor Jack Spratt
is done up at last!'

On *DEFIANCE* Colin Campbell, 19, from Woodhall in Lanarkshire
(like Spratt, a master's mate but referred to as a 'midshipman', a rate
now being ascribed to older 'young officers'), wrote to his father how:

We ran alongside of her and at 3.10 lashed ourselves to her,
where we had it pretty hot, till finding we had silenced her
guns – we boarded her and took possession of her poop and
forecastle. One of our men ran to her mast-head – hauled
down the French pendant and hoisted an English ensign
and pendant, but her men still keeping up a heavy fire of

musketry from her tops and lower deck and every now and
then firing some guns and throwing stink pots into the
ports which killed a number of our men – we recalled the
boarders, hauled off within pistol shot and turned to on her
again – every shot of ours going through and through her.

The unexpected destructive fire of musketry had been opened upon
the boarders from the forecastle, waist and tops of the *Aigle*, and the
British had been in possession of their prize for only five minutes or so,
before Captain Durham recalled them to the *DEFIANCE* rather than
lose any more of his men. The official French account suggested that
the French thought they had a fighting chance. However, Lieutenant
Classen's account was at variance with his known character, not least
because he later accused Collingwood of ordering *Aigle*'s cables to be
cut so as to leave him no chance of escape. He seemed to corrupt the
truth in order to cast a better light on himself afterwards:

We replied gallantly to her vigorous fire in spite of our
weakened crew, and at the end of three-quarters of an hour
we were hoping to subdue her or at least oblige her to
abandon us . . .

The *DEFIANCE* did cut loose, but only sheered off to half pistol-
shot distance – about 30 yards – and from this range kept up so well
maintained a broadside that in less than 20 minutes the battered
Aigle, whose fire had nevertheless been maintained, finally struck her
colours. Lieutenant Classen again sought to explain his capitulation,
this time referring to his isolated situation and overwhelming odds:

We were surrounded by three other ships, one – a three-
decker – on the larboard bow, a 74 astern, and a third on the
starboard beam. We held out for some time, but the enemy's
flaming sulphur-saturated wads having set the gun-room
on fire close to the cable tier and to the taffrail, the ship
being stripped of her rigging, most of the guns dismounted,

the captain and the commander killed, nearly all the naval officers wounded and two thirds of the crew disabled, the ship moreover – by what misfortune I know not – being isolated from the rest of the Fleet, we decided to haul down our colours in order to extinguish the flames and to preserve for the Emperor the scanty number of gallant defenders who remained.

Colin Campbell concluded the story:

About 4 they called for quarter which we instantly gave and sent a lieutenant and 20 men to take possession of her. The slaughter on board was horrid, the decks were covered with dead and wounded. They never heave their dead overboard in time of action as we do. We had 18 men killed amongst whom was our 2nd lieutenant, boatswain, and one midshipman. Captain Durham was slightly wounded in the leg by a splinter. Four of our midshipmen were also wounded and 50 men. By 5 the action was finished and nothing to be seen, but wrecks of masts and yards floating about and some hundreds of dead bodies.

It was common practice throughout the French and Spanish Navies to keep the dead on board, since Catholic widows needed evidence of burial of their husbands' bodies if they were to remarry. The carnage had been truly awful: the *DEFIANCE* had 70 killed and wounded. The *Aigle* had suffered 270 casualties and the *BELLEROPHON* close to half that number. Lieutenant Cumby of the *BELLEROPHON* concluded:

I must say I was astonished at the coolness and undaunted bravery displayed by our gallant and veteran crew, when surrounded by five enemy's ships, and for a length of time unassisted by any of ours. Our loss, as might be expected, was considerable, and fell chiefly on our prime seamen, who were foremost in distinguishing themselves; twenty-eight, including the Captain Master, and a Midshipman, were killed outright; and 127, including the captain of marines, who had eight balls in his body, and his right arm shot off, before he quitted the deck; Boatswain, and five Midshipmen, were badly wounded, and about forty more slightly, so as not to be incapable of duty; nineteen of the wounded had already died before we left Gibraltar. I consider myself as very fortunate in having escaped unhurt, as our class suffered so severely.

What of James Spratt? He survived his adventure and kept his leg! A few days after the battle the ship's Surgeon, Alexander Whyte . . .

. . . came to Captain Durham and asked for a written order to cut off Mr. Spratt's leg, saying that it could not be cured, and that he refused to submit to the operation. The Captain replied that he could not give such an order, but that he would see Mr. Spratt, which he managed to do inspite of his wounds. Upon the Captain remonstrating with him, Spratt held out the other leg and exclaimed, 'Never! If I lose my leg, where shall I find a match for this?'

Although too crippled to serve at sea, James Spratt was promoted to lieutenant and put in charge of the signal station at Dawlish, in Devon, where he invented the homograph, the predecessor of semaphore. After his retirement it is recorded that, 'Captain Spratt had a useless leg, yet he was a splendid swimmer, and when nearly sixty swam a fourteen mile race for a wager and won it.' He died in 1852, aged 80.

The *COLOSSUS*, under Captain James Nicholl Morris, came up behind the *BELLEROPHON* and opened fire at 12.50 p.m., breaking through the line some ten minutes later. She was engaged first by the *Argonaute* (74) and then on both sides by the *Bahama* (74) and the French *Swiftsure* (74). After a two-hour fight with the closing support of the *ORION*, from the rear of the Weather Column, who fired her first broadside of the battle into the *Swiftsure*, Captain Morris took them both. The *Bahama* struck after her captain, Commodore Don D A Galiano, had been killed by a shot in the head, one of 400 casualties – amongst the highest of any ship in the Combined Fleet. Morris was badly wounded in the leg and *COLOSSUS* had most of her rigging shot away and, much shattered, 'had become quite unmanageable'. To her fell the sad distinction of the highest casualties in the British fleet, with 40 killed and 160 wounded, a testament to the resoluteness of her opponents, and possibly to the difficulty she had penetrating the line because of the doubling up of ships. An unknown officer in the *CONQUEROR* (74) observed that:

> In the rear the line was in some places trebled; and this particularly happened where the *COLOSSUS* was, who, after passing the stern of the French *Swiftsure*, and luffing up under the lee of the *Bahama*, supposing herself to leeward of the enemy's line, unexpectedly ran alongside of the French *Achille* under cover of the smoke. The *COLOSSUS* was then placed between the *Achille* and the *Bahama*, being on board of the latter; and was also exposed to the fire of the *Swiftsure*'s guns. All these positions I believe to have been merely accidental; and to accident alone I attribute the concave circle of the fleet, or crescent line of battle.

Many of Collingwood's ships, because they were not in perfect line ahead, made a slanting approach at the enemy and picked their own, different, breakthrough points, unlike Nelson's Weather Column, where his following ships streamed through the same gap he had created. This meant that as the remainder of Collingwood's column – *ACHILLE, DREADNOUGHT, POLYPHEMUS, REVENGE, SWIFTSURE, DEFIANCE, THUNDERER, DEFENCE* and *PRINCE* – came into action there was a host of ship-to-ship and multi-ship struggles with, variously, the *Argonaute, Argonauta* (80), *Achille, Berwick* (74), *Principe de Asturias, San Ildefonso* (74) and *San Juan Nepomuceno*. Some of these engaged comparatively late, notably the *Argonaute, Principe de Asturias* and *San Ildefonso*, and one, the *Montanes* (74), did not fight at all.

Within two hours of *ROYAL SOVEREIGN* breaking through the allied line Collingwood's ships had effectively overwhelmed the enemy rear, and by the end of the battle they had taken ten prizes. Good gunnery mixed with a little luck had given them the upper hand.

Most, though not all, of the British ships held their fire until they had 'gone on board'. The *REVENGE* was commanded by one of the Navy's leading gunnery experts, Captain Robert Moorsom. He made a point of holding fire with dramatic results. His gun crews brought down the mizzen mast of the *Achille* before engaging simultaneously the *Principe de Asturias* and *San Ildefonso*, 'throwing them into disorder'. William Robinson, better known as 'Jack Nastyface', in the *REVENGE*, recollected the impatience that holding fire caused the gun crews:

> It fell to our lot to cut off the five stern-most ships; and, while we were running down to them, of course we were favoured with several shots, and some of our men were wounded. Many of our men thought it hard that the firing should be all on one side and became impatient to return the complement: but our Captain had given orders not to fire until we get close in with them, so that all our shots might tell; indeed these were his words, 'We shall want all our shot when we get close in; never mind their firing. When I fire a carronade from the quarter-deck, that will be the signal for you to begin, and I know you will do your duty like Englishmen.' In a few minutes the gun was fired, and our ship bore in and broke the line [between the *Achille* and the *San Ildefonso*], but we paid dear for our temerity, as those ships we had thrown into disorder turned round and made an attempt to board.

Collingwood had drilled his old ship the *DREADNOUGHT* to the point that it could fire three concentrated broadsides every three and a half minutes. This told to great effect when she set about Admiral Gravina's flagship the *Principe de Asturias* and Commodore Churruca's *San Juan Nepomuceno*. Within moments, Churruca was dead and the battering his ship sustained was so awful that her demoralized crew struck within ten minutes. The *Principe de Asturias* faired only slightly better. With Gravina mortally wounded, she managed to escape only because the *DREADNOUGHT* was such a slow sailer. The shock of three successive devastating broadsides at close range frequently proved overwhelming. By the time the British ships reached the enemy line the French and Spanish had already fired up to four broadsides, but at longer range. Their gun crews would have been tiring just as the weight of the British cannonade pounded them.

The *San Juan Nepomuceno* was hammered repeatedly in this way by the *TONNANT, BELLEROPHON, DEFIANCE* and *DREADNOUGHT*. The following account of Churruca's heroic resistance is based on the account by Don José Ruiz de Apodoca, Churruca's nephew, as written down by Perez Galdos:

> Five English vessels under Collingwood attacked our ship; two, however, passed on, and Churruca had only three to deal with.
>
> We held out bravely against these odds till two in the afternoon, suffering terribly, though we dealt double havoc on the foe. Our leader seemed to have infused his heroic spirit into the crew and soldiers, and the ship was handled and her broadsides delivered with wonderful promptitude and accuracy. The new recruits learnt their lesson in courage in no more than a couple of hours' apprenticeship, and our defence struck the English with astonishment. They were in fact forced to get assistance, and bring up no less than six against one. The two ships that had at first sailed past us now returned, and the *DREADNOUGHT* came alongside of us, with not more than half a pistol shot between her and our stern. You may imagine the fire of these six giants pouring balls and small shot into a vessel of 74 guns!
>
> Churruca, meanwhile, who was the brain of all, directed the battle with gloomy calmness. Knowing that only care and skill could supply the place of strength, he

economised our fire, trusting entirely to careful aim, and the consequence was that each ball did terrible havoc on the foe. He saw everything, settled everything, and the shot flew round him and over his head without his ever once even changing colour.

It was not the will of God, however, that he should escape alive from that storm of fire. Seeing that no one could hit one of the enemy's ships which was battering us with impunity, he went down himself to judge of the line of fire, and succeeded in dismasting her. He was returning to the quarter-deck when a cannon ball hit his right leg with such violence as almost to take it off, tearing it across the thigh in the most frightful manner. He fell to the ground, but the next moment he made an effort to raise himself, supporting himself on one arm. His face was as white as death, but he said, in a voice that was scarcely weaker than his ordinary tone: 'It is nothing – go on firing.'

He did all he could to conceal the terrible sufferings of his cruelly mangled frame. Nothing would induce him to quit the quarter-deck. At last he yielded to our entreaties and then he seemed to understand that he must give up the command. He called for Moyna, his second in command, but was told that he was dead. Then he called for the officer in command on the main deck. That officer, though himself seriously wounded, at once came to the quarterdeck and took command.

It was just before he went below that Churruca, in the midst of his agonies, gave the order that the flag should be nailed to the mast. The ship, he said, must never surrender as long as he breathed.

The delay, alas! could be but short. He was going fast. He never lost consciousness till the very end, nor did he complain of his sufferings. His sole anxiety was that the crew should not know how dangerous his wound was; that no one should be daunted or fail in his duty. He specially desired that the men should be thanked for their heroic courage. Then he spoke a few words to Ruiz de Apodoca [who a few hours earlier he had told with certainty that he would meet his death], and after sending a farewell message to his poor young wife, whom he had married only a few days before he sailed, he fixed his thoughts on God. Whose name was ever on his lips. So with the calm resignation of a good man and the fortitude of a hero, Churruca passed away.

After he was gone, it was too quickly known, and the men lost heart . . . Their courage was really worn out. It was but too plain that they must surrender . . . A sudden paralysis seemed to seize on the crew; their grief at losing their beloved leader apparently overpowered the disgrace of surrender.

Quite half the San Juan's crew were *hors de combat*, dead or wounded. Most of the guns were disabled. All the masts, except the main-mast, had gone by the board. The rudder was useless. And yet, in this deplorable plight even, they made an attempt to follow the *Principe de Asturias*, which had given the signal to withdraw, but the *San Juan Nepomuceno* had received the death blow. She could neither sail nor steer.

At last the *San Juan Nepomuceno* struck her colours (to the *DREADNOUGHT*). The official Spanish returns show that she had 250 casualties, 100 killed, out of a total complement of 693. Churruca's death was a bitter blow. He was idolized throughout Spain as a fine naval officer, and for his reputation as an explorer of the coasts of Patagonia and Chile.

The aggressiveness and good gunnery of Collingwood's leading ships, particularly the *BELLEISLE, MARS* and *COLOSSUS*, had been central to the destruction of the rear of the Combined Fleet. These three ships alone had managed to engage six, five and three of the enemy respectively and with help from the other 12 ships in the Lee Column had overcome 16 of the enemy. However, while they may have carried the day the latecomers ensured that the battle was won. The last in the Lee Column – and indeed the last ship in the British fleet – to get into the fray was the

98-gun *PRINCE*, commanded by Captain Richard Grindall. She should have been one of the first, but as Volunteer First Class Henry Browne Mason, born in Calcutta 16 years earlier, explained in his diary:

> We were unfortunately a very dull sailor, and in consequence, being unable to keep our station, were put out of the line, and when at daylight the combined fleet was discovered to leeward, and our fleet bore up in chase, we were astern of the whole fleet, and were totally unable to gain our place, though second to Collingwood on the lee line. It was poor satisfaction that we had a magnificent sight of the battle, but at length we passed through the disabled ships on both sides.

She came upon the *Principe de Asturias*, Admiral Gravina's flagship, which was now the only ship in the enemy's rear that had not struck her colours. The broadsides from the *PRINCE* mortally wounded Gravina but she was unable to overwhelm the ship and disengaged when the *San Justo* and the French *Neptune* came to the *Principe*'s aid.

After the battle Collingwood was careful to recognize the important role of the latecomers:

> People who cannot comprehend how complicated an affair a Battle at sea is, and who judge an Officer's conduct by the number of sufferers in his Ship, often do him a wrong. Though there will appear great difference in the loss of men, all did admirably well.

Nevertheless, some ships did achieve more than might be expected of them or suffered more severely than others, helping to explain expressions of animosity between some of the captains after the battle. Collingwood would have none of these criticisms and refused to answer them. He did not want anything, not even a rebuke of a cabin boy, to besmirch the character of Lord Nelson or tarnish the great victory.

7
THE BATTLE: THE WEATHER COLUMN

Having passed astern of the wounded *Bucentaure,* and been raked by Commodore Maistral's 84-gun *Neptune,* Captain Hardy had ordered the *VICTORY*'s helm hard a-starboard to take on Captain Jean-Jacques Lucas's 74-gun *Redoubtable,* whose effective enfilading cannonade was battering *VICTORY*'s starboard side, which with perfect timing he now smashed against the Frenchman's port side, their anchors striking, sides grinding, and their sails and yards fouling and locking the two ships together. The French lower-deck gunners managed to pull in their guns and close their ports before the collision, in order to prevent the British from boarding through them, but *VICTORY* kept hers open and her starboard guns pounded the *Redoubtable*'s hull at point-blank range with treble-shotted fire. The firemen were throwing buckets of water on to the sides of the enemy after every discharge. *Redoubtable* never fired her great guns at *VICTORY* again.

Marine Second Lieutenant Lewis Rotely from Glamorgan was aged 20 when he described the scene on *VICTORY*'s middle gun-deck, which would have been as dim as a cellar. The guns were loud enough to damage eardrums and to deafen their exhausted keepers, who would be swabbing and reloading, ramming and heaving, breathing smoke and dust, and slipping in blood as they hauled the guns out time and time again. *VICTORY*'s port-side guns were firing at the massive *Santissima Trinidad.* The whole ship would have been shuddering:

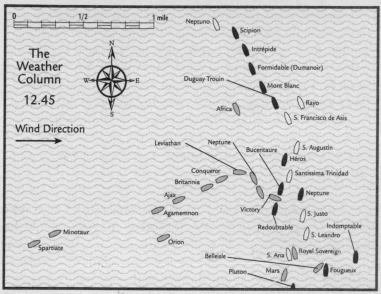

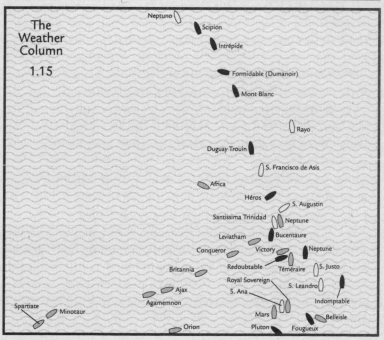

We were engaging on both sides; every gun was going off. A man should witness a battle in a three-decker from the middle deck, for it beggars all description; it bewilders the senses of sight and hearing. There was the fire from the deck I was upon, the guns recoiling with violence, reports louder than thunder, the decks heaving and the sides straining. I fancied myself in the infernal regions, where every man appeared a devil. Lips might move, but orders and hearing were out of the question; everything was done by signs.

Dr William Beatty elaborated. The *TÉMÉRAIRE* was close astern of the *VICTORY* and Captain Harvey was steering her on to the starboard side of the *Redoubtable*:

An incessant fire was kept up from both sides of the *VICTORY*; her larboard guns played on the *Santissima Trinidad* and the *Bucentaure*, and the starboard guns of the middle and lower decks were depressed and fired with a diminished charge of powder and three shot each, into the *Redoubtable*. This mode of firing was adopted by Lieutenants Williams, King, Yule, and Brown, to obviate the danger of the *TÉMÉRAIRE*'s suffering from the *VICTORY*'s shot passing through the *Redoubtable*; which must have been the case if the usual quantity of powder and common elevation, had been given to the guns. – A circumstance occurred in this situation, which shewed in a most striking manner the cool intrepidity of the Officers and men stationed on the lower deck of the *VICTORY*. When the guns on this deck were run out, their muzzles came into contact with the *Redoubtable*'s side; and consequently at every discharge there was reason to fear that the Enemy would take fire, and both the *VICTORY* and the *TÉMÉRAIRE* be involved in her flames. Here then was seen the astonishing spectacle of the firemen of each gun

standing ready with a bucket full of water, which as soon as
his gun was discharged he dashed into the Enemy through
the holes made in her side by the shot.

The men in *Redoubtable* were far from being vanquished. Those on
her upper deck had lashed the two ships together at the bow with
grapples. Captain Lucas had made a special study of boarding and
close combat and had trained his crew well while they were in Cadiz.
They were now responding perfectly. He described the nature of the
training. Every sort of drill was included:

> My thoughts ever turned on boarding my enemy in any
> action I fought, and I so counted on finding my opportunity
> that I made that form of attack part of our daily exercises,
> so as to ensure success when the hour arrived. I had canvas
> cartridge-cases made for each of the captains of the guns,
> each to hold two grenades apiece; with, attached to the
> shoulder-belts of the cartridge-cases in each case, a tube
> of tin holding a piece of quick-match. At all our drills on
> board ship I practiced the men at flinging dummy hand-
> grenades made of pasteboard, to ensure rapidity and
> expertness, and while at Toulon also I often landed parties
> to practice with iron grenades. By that means, in the end,
> they had so acquired the art of flinging the grenades that
> on the day of battle my topmen were able to fling two
> grenades at a time. I had a hundred muskets, fitted with
> long bayonets, sent on board also. The picked men to whom
> these were served out were specially trained at musketry
> and stationed in the shrouds. All the men with cutlasses
> and pistols were regularly trained at sword exercise, and the
> pistol became with them a very familiar weapon. My men
> also learnt to throw grappling irons with such skill that we
> could count on being able to grapple an enemy's ship before
> her sides had actually touched ours. On the drums beating
> *branle-bas de combat* [beat to quarters] before Trafalgar, every

man went to his post fully accoutred, and with his weapon loaded and they placed them at hand by their guns, in racks between the gun ports. My ship's company indeed, had themselves learned to have such confidence in the mode of fighting that I proposed for the *Redoubtable* that they, several times before the battle, asked me, of their own accord to lay the ship alongside of the first enemy we met.

Lucas noticed that VICTORY's upper-deck guns were virtually silent. This may have been because in Beatty's words 'her great guns however being silent, it was supposed at different times that she [the *Redoubtable*] had surrendered; and in consequence of this opinion, the VICTORY twice ceased firing upon her, by orders transmitted from the quarter-deck', or because the crews of her upper-deck 12-pounders had been killed or driven below deck. Whichever, with his lower gun ports closed he could amass his crew, and at the sound of a trumpet the men raced up from below, those armed with muskets and grenades climbing the ratlines. *Redoubtable*'s rigging was filled with men; the VICTORY's was empty. *Redoubtable*'s murderous fire cleared the flagship's decks but her size and the respective tumblehomes of the big British and smaller French ship presented too large a gap for Lucas's boarders to cross easily. The upper decks would have been 30 or more feet apart. The main yard was ordered cut down to form a bridge, but just as it looked possible, the *TÉMÉRAIRE* came along *Redoubtable*'s starboard side. Lucas wrote:

I perceived that they were preparing to board, the foe thronged up onto their upper decks. I ordered the trumpet to sound, it was the recognised signal to summon the boarding parties in our exercises; they came up in such perfect order with the officers and midshipmen at the head of their divisions that one would have said that it was only a sham fight. In less than a minute our decks swarmed with armed men, who rapidly hurled themselves on to the poop, the nettings and the shrouds; it was impossible to say who was the most courageous. Then there began a furious musketry fire in which Admiral Nelson was fighting at the head of his crew. Our fire was greatly superior that in less than fifteen minutes we had silenced that of the VICTORY. More than two hundred grenades were thrown on board the VICTORY with the utmost success; her decks were strewn with dead and wounded . . .

. . . but it was difficult to get aboard her owing to the rolling of the two ships and to the superior height afforded by her third deck. I gave the order to cut away the slings of the main yard and to lower it so that it might serve as a bridge. At the same time Midshipman Yon and four seamen sprang on board the VICTORY by means of the anchor and informed us that there was not a soul on her decks; but at the moment, when my brave fellows were just hurling themselves after them the three-decker – who had doubtless perceived that the VICTORY had ceased fire and would inevitably be taken – ran foul of the *Redoubtable* to starboard and overwhelmed us with the point-blank fire of all her guns. It is impossible to describe the horrible carnage produced by the murderous broadside of this ship. More than two hundred of our brave lads were killed or wounded by it. I was wounded also at the same time, but not so seriously as to warrant my leaving my post.

The air above the upper deck of VICTORY was filled with the crackling of muskets and the bee-like hum of musket balls that lashed down from the French masts, splintering the deck everywhere and felling those men fighting from it. Dr Beatty confirmed that 'the *Redoubtable* commenced a heavy fire of musketry from the tops, which was continued for a considerable time with destructive effect to the VICTORY's crew'. Lieutenant Rotely witnessed how:

> The poop became a slaughter-house, and soon the two
> senior lieutenants of marines and half the original forty

were placed hors de combat. Captain Adair's party was reduced to less than ten men, himself wounded in the forehead by splinters, yet still using his musket with effect. One of his last orders was, 'Rotely, fire away as fast as you can!' when a ball struck him on the back of the neck and he was a corpse in a moment.

Captain Charles William Adair, 39, from County Antrim, had only a short while before been in conversation with Nelson, who was concerned to give the Marines some shelter from the torrential fire sweeping the deck. When afloat, they still went into action drawn up in conspicuous ranks, according to Marine Lieutenant Paul Harris Nicholas:

> Though it seems that in many of the ships engaged, the Marines and Bluejackets had been ordered to lie down until the time came to return the enemy's fire, this precaution does not seem to have been adopted on board the flagship, and a double-headed shot from the *Santissima Trinidada* killed no less than eight Marines as they stood on the poop. Lord Nelson at once ordered Captain Adair, who was in command of the detachment, to abandon the usual formation, and to distribute his men around the ship under cover of the hammock nettings. Adair himself fell mortally wounded very soon afterwards – according to one account as he stood in the gangway encouraging his men as they repelled a desperate attempt of the *Redoubtable* to board. Another story is that seeing the eight Marines fall, Nelson ordered their officer to lead some of his men aloft in order that they might open fire from the tops. 'Come along', shouted Adair to the men, 'and I'll make sailors of you!' he jumped upon the ratlines and before he had got a fathom aloft he fell down dead upon the deck with eighteen musket balls in his body.

Nelson is known to have discouraged the use of musketry from the tops because of the extreme danger of fire to sails and yards, so this may be a fanciful account, or if true, an indication of the desperate situation the *VICTORY* was in. William Beatty confirmed Nelson's policy:

> The *VICTORY* had no musketry in her tops: as His Lordship had a strong aversion to small arms being placed there, from the danger of their setting fire to the sails; which was exemplified by the destruction of the French ship *L'Achille* in this battle. It is a species of warfare by which individuals may suffer, and now and then a Commander be picked off: but it never can decide the fate of a general engagement.

Nicholas went on to tell how:

> . . . one of the Corporals belonging to *VICTORY*'s detachment had his arm taken off by a cannon-ball. Determined not to leave the deck, he picked up Adair's sash, bound it around the stump, collected a party to board the French ship with which they were engaged at close quarters, placed himself at its head, and was the first on the enemy's deck . . . There is a story . . . that during the fight a portion of the rigging was shot away and fell upon a marine thoroughly entangling him. Nelson observing his unsuccessful attempts to extricate himself from his painful and uncomfortable position, drew a knife from his pocket and threw it to the struggling man, bidding him cut himself free.

'MR BEATTY, LORD NELSON IS HERE'

Nelson and Hardy had been pacing the 21-foot stretch of *VICTORY*'s quarter-deck ever since the action began. Many had fallen around them and they had witnessed every minute of the horrifying carnage. Sometime after 1.00 p.m. Walter Burke, the 67-year-old Purser, came out on deck from the horrible scene of suffering in the gloom of the cockpit, now crowded with wounded and dying men – 'it was like a butcher's shambles' according to the chaplain, Alexander Scott. Nelson caught sight of him and said assertively, 'Mr. Burke, I expect every man to be upon his station!' Burke took the hint, and returned to his proper station in the cockpit. Nelson had also lost his secretary, John Scott, who while talking with an officer on the quarter-deck, had been almost cut in two by round shot. Nelson himself was about three yards from the stern and in the act of turning to accompany Hardy, with his face towards the *Redoubtable*, when he was mortally wounded by a musket ball and fell to his knees into the pool of John Scott's blood. William Beatty gave the best account:

About fifteen minutes past one o'clock, which was in the heat of the engagement, he was walking the middle of the quarterdeck with Captain Hardy, and in the act of turning near the hatchway with his face towards the stern of the *VICTORY*, when the fatal ball was fired from the Enemy's mizzen-top; which from the situation of the two ships (lying on board of each other), was brought just abaft, and rather below, the *VICTORY*'s main-yard, and of course not more than fifteen yards distant from the part of the deck where His Lordship stood. The ball struck the epaulette on the left shoulder, and penetrated the chest. He fell with his face on the deck. Captain Hardy, who was on his right (the side furthest from the Enemy) and advanced some steps before His Lordship, on turning around saw the Serjeant Major (Secker) of Marines with two seamen raising him from the deck; where he had fallen on the same spot on which, a little before, his Secretary had breathed his last, with whose blood His Lordship's clothes were much soiled. Captain Hardy expressed a hope that he was not severely wounded; to which the gallant Chief replied: 'They have done for me at last, Hardy.' – 'I hope not', answered Captain Hardy. 'Yes,' replied His Lordship; 'my backbone is shot through.'

Captain Hardy ordered the Seamen to carry the Admiral to the cockpit; and now two incidents occurred strikingly characteristic of this great man, and strongly marking the energy and reflection which in his heroic mind rose superior even to the immediate consideration of his present awful condition. While the men were carrying him down the ladder from the middle-deck, His Lordship observed that the tiller-ropes were not yet replaced; desired one of his Midshipmen stationed there to go upon the quarter-deck and remind Captain Hardy of the circumstance, and request that new ones should be immediately rove. Having delivered this order, he took his handkerchief from his pocket and covered his face with it, that he might be conveyed to the cockpit at this crisis unnoticed by the crew.

Several wounded Officers, and about forty men, were likewise carried to the Surgeon for assistance just at this time; and some others had breathed their last during their conveyance below. Among the latter were Lieutenant William Andrew Ram, and Mr Whipple Captain's Clerk. The Surgeon had just examined these two Officers and found that they were dead, when his attention was arrested by several of the wounded calling to him, 'Mr Beatty, Lord Nelson is here: Mr Beatty, the Admiral is wounded.' The Surgeon now, on looking round saw the handkerchief fall from His Lordship's face; when the stars of his coat, which also had been covered by it, appeared. Mr Burke the Purser, and the Surgeon, ran immediately to the assistance of His Lordship, and took him from the arms of the Seamen who had carried him below. In conveying him to one of the Midshipmen's births, they stumbled, but recovered themselves without falling. Lord Nelson then inquired who were supporting him; and when the surgeon informed him, His Lordship replied, 'Ah, Mr Beatty! You can do nothing for me. I have but a short time to live: my back is shot through.' The Surgeon said, 'he hoped the wound was not so dangerous as His Lordship imagined, and that he might still survive long to enjoy his glorious victory.' The Reverend Doctor Scott, who had been absent in another part of the cockpit administering lemonade to the wounded, now came instantly to His Lordship; and in the anguish of grief wrung his hands and said: 'Alas, Beatty, how prophetic you were!' alluding to the apprehensions expressed by the Surgeon for His Lordship's safety previous to the battle.

His Lordship was laid upon a bed, stripped of his clothes, and covered with a sheet. While this was effecting, he said to Doctor Scott, 'Doctor, I told you so. Doctor, I am gone;' and after a short pause he added in low voice, 'I have to leave Lady Hamilton, and my adopted daughter Horatia, as a legacy to my Country.' The Surgeon then examined the wound, assuring His Lordship that he would not put him to much pain in endeavouring to discover the course of the ball; which he soon found had penetrated deep into the chest, and had probably lodged in the spine. This being explained to His Lordship, he replied, 'he was confident his back was shot through.' The back was then examined externally, but without any injury being perceived; on which His Lordship was requested by the Surgeon to make him acquainted with all his sensations. He replied, that 'he felt a gush of blood every minute within his breast: that he had no feeling in the lower part of his body: and that his breathing was difficult, and attended with very severe pain about that part of the spine where he was confident that the ball had struck; for,' said he, ' I felt it break my back.' These symptoms, but more particularly the gush of blood which His Lordship complained of, together with the state of his pulse, indicated to the Surgeon the hopeless situation of the case; but till after the victory was ascertained and announced to His Lordship, the true nature of his wound was concealed by the Surgeon from all

on board except only Captain Hardy, Doctor Scott,
Mr Burke, and Messrs. Smith and Westemburg the
Assistant Surgeons.

As to the true nature of Nelson's wound, Beatty wrote on 15 December
1805, after the post mortem he carried out in *VICTORY* once she had
returned to England:

> Course and site of the ball ascertained since death, by
> William Beatty:
> The ball struck the fore part of his Lordship's epaulette,
> and entered the left shoulder immediately before the
> *processus acromium scapulae*, which it slightly fractured; it
> then descended obliquely into the thorax, fracturing the
> second and third ribs; and after penetrating the left lobe
> of the lungs, and dividing in its passage a large branch of
> the pulmonary artery, it entered the left side of the spine,
> between the sixth and seventh dorsal vertebra; fractured the
> left tranverse process of the sixth vertebra, wounded the
> *medulla spinalis*, and fracturing the right tranverse process
> of the seventh vertebra, it made its way from the right side
> of the spine, directing its course through the muscles of
> the back, and lodged therein, about two inches below the
> inferior angle of the eighth scapula.
> On removing the ball, a portion of the gold lace, and pad
> of epaulette, with a small piece of his Lordship's coat was
> found firmly attached to it.

The French musket that fired the fatal ball would have been similar
to the British 39-inch sea service musket although a little shorter and
possibly rifled. The sea service musket was a cheaper version of the
army's Brown Bess or India pattern smooth bore flintlock musket,
only three inches shorter. Sea muskets used wooden ramrods because
iron ones would have rusted at sea. Seamen usually had blackened
barrels to prevent corrosion whereas the Royal Marines, who would

have had a little more time to keep their kit clean, had 'bright' models. Both types were highly inaccurate and subject to misfires, especially if the powder was damp. At one hundred yards even a good shot would miss three times out of four. However, at Trafalgar the range was *very* close. Nelson was shot from a distance of about 20 yards, maybe less. The French musket ball weighed about an ounce and was fractionally smaller than the British 0.76-inch calibre. At close range either size could inflict terrible injuries since they flattened slightly on impact, which helped them to smash bones, rip huge holes in muscle and cause massive bleeding and clinical shock.

Whether Nelson was hit by an aimed shot remains a mystery. Beatty thought it was highly likely, but the ferocity of the musketry at such close range and the many other casualties on the upper deck of *VICTORY* that early afternoon suggest that it was more than likely an unaimed lucky shot. It is probably more surprising that Hardy survived unscathed. Beatty wrote that:

> It is by no means certain, though highly probable, that Lord Nelson was particularly aimed at by the Enemy. There were only two Frenchmen left alive in the mizzen-top of the *Redoubtable* at the time of His Lordship's being wounded, and by the hand of one of these he fell. These men continued firing at Captain Hardy and Adair, Lieutenant Rotely of the Marines, and some of the Midshipmen on the *VICTORY*'s poop, for some time afterwards. At length one of them was killed by a musket ball: and on the other then attempting to make his escape down the rigging, Mr Pollard (Midshipman) fired his musket at him, and shot him in the back; when he fell dead from the shrouds, on the *Redoubtable*'s poop.

Up until about 1863 a 21-year-old able seaman, Edward Francis Collingwood of Milford Haven, was believed to be the man who had avenged Nelson, but then a Cornishman, Midshipman John Pollard, also aged 21 at the battle, came from the wings with this convincing account, which has a nice symmetry with Beatty's, although he gave his age as two years younger than that recorded in VICTORY's muster book.

> I was on the poop of the VICTORY from the time the men were beat to quarters before the action till late in the evening. I was the first struck, as a splinter hit my right arm, and I was the only officer left alive of all who had been originally stationed on the poop. It is true my old friend Collingwood came on the poop for a short time. I had for some time discovered the men in the top of the Redoubtable; they were in a crouching position, and rose breast high to fire. I pointed them out to Collingwood as I made my aim; he took up a musket, fired once, and then left the poop, I concluded to return to the quarter-deck, which was his station during the battle. I remained firing at the top till not a man was to be seen; the last one I discovered coming down the mizzen rigging, and from my fire he fell also. King [John King, age 56 from Sunderland], a quarter-master, was killed while in the act of handing me a parcel of ball cartridge long after Collingwood had left the poop. I remained there till after the action was over, and assisted in superintending the rigging of the jury mast. Then I was ushered into the ward-room where Sir Thomas Hardy and other officers were assembled, and complimented by them on avenging Lord Nelson's death, which fact afterwards appeared in the Gazette. I did not go on board the Redoubtable with Mr. Collingwood at all, therefore could not have discovered the man 'lying in the mizentop, with one ball in his head, and another in his breast.' At the time of the action I was nineteen years of age.

Curiously, some 20 years after the battle an account came out of France from 'the man who shot Nelson'. The narrative by Sergeant

Robert Guillemard is widely regarded as a falsification. There is no evidence that Guillemard ever existed and part of his story gives him away since he says, 'When the English top-men, who were only a few yards distant from us, saw us appear, they directed a sharp fire on us, which we returned.'

THE FIGHTING *TÉMÉRAIRE*

Away from the gloom and misery of the cockpit where Nelson lay dying, the battle raged on. So destructive was the fire kept up from the *Redoubtable*'s tops, as well as from her second deck guns, occasionally pointed upwards, that within a few minutes of Nelson's wounding, several officers and 40 men, nearly the whole of them upon the third or upper deck, were killed or wounded. Unfortunately, the *VICTORY* had no guns mounted on her poop and could not return fire on the *Redoubtable*'s mizzen-top, and her 68-pounder carronades could not be laid to get the required elevation. About 15 minutes after Nelson had been shot and just as the Frenchman was about to board, the 'fighting' *TÉMÉRAIRE* crashed into the battered *Redoubtable*'s starboard side, the French bowsprit passing over Captain Harvey's main entry port, which his crew quickly lashed to his ship. Trapped between the two British three-deckers, while *TÉMÉRAIRE* put much shot into her bows, Lucas's crew fought on, mostly with small fire and grenades. In Beatty's words,

> A few minutes after this the *TÉMÉRAIRE* fell likewise on board of the *Redoubtable*, on the side opposite to the *VICTORY*, having also an Enemy's ship, said to be *La Fougueux*, on board of her on *her* other side: so that the extraordinary and unprecedented circumstances occurred here, of *four* ships of the line being *on board of each other* in the heat of battle; forming as compact a tier as if they had been moored together, their heads lying all the same way.

Rotely, now in command of the Marines, spent five minutes or so clearing the mizzen-top until 'not a man was left alive in it'. He described how:

> Another French ship, the *Fougueux*, fell on board the
> *TÉMÉRAIRE* on her starboard side, so that four ships of the
> line were rubbing sides in the heat of the fight, with their
> heads all lying the same way, as if moored in harbour. It
> consequently became a great nicety in directing the fire of
> the musketry lest we should shoot our own men over the
> decks of the *Redoubtable*. I therefore directed the fire of the
> marines to the main and fore tops of that devoted ship, and
> but few of their men escaped.

Aboard the *Redoubtable*, Captain Lucas, seeing he could do nothing more on his port side against *VICTORY,* ordered the rest of his crew to go as quickly as possible to the lower gun decks to man whatever starboard guns had not been dismounted during the collision with the *TÉMÉRAIRE*. He picked up the story:

> There were so few guns fit for service, that the *TÉMÉRAIRE*
> replied with great advantage . . . In less than half an hour
> our ship had been so fearfully mauled that she looked like
> little more than a heap of debris. Judging by appearances,
> no doubt, the *TÉMÉRAIRE*, now hailed us to surrender and
> not prolong a useless resistance. My reply was instantly to
> order some soldiers who were near me to fire back; which
> they did with great alacrity. At the same moment almost,
> the main mast of the *Redoubtable* fell on board the English
> ship. The two topmasts of the *TÉMÉRAIRE* then came
> down, falling on board of us. Our whole poop was stove in,
> helm rudder and stern post all shattered to splinters, all the
> stern frame, and the decks shot through. All our own guns
> were either smashed or dismounted by the broadsides of
> the *VICTORY* and *TÉMÉRAIRE*. In addition an 18-pounder

gun on the lower deck, and a 32-pounder carronade on the forecastle had burst killing and wounding a great many men. The hull itself was riddled, shot through from side to side; deck beams were shattered; port lids torn away or knocked to pieces. Four of our six pumps were so damaged as to be useless. The quarter-deck ladders were broken, which rendered communication with the rest of the ship very difficult. Everywhere the decks were strewn with dead men, lying beneath the debris. Out of a crew of 634 men we had 522 *hors de combat*; of whom 300 were killed and 222 wounded nearly all the officers among them. A number of the wounded were killed on the orlop deck below the waterline. Of the remaining 121, a large number were employed in the storerooms and magazines. The batteries and upper decks were practically abandoned – bare of men, and were unable longer to offer any resistance. No one who had not seen the state of the *Redoubtable* could ever form an idea of her awful condition. Really I know of nothing on board that had not been hit by shot. In the midst of this horrible carnage and devastation my splendid fellows who had not been killed, and even, too, the wounded below on the orlop, kept cheering '*Vive l'Empereur*! We're not taken yet; is our Captain still alive?'

The French would not give in and still made attempts to board. Yet, after some of their fire-balls and grenades had fallen short and set fire to her starboard rigging – the flames spreading to the *TÉMÉRAIRE*'s foresail – men on both sides dropped their weapons in order to man the pumps together to douse the fires, since left unattended they would have fuelled a raging inferno. A small British boat party entered through the *Redoubtable*'s stern ports to help fight the fires and were well received by their enemy, such is the power of the 'brotherhood of the sea'. One of *Redoubtable*'s fire-balls is reported as entering the powder screen on the quarter deck where it 'caused a destructive explosion on the main deck below. Had it not been for the presence of mind of the Master-At-Arms, John Toohig from Cork, quartered in the light room, the fire would have communicated to the after magazine, and probably have occasioned the loss not only of the *TÉMÉRAIRE* but of the ships near her.'

Lucas was wounded and exhausted: 'Not being able to reply and not seeing any of our ships – which were far away to leeward – coming to our assistance, I only awaited the certain knowledge that the leaks which the ship had sprung were so considerable that it could not be long before she foundered.' He adds:

> I no longer hesitated about surrendering; the leaks were serious enough to sink the ship, so the enemy would not have her long. I warned the *TÉMÉRAIRE* that if she did not at once send help and spare parts for the damaged pumps, I would have to set fire to the ship, and this would involve the *TÉMÉRAIRE*. Two officers with some seamen and marines then came on board to take possession. One of our wounded seamen, armed with a musket and bayonet, cried out, 'I must kill another of them!' As one of the English marines was climbing in through a lower deck port, this sailor bayoneted him in the thigh, and he fell between the ships. Because of this, the English were about to go back to their ship and leave us; but in spite of it I prevailed on them to remain.

He at last surrendered to the *TÉMÉRAIRE* to prevent any further slaughter of his men. It was 2.30 in the afternoon. However, his brave ship did not haul down her colours when Lucas ordered; they came down of themselves with the fall of her mizzen-mast. Of the original complement of 643, 474 had been killed and 70 wounded; the highest number of casualties in any ship at the Battle of Trafalgar. *Redoubtable* now had two claims to fame.

As the interlocked *VICTORY*, *Redoubtable* and *TÉMÉRAIRE* had drifted on to the *Fougueux*, Captain Harvey wasted no time in ordering his tired crew to 'Away boarders!' His first Lieutenant, Thomas

Kennedy, led around 20 sailors and marines – all he could muster – on to the *Fougueux*'s deck. When they had fought their way to the quarterdeck they found Captain Louis Beaudouin in a pool of his own blood, his sword close by. His crew had been so badly mauled repelling the boarders from the *BELLEISLE* that their power to resist was exhausted and Beaudouin's once superb ship was now a complete wreck. Captain Pierre Servaux in the *Fougueux,* who had been proud that her flag was still flying even though it was 'the only thing left above the deck', gave his account of her final moments:

Now, however, yet another English ship, the *TÉMÉRAIRE,* of 100 guns came down to attack us. Borne down alongside of us with the current, she fell on board us. At once a broadside burst from her upper-deck guns and main battery, with a hot small arms fusillade, fired right down into us. It swept our decks clear. Even then, though our men rallied. With cries of *à l'abordage* repeated all over the ship, some sixty to eighty of them swarmed up on deck, armed with sabres and axes. But the huge English three-decker towered high above the *Fougueux,* and they fired down on us as they pleased with their musketry, until, at length, they themselves boarded us. From two to three hundred of them suddenly rushed on board us, entering the ship from their chains and main-deck ports. Our captain fell dead, shot through the heart with a musket bullet. The few men who were left could make no resistance in the face of numbers. Resistance was out of the question, while still the enemy's murderous fire from the gangways continued. We were obliged to give back and yield, though we defended the decks port by port. So the *Fougueux* fell into the power of the English.

Yet we had in the end the proud consolation of not hauling down our own colours. The doing that we left to the enemy, who carried the colour off after they had taken possession of the ship. Thus ended one of the most murderous of battles. For nearly four hours we had not ceased firing once, and at the same time we had stood up against four ships, each one of them more powerful at all points than the *Fougueux*. Indeed, the *Fougueux* was a very weakly built vessel. We lost in the combat our captain, more than half the ship's company, two lieutenants, three mates, two midshipmen, and three warrant officers.

On their approaches the *NEPTUNE, LEVIATHAN, CONQUEROR* and *BRITANNIA* all passed under the *Bucentaure*'s pulverized stern and added the full weight of their broadsides to the devastation. The log of the *CONQUEROR* records: 'At 2, shot away the *Bucentaure*'s main and mizzen masts . . . Shot away the *Bucentaure*'s foremast.' Captain Magendie wrote in his official report that all the men at the upper-deck guns were either killed or wounded; the 24-pounder battery was 'entirely dismounted and heaped up with dead and wounded'. And the starboard upper deck was 'blocked with wreckage from aloft so that it was impossible to fire again'. Major General de Contamine later wrote to Napoleon:

It was impossible to meet the *VICTORY* as she came on with our broadside, because the *Santissima Trinidad*, which in the light breeze would not answer her helm, was leeward of us, almost touching us. Indeed we received several broadsides from the enemy without power of reply.

The *VICTORY, TÉMÉRAIRE,* and *NEPTUNE,* three-deckers, took post, one on our quarter, and the other two astern. They fired into us for nearly two hours at half pistol-shot. By 3 o'clock the *Bucentaure* had received the first of 11 English ships, most of which passed by and raked us ahead and astern. The ship was dismasted, '*ras comme un pontoon,*' and the masts and sails fell over to starboard, blocking up the batteries and rendering it impossible to move. The 24-pounder battery was left without a man at the guns; only nine men were left on the forecastle and the poop. With about 400 killed and wounded, beyond reach of assistance or rescue, surrounded by the enemy, the admiral had to order the flag to be lowered.

One of Villeneuve's officers told of the Admiral's plight, isolated as he was from the rest of the battle:

By now the upper decks and gangways of the *Bucentaure*, heaped with the dead and the wreckage from overhead, presented an appalling spectacle. All this time, amid all this scene of disaster, Admiral Villeneuve, who from the first had displayed the calmest courage, continued tranquilly pacing up and down the quarter-deck. At length he saw his ship totally dismasted, and no hope of succour coming from any quarter. With bitter sorrow he exclaimed, 'The *Bucentaure* has played her part; mine is not yet over.'

He gave orders for his boat to be got ready at once to take him with his flag on board one of the ships of the van squadron. He still cherished the hope that he might be able, with ten fresh ships of the van, to make a supreme effort, and even yet snatch victory from the enemy. But the unfortunate Admiral's illusion did not last long. Word was soon brought him that his barge, which before the battle had been got ready against this very possibility, had early in the action had several holes made in it by the enemy's shot; and as a finale, had been crushed to pieces under a mass of fallen spars and rigging. Every single one of the ship's other boats had also been destroyed. On that they hailed from the *Bucentaure* across to the *Santissima Trinidad* for them to send a boat, but no reply was made and no boat was sent. Bitterly did Admiral Villeneuve realise his desperate position, and the hard fate that was in store for him! He saw himself imprisoned on board a ship that was unable to defend herself, and this too, while a great part of his fleet was in action and fighting hard. He cursed the destiny that had spared him in the midst of all the slaughter round about. Compelled by force of circumstances to think no more about his fleet, he had now only to think of the ship he was in. All he could do now was to see after the lives of brave men left fighting with him. Humanity forbade him to allow them to be shot down without means of defending themselves. Villeneuve looked away and allowed the captain of the *Bucentaure* to lower the colours.

'I had to yield to my fate,' accepted Villeneuve. Magendie also recognized that it really was all over:

All rigging gone, entirely dismasted, having lost all the men on the upper decks, the battery of 24-pounders left totally dismounted and unmanned by dead and wounded, the starboard guns covered by fallen rigging, spars and timber and close to 450 casualties and no longer even being in a state to defend ourselves . . . surrounded by 5 enemy ships, with no help in sight, Admiral Villeneuve had no choice but to put an end to this, to prevent the further useless killing of any more brave people, which he then did after three and a quarter hours of fighting, after first throwing the debris of the Imperial eagle into the sea along with the ship's signals.

The log of the BRITANNIA noted that, 'Her colours being shot away, someone waved a white handkerchief from the remains of the larboard gallery in token of surrender.' Midshipman William Hicks, the 21-year-old aide-de-camp to Captain Israel Pellew of the CONQUEROR, described the surrender from her quarterdeck:

We engaged her single-handed for an hour, and she struck to us; after her colours were hauled down two guns from her starboard side began to play on us. Sir Israel Pellew, thinking that they were disposed to renew the fight, ordered the guns which could bear on her foremast to knock it away, and her masts were cut away successfully in a few minutes. The officers of the French ship waving their handkerchiefs in sign of surrender, we sent a cutter and took possession of the *Bucentaure*. Then we moved on.

Captain Pellew was unaware that the Commander-in-Chief had surrendered because Villeneuve's flag was not to be seen. Otherwise he would have given Lieutenant James Couch the honour of boarding the prize, but, unable to spare him, Pellew ordered Captain of Marines James Atcherley aboard the *Bucentaure* instead. Atcherley took with him a corporal and two privates of his corps, and two seamen. One can only imagine his surprise when, on reaching the quarterdeck, four French officers stepped forward, Captain Magendie, Flag-Captain Prigny, Major General de Contamine, in a brilliant but powder-smoked red uniform (he commanded the 4,000 troops in the Combined Fleet), and the commander in chief, Admiral Pierre de Comte de Villenueve himself.

'To whom,' asked Villeneuve, in good English, 'have I the honour of surrendering?'
'To Captain Pellew of the *CONQUEROR*.'
'I am glad to have struck to the fortunate Sir Edward Pellew.'
'It is his brother, Sir,' said Captain Atcherley.
'His brother! What! Are there two of them? Hélas!'

Captain Magendie is believed to have shrugged his broad shoulders and said laconically, *'Fortune de la guerre.'* It was the third time in his career he had been captured by the Royal Navy. Believing that it more properly belonged to Captain Pellew to disarm officers of such exalted rank, Atcherley declined the honour, secured the magazine and put the key in his pocket, placed two of his men as sentries, one at each cabin door, and then escorted Villeneuve and his 'retinue' to the *MARS*, since the *CONQUEROR* had moved off. Aboard *MARS*

Villeneuve's sword was received by Lieutenant William Hennah, who had assumed command when Captain George Duff had been killed. After the battle the sword was sent to Collingwood. Three days later Villeneuve, who had amazingly survived the action without a scratch, would meet Collingwood aboard the *EURYALUS*. Captain Prigny wrote in his report, 'Admiral Villeneuve complained most bitterly having been spared in the midst of that hail of bullets and bursting shells.'

While securing the magazine, Atcherley could not but take in the awful scene on the French ship's gundecks:

> The dead, thrown back as they fell, lay along the middle of the decks in heaps, and the shot, passing through these, had frightfully mangled the bodies . . . More than four hundred had been killed and wounded, of whom an extraordinary proportion had lost their heads. A raking shot, which entered in the lower deck, had glanced along the beams and through the thickest of the people, and a French officer declared that this shot alone had killed or disabled nearly forty men.

Meanwhile, while he had been away from the *CONQUEROR*:

> Lieutenant [Robert] Lloyd was struck in the mouth, the bullet passing through the back of his head. So little was his countenance changed . . . that an officer who just then reached the quarterdeck with a party of boarders, and ran to assist him, thought he had only been stunned by the wind of a shot. Lieutenant [William Molyneaux] St. George was shot through the neck. He had gone into action with a strong impression that that he should fall; and that morning, when his brother officers proposed to him to take some refreshment in the wardroom, with the half-serious, half-jocular remark that it might be the last time, he replied that he felt that it would indeed be so. Just after the death

of these officers, Captain Pellew reeled and fell stunned by the wind of a shot. He recovered immediately, but it was found afterwards that he had received permanent injury. [Although he was not listed as a casualty.]

The 98-gun *NEPTUNE* was under the command of Captain Thomas Fremantle, one of Nelson's original 'band of brothers', who had been sailing astern of the *TÉMÉRAIRE*. He had brought his ship under the stern of the magnificently imposing four-deck Spanish *Santissima Trinidad*, 'with her rich display of sculpture, figures, ornaments and inscriptions with which she was adorned', and then luffed up to come alongside, from where he fought her into submission. *NEPTUNE* was carrying an additional 14 32-pound carronades, and her gunnery was so effective that while Captain Henry Bayntun's *LEVIATHAN* was poised to open fire on the *Santissima Trinidad* there was a loud and terrible tearing noise as both the main and mizzen masts came crashing down together.

Don Perez Galdos illustrated in his account of the battle the dreadful results of the British cannonade:

> The scene on board the *Santissima Trinidad* was simply infernal. All attempts at working the ship had to be abandoned and she could not move. The only thing to be done was serve the guns as fast as we could and damage the enemy all we could.
>
> The English shot had torn our sails to tatters. It was as if huge invisible talons had been dragging at them. Fragments of spars, splinters of wood, thick hempen cables cut up as corn is cut by the sickle, fallen blocks, shreds of canvas, bits of iron, and hundreds of other things that had been wrenched away by the enemy's fire, were piled along the deck, where it was scarcely possible to move about . . . Blood ran in streams about the deck, and in spite of the sand, the rolling of the ship carried it hither and thither until it made strange patterns on the planks. The enemy's shot, fired as

they were from very short range caused horrible mutilations
... The ship creaked and groaned as she rolled, and through
a thousand holes and crevices in her hull the sea spurted in
and began to flood the hold.

There was hardly a man to be seen who did not bear
marks, more or less severe, of the enemy's iron and lead.

At 2.30 p.m. the foremast, the last remaining, came thundering
down, leaving only a stump. At this point Captain Henry Digby in
command of *AFRICA*, the smallest ship of the 50 ships of the line
present, which had been far to the north at the start of the battle and
had exchanged broadsides with every French and Spanish ship that
she passed on her way towards the heart of the action, arrived within
range of the biggest warship in the world at the time. The *Santissima
Trinidad* towered over the little 64-gun ship. Unperturbed by her size,
and by the fact that she mounted twice as many guns, Digby opened
fire. The *Santissima Trinidad* did not reply. Seeing that the injured giant
was not showing any colours, Digby lowered a boat and sent a party
aboard to ask for the captain's sword and to take possession of her.
However, the Spanish had not struck and told 37-year-old Lieutenant
John Smith, who led the boarding party, that they had no intention
of doing so. They had only ceased firing because they were getting up
fresh ammunition from the magazines. With true Castillian courtesy,
they allowed Smith and his men to return to the *AFRICA* unharmed,
after which they recommenced firing. This defiance did not last long.
The ship was an unmanageable wreck drifting in the heaving swell.
She remained with her colours down, taking no further part in the
battle all round her.

The *Bucentaure, Fougueux* and *Redoubtable* had all struck their colours
by the time the *BRITANNIA* cut the line at about 3.00 p.m. She had
been pounding away for most of the early afternoon but at too far
a range to do any damage and was getting close to running out of
ammunition. The *LEVIATHAN* had started to engage the *San Agustin*
(74), which struck within a half hour after Lieutenant John Baldwin,
at the head of a party of seamen and marines, 'leapt on board and

carried her'. The little *AFRICA* had passed on to fight Captain Louis Antoine Cyprian Infernet's *Intrépide*, to be relieved by Captain Edward Codrington in the *ORION* – the last of Nelson's ships to engage in the battle – about three quarters of an hour later. These ships were scattered across the ocean and the mêlée was general.

The unequal duel between the *AFRICA* and the *Intrépide* silenced Digby's guns and so damaged *AFRICA*'s lower yards that they eventually collapsed. However, he unfalteringly refused to surrender, and in the end Codrington's ship pounded the *Intrépide* into surrender. The *ORION*'s log states:

> Passed close athwart the *LEVIATHAN*'s stern, so as to
> close with the French 74. At 4, opened our fire close on
> his starboard quarter, wore round his stern, and brought
> to on his lee bow betwixt the *AFRICA* and the above ship,
> keeping up such a well-directed fire as carried away his
> three masts and bitts [this word is nearly illegible: it may
> be a contraction of bowsprit] and prevented his returning
> us more than one or two broadsides. At 4.45, he struck his
> colours. Sent the first lieutenant, Mr Croft, and a party of
> men to [take] possession of her. At 6 stood under her stern
> with a rope to take her in tow, but they slipped it. At 8 the
> *AJAX* took her in tow.

The *Intrépide* was the last French ship to strike her colours. In his account Sub-Lieutenant Gicquel des Touches painted a fascinating picture of the engagement that reveals a brief humorous moment between friends:

> At the height of the action the British *ORION* crossed our
> bows in order to pour in a raking fire. I got my men ready
> to board, and pointing out to a midshipman her position
> and what I wanted to do, I sent him to the captain with
> a request to have the ship laid on board the *ORION*. I
> already imagined myself master of the British seventy-four

There are many representations of Nelson collapsing on the quarterdeck after being shot. This naïve engraving is rarely seen but perpetuates the myth that he was wearing a splendidly decorated coat when he was shot. An officer is seen pointing to the top from which the fatal bullet was fired while Nelson is supported by the solid Captain Hardy as sailors look on in disdain.

In this accurate Victorian picture Nelson stands on the poop deck of VICTORY with Hardy and Blackwood as his most famous signal, reading 'England expects that every man will do his duty', is hoisted. He was the first to appreciate that a new signal code could be used to send ordinary messages. The flags on the deck spell his last signal, 'Engage the enemy more closely'.

'Grand Naval Action: The Battle of Trafalgar'. This is one of the first published charts of the battle and appeared in November 1805. It reverses the weather and lee columns, but is otherwise reasonably accurate. It shows the close proximity of the battle to both Cadiz and the coast that claimed many of the battle-damaged ships during the subsequent storm.

BELOW This oblique drawing, published in November 1805, is one of the earliest published representations of the battle. Nelson's Weather Column is to the left of the picture. Although neither of the columns were this perfectly formed, the picture shows the studding sails set, the ROYAL SOVEREIGN engaging before VICTORY, the concave formation of the Combined Fleet and the AFRICA joining the battle from the north.

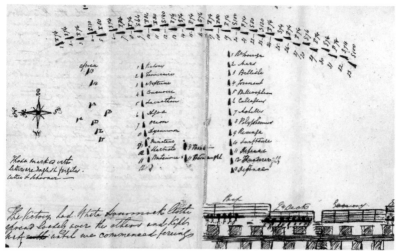

ABOVE *An anonymous account of the battle is illustrated with a sketch of the elevation of the starboard side of the* VICTORY *from the poop to the fore deck descending as far as the second row of guns. Alongside, the text reads, 'The* VICTORY *had White Hammock Clothe spread loosely over the others and kept wet until we commenced firing.' The letter is also illustrated with a stylized sketch plan of the battle.*

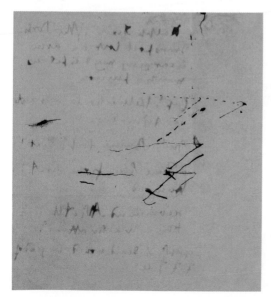

A rough but remarkable 'back of an envelope' diagram by Nelson indicating his tactical thinking for Trafalgar. Sketched in September 1805, the lower part shows the British fleet in three divisions: two to cut the enemy line, indicated by the continuous diagonal, and one ranging alongside the enemy's van, in order to contain it. This diagram was clearly drawn with enthusiasm since the nib has been pressed firmly into the paper allowing the ink to flow freely at the point where the 'weather column' cuts the line.

The Ball

which mortally wounded

The *LAMENTED NELSON* of

Glorious & Immortal Memory

*This engraving shows 'the Ball in the exact
state in which it was extracted' and in its
presentation oval glass locket. The portion of
gold lace, pad of epaulette and piece of coat that
fused to the lead ball are clearly visible. Beatty
found that, after entering the left shoulder, the
ball had divided a major part of the pulmonary
artery and the spinal cord; for 'I felt it break
my back' said Nelson.*

*BELOW 'Captain Harvey of the TÉMÉRAIRE,
with part of his brave ship's company, clearing
the deck of the French and Spaniards who
had succeeded in boarding and striking the
British flag.' This mezzotint was based on
Collingwood's first dispatch, which incorrectly
refers to the TÉMÉRAIRE being boarded. The
picture is pure fiction. Collingwood's account
owes itself to Harvey's boastfulness.*

'Key to a large historical engraving of the Death of Lord Nelson' by Edward Orme, showing clockwise from bottom left: a sailor, Lieutenant Ram, Captain Hardy, Lord Nelson, one of the sailors who left his gun to assist Lord Nelson, Mr Scott (Nelson's secretary) and Captain Adair of the Marines.

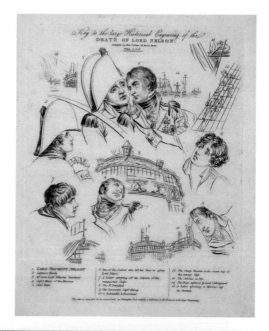

This picture is an interpretation of the more famous 'Death of Nelson' by Arthur Davis depicting the scene in the cockpit of VICTORY. The men gathered around the dying Nelson include Reverend Dr Sutt, Dr Beatty who is holding Nelson's wrist, and Captain Hardy who is standing over them. In contrast to the Davis picture most of the officers are wearing hair.

The second of the Robert Dodd panoramas portrays the victory over the allied van. The left half shows the French Admiral Dumanois in the Formidable *with the remaining five ships of his division making their escape under full shot-turn sail to windward. The* PRINCE *and* MINOTAUR *can be seen between the second and third of his ships bearing up to intercept them. To the right we see the battered British and allied ships with the dismasted* BELLEROPHON *in the foreground.*

BELOW As Nelson lay dying he realized that a storm was brewing and issued the order to anchor; Collingwood chose not to. This dramatic oil painting, after the style of Tudgay, shows one of the Spanish prizes caught in the gale that followed the battle, possibly the Santissima Trinidad.

LEFT This painting depicts Jeannette being rescued from the Achille, which blew up with an incredible explosion as the battle was coming to an end. A woman in her mid-20s working in the powder room, she made a dramatic escape through the gun room port and was eventually reunited with her husband.

The badly damaged VICTORY, with most of her masts shot away, is towed into Gibraltar by Nelson's old friend Fremantle commanding the NEPTUNE. After temporary repairs she took a month to sail back to England with Nelson's body preserved in a cask of brandy.

Nelson's ornate funeral car arrives at St Paul's Cathedral. It was built to resemble the hull of VICTORY, with a representation of Fame as its figurehead and was decorated with large plumes, heraldic devices and trophies. The vast crowds fell silent as it passed apart from a noise like the rushing of leaves as the men removed their hats.

and taking her into Cadiz with her colours under ours! With keen anxiety I waited; but there was no change in the *Intrépide*'s course. Then I dashed off for the quarter-deck myself. On my way I found my midshipman lying flat on the deck, terrified at the sight of the *TÉMÉRAIRE*, which ship had come abreast of us within pistol-shot and was thundering into us from her lofty batteries. I treated my emissary as he deserved – I gave him a hearty kick – and then I hurried aft to explain my project personally to the captain. But it was too late. The *ORION* swept forward across our bows, letting fly a murderous broadside.

At the moment I reached the poop the brave Infernet was brandishing a small curved sabre which struck off one of the pieces of wooden ornamental work by the rail. The sword-blade went close to my face, and I said laughingly, 'Do you want to cut my head off, Captain?' 'No certainly not you, my friend,' was the reply, 'but that's what I mean to do to the first man who speaks to me of surrender.' Nearby was a gallant colonel of infantry, who had distinguished himself at Marengo. He was terribly perturbed at the broadside from the *TÉMÉRAIRE*. In vain he tried to dodge the shelter behind the stalwart form of the captain, 'do you think I am sheathed in metal then?' In spite of the gravity of the moment we could not help laughing.

But by now the decks had been almost swept clear; our guns were disabled, and the batteries heaped up with dead and dying. It was impossible to keep up a resistance which meant the doom of what remained of our brave ship's company. Our flag was hauled down . . . the only one still flying, the *Intrépide* was dismasted, had lost two thirds of her crew and, riddled with round shot, the port covers ripped away, she was making water everywhere. But at least honour had been saved, the task accomplished, duty fulfilled to the very end.

Codrington later wrote to his wife saying, 'He said he would not strike till his masts and rudder were shot away; and this we did for him in so handsome a way that he had no time to do us much injury.'

Before surrendering the *Bucentaure*, Villeneuve had been signalling Rear Admiral Dumanoir Le Pelley to wear the van, with its seven fresh ships of the line, in order to alleviate the crisis at the Combined Fleet's centre. From the start of the action this had been niggling Commodore Churruca in the *San Juan Nepomuceno*. After the morning's tedious wearing an exasperated Churruca found himself at the southerly tail end of the Combined Fleet. He could nevertheless see the whole panorama and how the battle was unfolding. Moreover, he had decided in his own mind how to foil the British attack. He was impatient for Villeneuve to see this as well as he kept his telescope trained on the *Bucentaure*'s main mast in the vain hope of seeing a signal to act. Lowering his glass for a moment he declared to one of his officers:

> Our van will be cut away from the main body and our rear will be overwhelmed. Half the line will be compelled to remain inactive. The French Admiral does not – will not – grasp it. He has only to act boldly, only to order the van ships to wear round at once and double on the rear squadron. That will place the enemy themselves between two fires.

He looked repeatedly to the *Bucentaure* for the signal that it seemed Villeneuve had no intention of sending, before giving up at last, muttering '*Perdidos*! – *Perdidos*! – *Perdidos*!' (All is lost!)

However, Villeneuve *had* appreciated the situation and did make the signal to Rear Admiral Dumanoir to support the centre. Unfortunately, not only did Churruca miss it, but Dumanoir did also. As did the other ships in the van squadron of the Combined Fleet, even though the French frigate, *Hortense*, repeated it. Not one of them put about. When the battle was under way Villeneuve repeated the signal and eventually Dumanoir responded, but his manoeuvre was hindered by the lack of wind and sweeps had to be used to turn his ship's heads around. Sub-Lieutenant Gicquel des Touches, in the *Intrépide*, explained:

> Happily, Captain Infernet took another view of his duty, and his honour. Although we were immediately under the orders of M. Dumanoir, we had already made several unsuccessful attempts to put about; but the wind had been entirely stilled by the cannonading. In the end, after incessant efforts and by the aid of the only boat we had available, we were able to wear round, whereupon the captain shouted in a stirring voice, 'Lay her head for the *Bucentaure*.' It was now the hottest moment of the battle.
>
> We could hardly make out in the midst of the smoke and confusion of the battle, the situation of our flagship, surrounded as she was by the enemy, and having near her only the *Redoubtable*, a small 74, crushed by the overpowering mass of the *VICTORY*, but still resisting with such valour that she almost took Nelson's ship by boarding. Everywhere the English had the advantage of numbers over us. Not one of them was idle. Having the wind, they were able to go anywhere where they were most needed, taking no notice of the leeward ships which were too far away to take part and which were destined to succumb one by one in useless combats. Moreover the superiority of our adversaries gunnery meant that in a very short time, our crews were decimated, while on their side the losses were comparatively trivial.
>
> When at length we drew near the *Bucentaure* and *Redoubtable,* their masts had fallen and their guns were almost silenced; yet the heroism of those on board kept up an unequal and hopeless struggle, fighting against ships that were practically undamaged, from the ports of which broadside after broadside flashed incessantly. It was into the thick of this fray that Captain Infernet led us. He

wanted, he said, to relieve the Admiral, take him on board, and rally around us the ships which could still fight. It was noble madness, but, though we knew it, we all supported him with joyful alacrity – and would that others had imitated his example!

We had the honour of attracting numerous opponents: the *LEVIATHAN*, *AFRICA*, *AGAMEMNON*, *ORION* and *TÉMÉRAIRE* [he meant the *BRITANNIA*] of 100 guns. They all set on us fiercely.

By the time Dumanoir's squadron could start engaging, at about 3.00 p.m., the battle was already decided. Meanwhile, Nelson had been in *VICTORY*'s dark cockpit for nearly one and a half hours. *The Naval Chronicle* printed a report of his symptoms:

On his being brought below, he complained of acute pain about the sixth or seventh dorsal vertebra; of privation of sense, and motion of the body, and inferior extremities; his respiration short and difficult; pulse weak, small and irregular. He frequently declared his back was shot through; that he felt every instant a gush of blood within his breast; and that he had symptoms which indicated to him the approach of death. In the course of an hour his pulse became indistinct, and was gradually lost in the arm; his extremities and forehead became soon afterwards cold; he retained his wonted energy of mind, and exercise of his faculties, until the last moment of his existence; and when victory, as signal as decisive, was announced to him he expressed his pious acknowledgements thereof, and heartfelt satisfaction at the glorious event, in the most emphatic language. He then delivered his last orders with his usual precision; and in a few minutes afterwards expired without a struggle.

Dr William Beatty's account continues:

The *VICTORY*'s crew cheered whenever they observed an
Enemy's ship surrender. On one of these occasions, Lord
Nelson anxiously inquired what was the cause of it; when
Lieutenant Pasco, who lay wounded at some distance
from His Lordship, raised himself up, and told him that
another ship had struck, which appeared to give him much
satisfaction. He now felt an ardent thirst; and frequently
called for drink, and to be fanned with paper, making
use of these words: 'Fan. Fan' and 'Drink, drink.' This
he continued to repeat, when he wished for drink or the
refreshment of cool air, till a very few minutes before he
expired. Lemonade, and wine and water, were given to him
occasionally. He evinced great solicitude for the event of
the battle, and fears for the safety of his friend Captain
Hardy. Doctor Scott and Mr Burke used every argument
they could suggest, to relieve his anxiety. Mr Burke told him
'the enemy were decisively defeated, and that he hoped His
Lordship would still live to see himself the bearer of the
joyful tidings to his country.' He replied, 'It is nonsense,
Mr Burke, to suppose I can live: my sufferings are great,
but they will all soon be over.' Doctor Scott entreated His
Lordship 'not to despair of living,' and said 'he trusted that
Divine Providence would restore him once more to his dear
Country and friends.' 'Ah, Doctor!' replied his Lordship, 'it
is all over; it is all over.'

Many messages were sent to Captain Hardy by the
Surgeon, requesting his attendance on His Lordship; who
became impatient to see him, and often exclaimed: 'Will
no one bring Hardy to me? He must be killed; he is surely
destroyed.' The Captain's Aide-de-camp, Mr Bulkley, now
came below, and stated that 'circumstances respecting the
Fleet required Captain Hardy's presence on deck, but that
he would avail himself of the first favourable moment to
visit His Lordship.' On hearing him deliver this message to
the Surgeon, His Lordship inquired who had brought it.

Mr Burke answered, 'It is Mr Bulkley, my Lord.' 'It is his voice,' replied His Lordship: he then said to the young gentleman, 'Remember me to your father.'

An hour and ten minutes however elapsed, from the time of His Lordship's being wounded, before Captain Hardy's first subsequent interview with him; particulars of which are nearly as follow. They shook hands affectionately, and Lord Nelson said: 'Well, Hardy, how goes the battle? How goes the day with us?' 'Very well, my Lord,' replied Captain Hardy: 'we have got twelve or fourteen of the Enemy's ships in our possession; but five of their van have tacked, and show an intention of bearing down upon the VICTORY. I have therefore called two or three of our fresh ships round us, and have no doubt of giving them a drubbing.' 'I hope,' said His Lordship, 'none of our ships have struck, Hardy.' 'No my Lord' replied Captain Hardy; 'there is no fear of that.' Lord Nelson then said: 'I am a dead man, Hardy. I am going fast: it will be all over with me soon. Come nearer to me. Pray let my dear Lady Hamilton have my hair, and all other things belonging to me.' Mr Burke was about to withdraw at the commencement of this conversation; but His Lordship, perceiving his intention, desired he would remain. Captain Hardy observed, that 'he hoped Mr Beatty could yet hold out some prospect of life.' 'Oh! No,' answered His Lordship; 'it is impossible. My back is shot through. Beatty will tell you so.' Captain Hardy then returned on deck, and at parting shook hands again with his revered friend and commander.

His Lordship now requested the Surgeon, who had been previously absent a short time attending Mr Rivers, to return to the wounded, and give his assistance to such of them as he could be useful to; 'for,' said he, 'you can do nothing for me.' The Surgeon assured him that the Assistant Surgeons were doing everything that could be affected for those unfortunate men; but on His Lordship's

several times repeating his injunctions to that purpose, he
left him surrounded by Doctor Scott, Mr Burke, and two
of His Lordship's domestics. After the Surgeon had been
absent a few minutes attending Lieutenants Peake and
Reeves of the marines, who were wounded, he was called by
Doctor Scott to His Lordship, who said: 'Ah, Mr Beatty! I
have sent for you to say, what I forgot to tell you before, that
all power of motion and feeling below my breast are gone;
and you,' continued he, 'very well know I can live but a
short time.' The emphatic manner in which he pronounced
these last words, left no doubt in the Surgeon's mind, that
he adverted to the case of a man who had some months
before received a mortal injury of the spine on board the
VICTORY, and had laboured under the similar privations
of sense and muscular motion. The case had made a great
impression on Lord Nelson: he was anxious to know the
cause of such symptoms, which was accordingly explained
to him; and he now appeared to apply the situation and
fate of this man to himself. The Surgeon answered, 'My
Lord, you told me so before:' but he now examined the
extremities, to ascertain the fact; when His Lordship said,
'Ah Beatty! I am certain of it: Scott and Burke have tried
it already. You know I am gone.' The Surgeon replied: 'My
Lord, unhappily for our Country, nothing can be done for
you;' and having made this declaration he was so much
affected, that he turned round and withdrew a few steps to
conceal his emotions. His Lordship said: 'I know it. I feel
something rising in my breast,' putting his hand on his left
side, 'which tells me I am gone.' Drink was recommended
liberally, and Doctor Scott and Mr Burke fanned him with
paper. He often exclaimed, 'God be praised, I have done my
duty;' and upon the Surgeon's inquiring whether his pain
was still very great, he declared, 'it continued so very severe,
that he wished he was dead. Yet.' said he in a lower voice,
'one would like to live a little longer, too:' and after a pause

of a few minutes, he added in the same tone, 'What would become of poor Lady Hamilton, if she knew my situation!'

The Surgeon finding it impossible to render His Lordship any further assistance, left him, to attend Lieutenant Bligh, Messrs Smith and Westphall Midshipmen, and some Seamen, recently wounded. Captain Hardy now came to the cockpit to see his Lordship a second time, which was after an interval of about fifty minutes from the conclusion of his first visit. Before he quitted the deck he sent Lieutenant Hills to acquaint Admiral Collingwood with the lamentable circumstance of Lord Nelson's being wounded.

Lieutenant James Hills, 25, from Hampshire, was rowed across to the *ROYAL SOVEREIGN*. Collingwood noted:

When my dear friend received his wound, he sent an officer to me to tell me of it, and gave his love to me. Though the officer was directed to say the wound was not dangerous, I read in his countenance what I had to fear.

Beatty's account continues:

Lord Nelson and Captain Hardy shook hands again; and while the Captain retained His Lordship's hand, he congratulated him even in the arms of Death on his brilliant victory; 'which', he said, 'was complete; though he did not know how many of the enemy were captured, as it was impossible to perceive every ship distinctly. He was certain however of fourteen or fifteen having surrendered.' His Lordship answered, 'That is well, but I had bargained for twenty:' and then emphatically exclaimed, "Anchor, Hardy, *anchor*!' To this the Captain replied: 'I suppose my Lord, Admiral Collingwood will now take upon himself the direction of affairs.' 'Not while I live, I hope, Hardy!' cried the dying Chief; and at that moment endeavoured ineffectually to raise himself from the bed. 'No,' added he; 'do *you* anchor Hardy.' Captain Hardy then said: 'Shall we make the signal, Sir?' 'Yes,' answered His Lordship; 'for if I live, I'll anchor.' The energetic manner in which he uttered these his last orders to Captain Hardy, accompanied with his efforts to raise himself, evinced his determination never to resign the command while he retained the exercise of his transcendent faculties, and that he expected Captain Hardy still to carry into effect the suggestions of his exalted mind; a sense of his duty overcoming the pains of death. He then told Captain Hardy, 'he felt that in a few minutes he should be no more;' adding in a low tone, 'Don't throw me overboard, Hardy.' The Captain answered: 'Oh! no, certainly not.' 'Then,' replied His Lordship, 'you know what to do: and,' continued he, 'take care of my dear Lady Hamilton, Hardy; take care of poor Lady Hamilton. Kiss me, Hardy.' The Captain now knelt down, and kissed his cheek; when His Lordship said, 'Now I am satisfied. Thank God, I have done my duty.' Captain Hardy stood for a minute or two in silent contemplation: he then knelt down again, and kissed His Lordship's forehead. His Lordship said: 'Who is that?' The Captain answered: 'It is Hardy;' to which His Lordship replied, 'God bless you, Hardy!' After this affecting scene Captain Hardy withdrew, and returned to the quarter-deck, having spent about eighteen minutes in this his last interview with his dying friend.

Lord Nelson now desired Mr Chevalier, his steward, to turn him upon his right side; which being effected, His Lordship said: 'I wish I had not left the deck, for I shall soon be gone.' He afterwards became very low; his breathing was oppressed, and his voice faint. He said to Doctor Scott, 'Doctor, I have not been a great sinner,' and after a short pause, '*Remember*, that I leave Lady Hamilton and my Daughter Horatia as a legacy to my Country: and,' added he, 'never forget Horatia.' His thirst now increased;

and he called for 'Drink, drink,' 'Fan, fan,' and 'Rub, rub:' addressing himself in the last case to Doctor Scott, who had been rubbing His Lordship's breast with his hand, from which he found some relief. These words he spoke in a very rapid manner, which rendered his articulation difficult: but he every now and then, with evident increase in pain, made a greater effort with his vocal powers, and pronounced distinctly these last words: 'Thank God, I have done my duty;' and this great sentiment he continued to repeat as long as he was able to give it utterance.

The final, moving exchange of words at what has become the most celebrated death in British history was recorded by others present, including Mr Burke, the purser of the VICTORY and the chaplain Dr Alexander Scott. There are slight variations in the accounts, as the extracts show. However, it is beyond doubt that Nelson said 'Kiss me', since it was written down independently by the three witnesses. 'Kismet' and 'Promise me' have been put forward as plausible options, but they reflect the prurience of the later Victorian age. *The Naval Chronicle* reported:

When Bourke [*sic*] returned into the cockpit with Captain Hardy, Lord Nelson told the latter to come near to him. 'Kiss me, Hardy!' he exclaimed. Captain Hardy kissed his cheek. 'I hope your Lordship,' he said, 'will live to enjoy your triumph.' 'Never, Hardy!' he exclaimed; 'I am dying – I am a dead man all over – Beatty will tell you so – bring the fleet to an anchor – you have all done your duty – God bless you!' Captain Hardy now said, 'I suppose Collingwood, my dear Lord, is to command the fleet?' – 'Never,' exclaimed he, 'whilst I live;' – meaning doubtless, that so long as his gallant spirit survived, he would never desert his duty.

What passed after this was merely casual: his lordship's last words were to Mr Beatty, whilst he was expiring in his arms, 'I could have wished to have lived to enjoy this; but

God's will be done!' – 'My Lord,' exclaimed Hardy, 'you
die in the midst of triumph!' – 'Do I, Hardy?' – he smiled
faintly – 'God be praised!' These were his last words before
he expired.

Dr Scott's description of Nelson's last moments was recorded in a
letter dated 22 December to George Rose, who had promised his
friend Nelson that he would take care of Emma Hamilton if he
should die.

> It is my intention to relate everything Lord Nelson said, in
> which your name was any way connected. He lived about
> three hours after receiving his wound, was perfectly sensible
> the whole time, but compelled to speak in broken sentences,
> which pain and suffering prevented him always from
> connecting. When I first saw him, he was apprehensive he
> should not live many minutes, and told me so; adding, in a
> hurried agitated manner, though with pauses, 'Remember
> me to Lady Hamilton! Remember me to Horatia! Remember
> me to all my friends. Doctor, remember me to Mr. Rose:
> and tell him I have made a will, and left Lady Hamilton and
> Horatia to my Country.' He repeated his remembrances to
> Lady Hamilton and Horatia, and told me to mind what he
> said several times.
>   Gradually he became less agitated, and at last calm
> enough to ask questions about what was going on; this
> led his mind to Captain Hardy, for whom he sent and
> inquired with great anxiety, exclaiming aloud, he would not
> believe he was alive, unless he saw him. He grew agitated
> at the Captain's not coming, lamented his being unable
> to go on deck, and do what was to be done, and doubted
> every assurance given him of the Captain being safe on the
> quarter-deck.
>   At last the Captain came, and he instantly grew more
> composed, listened to his report about the state of the

Fleet, directed him to anchor, and told him he should die, but observed, he should live half an hour longer. 'I shall die, Hardy.' Said the Admiral. 'Is your pain great, Sir?' 'Yes, but I shall live half an hour yet – Hardy, kiss me!' The Captain knelt down by his side, and kissed him. Upon the Captain leaving him to return to the deck, Lord Nelson exclaimed very earnestly more than once 'Hardy, if I live I'll bring the Fleet to an anchor; if I live I'll anchor;' and this was earnestly repeated even when the Captain was out of hearing. I do not mean to tell you everything he said.

After this interview, the Admiral was perfectly tranquil, looking at me in his accustomed manner when alluding to any prior discourse. 'I have not been a great sinner, Doctor,' said he. 'Doctor, I was right – I told you so – George Rose has not yet got my letter: tell him' – he was interrupted here by pain. After an interval, he said, 'Mr Rose will remember – don't forget, Doctor: mind what I say.'

Returning again to Beatty's more famous account of Nelson's death:

His Lordship became speechless in about fifteen minutes after Captain Hardy had left him. Doctor Scott and Mr Burke, who had all along sustained the bed under his shoulders (which raised him in a nearly semi-recumbent posture, the only one that was supportable to him), forbore to disturb him by speaking to him; and when he had remained speechless about five minutes, His Lordship's Steward went to the Surgeon, who had been a short time occupied with the wounded in another part of the cockpit, and stated his apprehensions that His Lordship was dying. The Surgeon immediately repaired to him, and found him on the verge of dissolution, he knelt down by his side, and took up his hand; which was cold, and the pulse gone from the wrist. On the Surgeon's feeling his forehead, which was likewise cold, His Lordship opened his eyes, looked up, and

shut them again. The Surgeon again left him, and returned
to the wounded who required his assistance; but he was not
absent five minutes before the steward announced to him
'that he believed His Lordship had expired.' The Surgeon
returned, and found that the report was too well founded:
His Lordship had breathed his last, at thirty minutes past
four o'clock; at which period Doctor Scott was in the act of
rubbing His Lordship's breast, and Mr Burke supporting
the bed under his shoulders.

Thus died the matchless Hero, after performing, in a
short but brilliant and well-filled life, a series of naval
exploits unexampled in any age of the world.

The midshipman of the watch, 'a boy in his early teens' who is
believed to have been James Poad, aged 16, used the stub of a pencil
to write in *VICTORY*'s log:

Partial firing continued until 4.30, when a victory having
been reported to the Right Hon. Lord Viscount Nelson,
K.B., and Commander-in-Chief, he died of his wound.

8

THE BATTLE: 'PARTIAL FIRING
CONTINUED UNTIL 4.30'

Throughout 'that dreadful Monday afternoon' throngs of people in Cadiz crowded the city ramparts, packed the merchants' *miradores* and *azoteas* and sat on house roofs, all gazing, many with telescopes, at the low, grey smoke cloud that rose like a mound on the horizon to the south-west. 'The combined fleet was scarcely visible,' according to Commodore Alcalá-Galiano's son. Hour after hour, they heard the dull reverberating thunder of the guns. Far and wide the heavy booming of the cannonade re-echoed inland across large parts of Andalusia: over the orange groves and cork woods of Medina Sidonia, along the hillside of Conil, and as far away as the mountain caves of Ronda. From Tangier they saw smoke and heard distant firing, but at Gibraltar they heard nothing all day. Across the water the struggle continued, the fearful and anxious watchers on land yet unaware of the human horror, maiming and slaughter that was taking place, producing a list of casualties unequalled by any naval battle hitherto. Commodore Galiano was among those killed.

As Nelson's life slowly ebbed away so did the ability of the French and Spanish to resist the overwhelming impact of his strategy. Collingwood, who had now taken command, seeing Dumanoir's squadron to the north, signalled the rear of the Weather Column to come to windward on the port tack. Not many ships could respond, either because they were already engaged or because they failed to see the signal flags through the smoke that draped the battle. Those ships that did see the signal, the *MINOTAUR* and the *SPARTIATE*

(74), worked together to form a rough line-of-battle with four other ships, which for all its imperfections prevented Dumanoir from supporting his friends in the centre. Only Infernet's 'noble madness' in the *Intrépide* made any impact. She bore the fire of five ships in succession – *AFRICA, LEVIATHAN, AJAX, AGAMEMNON* and *ORION*. Lieutenant Humphrey Stenhouse in the *CONQUEROR* said his exploit 'deserves to be recorded in the memory of those who admire true courage'. Dumanoir turned his attention to the rear, but his resolve to support it fizzled away when he sighted Gravina's crippled flagship, the *Principe de Asturias,* bearing away and making off for Cadiz and signalling the remaining allied ships around her to follow; ten did so. Dumanoir sailed away from the battle site and set a safe course for Rochefort. Rear Admiral Don Antonio de Escano explained Gravina's retreat:

> At 4 o'clock we were continuing to engage in this manner, when an English three-decker [the *PRINCE*] passed a group of those that were on our larboard quarter and discharged all her guns, at grape-shot range, into our stern. The Major (General) [Gravina] was wounded in the left leg [Escano meant arm]; he was obliged to go below but while it was being temporarily dressed, he gave orders that he should be conveyed back and placed sitting at his post on deck. Weakened by loss of blood, he fell fainting; but quickly coming to himself and not perceiving the national colours, he ordered them to be hoisted without delay and he resumed command. It was very nearly five o'clock and the three-decker that had wounded the Major (General) was still continuing to engage us with advantage, and a smaller ship was also firing into us to larboard. In this critical position we sighted the *Neptune* and the *San Justo* that were coming to our aid.

By the time these two ships arrived the *Principe de Asturias* was hopelessly crippled. Nevertheless, Gravina was able to collect together

11 sail of the line and make for Cadiz, where he was put ashore. His left arm had been shattered. He lingered on in great pain for four and a half months and died on 9 March 1806. His unnecessary death was due largely to the poor advice of his many doctors. Some had pressed for the arm to be saved; others thought it should be amputated. While they debated Gravina was overwhelmed by toxic infection. An immense gathering attended a requiem mass in his honour, including Admirals Álava and Rosily, and the following tribute appeared in the *Gibraltar Chronicle*:

> We lament to hear that the brave Admiral Gravina is dead.
> His friends had long entertained the hopes of his recovery;
> but they have been unfortunately disappointed. Spain
> loses in him the most distinguished officer in her navy;
> one under whose command her fleets, though sometimes
> beaten, always fought in such a manner as to merit the
> encomiums of their conquerors.

Other incidents illustrate the closing stage of the battle. For instance, the *Argonauta*, according to Gravina the 'most perfect man-of-war in both fleets', had been the first ship in the Combined Fleet to strike – to the *ACHILLE*. However, it was the unmanageable *BELLEISLE* that accepted her surrender nearly two hours later. Out of 780 officers and men in the *Argonauta*, 300 had been killed and wounded. One of the *BELLEISLE*'s Marine officers sent to receive the surrender found:

> A beaten Spanish 80-gun ship having about this time,
> hoisted English colours, the Captain was good enough to
> give me the pinnace to take possession of her. The Master
> accompanied me, with eight or ten seamen or Marines,
> who happened to be near us. On getting up the *Argonauta*'s
> side, I found no living person on her deck; but on making
> my way, over numerous dead and a confusion of wreck,
> across the quarter-deck, I was met by the second captain at
> the cabin door, who gave me his sword, which I returned,

desiring him to keep it for Captain Hargood, to whom I should soon introduce him. With him I accordingly returned to the *BELLEISLE*, leaving the Master in charge of the prize.

The First Captain, Don Antonio Pareja, continued the story:

I handed over the command to the Second Captain. At this hour my ship had all the guns on the quarter-deck and poop dismounted, a great number of the guns in the batteries were out of action, as much on account of the pieces (being damaged) as from the want of crews, the result of the numerous dead and wounded among them, according to the report of their officers. The whole rigging was utterly destroyed, so that there were no shrouds left to the masts – save one to the main-mast – and they were threatening to fall every minute, being shot through; in this situation it was very evident that this ship could make but slight and feeble resistance, having continually engaged with the same superior force; with these inexpressible feelings I was taken below to have my wounds dressed, expecting every minute to find myself brought to the grievous point of having to surrender, which in fact took place when, my second having sent half an hour later to inform me that over and above the injuries that we had already sustained, the ship was making much water from further ones that had occurred, and had lost her rudder, which fresh increase of damage in addition to the previous ones, held out no further prospect – the ship being disabled – save that of the sacrifice of those men who with the greatest spirit, courage and fearfulness of death, had rendered the greatest service and honour to the King's colours. Consequently, I replied to my second that – given the absolute impossibility of being able to do otherwise – he must act in accordance with the regulations, and at 3.30

in the afternoon he gave orders to haul down the colours; such being the grievous condition of the *Argonauta* that in spite of the great efforts of the enemy to save her, they were unable to achieve it. It is not possible for me to state precisely the number of dead and wounded, and I can only affirm it was excessive, especially that of the former.

Lieutenant Philibert, Flag Lieutenant to Admiral Charles Magon de Médine in the 74-gun *Algésiras*, which had been battered into submission by the *TONNANT,* gave his account of the scene around him as the afternoon wore on:

When we ceased fire we were in the midst of four English ships, including the *TONNANT*; of which one, a three-decker, had her three masts gone by the board, another, a 74, had lost her mizzen-mast and fore-topmast, and the *TONNANT*, whose fore-mast alone remained standing; the fourth had her rigging cut to pieces but no mast standing.

The smoke which up to that time had enveloped us having dispersed, our first glances were turned towards our Fleet; there no longer existed any line on either side, we saw only groups of ships in the most dreadful plight about the place or very nearly so where we deemed that our *corps de bataille* ought to be. We counted 17 ships of the two fleets totally dismasted – their masts gone by the board – and many others partially so. Several vessels were at that time in action in the van, where we made out five or six ships still in line, but the firing did not last long; at 4.30 it slackened. Several ships that we supposed to belong to our Fleet were not engaging at all although they appeared to be in good condition, judging by their masts and canvas. Two French ships were hugging the wind in order to proceed towards the van but afterwards they joined Admiral Gravina's ship the *Principe*, which, as far as we could see, was flying the flag for the general and unconditional recall.

One ship that was not in good condition was the *Santissima Trinidad*. Her second and third lieutenants and 22 other officers had been wounded, seven of whom later died. Her casualties amounted to 254 killed, and 173 wounded. Rear Admiral Cisneros was among them, but recovered within a few weeks. The *PRINCE* took her surrender at about 5.30 p.m. One of her officers wrote that 'our first night's work on board the *Trinidad* was to heave the dead overboard'.

At about 4.00 p.m. the *PRINCE* had come alongside the French *Achille* drifting to leeward after she had done battle with Captain Robert Moorsom's *REVENGE*. Both ships suffered badly from the encounter, but in an attempt to come under the *REVENGE*'s stern, Moorsom's gunners had raked the *Achille* and she lost her mizzen mast. Her wheel was shot to pieces and Captain G Denieport was killed. The *PRINCE* fired a broadside into her that brought her mainmast tumbling down along the centre-line of the ship, smashing boats and leaving her with only the foremast standing. Lieutenant Cauchard, now in command of the *Achille*, was horrified to see flames spreading rapidly along the canvas and ropes. While men frantically hacked away at the burning wreckage the *PRINCE* unleashed another broadside, which brought down the foremast directly over the flames and destroyed the fire engine. Fearing a conflagration as embers were seen falling down the hatches, Captain Richard Grindall steered the *PRINCE* out of harm's way, but ordered boats to be lowered to rescue the French crew. The whole of the upper deck was soon like a bonfire and Lieutenant Cauchard ordered the bilge cocks to be opened to flood the ship. Lieutenant Lachasse said:

> All hands then came on deck and losing all hope of
> extinguishing the fire, we no longer attended to anything
> except saving the ship's company, by throwing overboard
> all the debris that might offer them the means of escaping
> from almost certain death and awaiting the aid that the
> neighbouring ships might send them.

The crew started to leap over the side and swam for *PRINCE*'s boats and those sent by the *ENTREPRENANTE* cutter and the schooner

PICKLE. The *Achille*'s abandoned but loaded guns were going off in the intense heat and at about 5.45 p.m. she blew up with an incredible explosion. Through his telescope in Cadiz, Commodore Galiano's son was captivated when 'Suddenly a bright flame on the horizon lit the sea. Soon after a tremendous bang let us know that a ship had blown up.' Lieutenant Frederick Hoffman in the *TONNANT* said, 'The explosion she made was sublime and awful.' An officer in the *DEFENCE* wrote:

It was a sight the most awful and grand that can be conceived. In a moment the hull burst into a cloud of smoke and fire. A column of vivid flame shot up to an enormous height in the atmosphere and terminated by expanding into an immense globe representing, for a few seconds, a prodigious tree in flames, speckled with many dark spots, which the pieces of timber and bodies of men occasioned while they were suspended

How well I remember the *Achille* in the clouds.

An eyewitness in the *BELLEISLE* noticed how the partial firing referred to in *VICTORY*'s log stopped at about the time the *Achille* blew up:

Before sunset all firing ceased. The view of the fleet at this period was highly interesting, and would have formed a beautiful subject for a painter. Just under the setting rays were five or six dismantled prizes; on the one hand lay the *VICTORY* with part of our fleet and prizes, and on the left hand the *ROYAL SOVEREIGN* and a similar cluster of ships. To the northward, the remnant of the combined fleets was making for Cadiz. The *Achille*, with the tricoloured ensign still displayed, had burnt to the water's edge about a mile from us, and our tenders and boats were using every effort to save the brave fellows who had so gloriously defended her; but only two hundred and fifty were rescued, and she blew up with a tremendous explosion.

JEANETTE IS RESCUED

The destruction of the *Achille* was a dramatic and symbolic end to the Battle of Trafalgar. Attention now turned to saving ships and rescuing those still in the water. Midshipman Hercules Robinson wrote:

> I got hold of a dozen of her men, who were hoisted into
> the air out of the exploding ship, cursing their fate, tearing
> their hair, and wiping the gunpowder and salt water from
> their faces . . . These same fellows, having got their supper
> and grog and dry clothes, danced for the amusement of
> our men under the half deck . . . I helped to save a black pig
> which swam over; and what a glorious supper of pork chops
> appeared instead of our usual refection of cheese, biscuit
> and salt junk.

Those rescued from the *Achille* included Jeanette Caunant, the young wife of a topman. Her story crops up in many accounts and her rescue as an incident in the battle is as well explained as many of the fighting aspects. The Dorset poet and novelist Thomas Hardy, in his expansive poem about the Napoleonic Wars, *The Dynasts*, was later captivated – or was it titillated? – by her story, describing Jeanette's 'breasts bulging on the brine'. Maybe her nakedness had something to do with the reportage, but more likely it was her pluck, the diversion her rescue brought from the horrors of the battle and the happy ending, that all secured her a place in the Trafalgar story. All the known accounts vary in detail, which suggests they were more than likely passed on by word of mouth, such as this account by 'Jack Nastyface' Robinson, a romanticized version that records incorrectly that Jeanette's husband had been killed.

> Whilst we were engaging the combined fleets, a French ship
> caught fire, the crew of which made every effort to escape
> from the flames, and as 'Britons fight to conquer, and
> conquer to save,' our frigates and schooners, which had been

laying off during the battle, sent their boats to endeavour to save as many lives as possible. Amongst those who were thus preserved was a young French woman, who was brought on board our ship in a state of complete nakedness. Although it was in the heat of battle, yet she received every assistance which at the time was in our power; and her distress of mind was soothed as well as we could, until the officers got to their chests, from whence they supplied her with needles and thread, to convert sheets into chemises, and curtains from their cots to make somewhat of a gown, and other garments, so that by degrees she was made as comfortable as circumstances would admit; for we all tried who would be most kind to her; and as the history of this adventurer may acquire some interest from the account she gave of it, the following is a statement, as collected from herself:–

'The combined fleets, (she says) were ordered to proceed from Cadiz, where they lay, to make an attack and take that of the British; for, from their superior force they were confident of success, and elated at the time with the idea that it would be an easy task. That no impediment might be in the way, all the females were ordered to go on shore; she was married, and quit her husband could not endure the thought; she was therefore resolved to share his glory or his death. No time was lost in carrying her plan into execution; for, having rigged herself out in a suit of sailor's clothes, thus disguised, she entered on board, and went in the same ship with him, as a seaman. In this state she remained, doing duty, during the engagement, when, whilst fighting by the side of her husband, a ball killed him on the spot. On seeing him fall dead, the conflict was too great: nature displayed itself; she became overwhelmed with grief, and by it, betrayed her sex.

To add to the distress which this discovery occasioned, an alarm was now spread that the ship was on fire; she seemed to care very little about it; life to her was not desirable, whilst all hands were employed in the endeavour to check the fire's progress. This seemed to be impossible, and it became necessary to think of the means to escape; for the fire raged with great fury, and there was every probability that, in a few minutes, the ship would be blown into the air, as the fire was fast approaching the magazines. The resolution to take to the water being now unavoidable, the men commenced to undress themselves and in this dreadful situation she was strongly urged to do the same, that it was a duty to make every effort for self-preservation, and it being the only chance she could possibly have. After much entreaty, persuasion, and remonstrance, she summoned up sufficient resolution and prepared herself to endure the agonising alternative for the only choice which her unfortunate case presented was, either to strip, or perish in the flames. She was then lowered into the ocean by a rope on the taffrail, the lead of which was melting at the time, and burned the back of her neck. On reaching the water, one of her shipmates was a good swimmer, staid by her side, and supported her until she was picked up by a boat belonging to the *PICKLE* schooner, and brought on board the ship she was then in.' (Here let the reader pause, and paint to himself if he can, what were the inward workings and heartfelt sufferings of this extraordinary heroine, and bright instance of conjugal fidelity and attachment).

Her name was Jeanette, of French Flanders, and she remained with us until our arrival in Gibraltar, when a cartel took her to a Spanish port. On leaving our ship her heart seemed overwhelmed with gratitude; she shed abundance of tears, and could only now and then, with deep sigh, exclaim, *'les bons Anglois'.*

Captain Robert Moorsom, the 45-year-old Commanding Officer of the *REVENGE*, wrote about Jeanette in a private letter to his father, and confirmed the happy ending:

I must tell you an anecdote of a French woman – the *PICKLE* schooner sent to me about fifty people saved from the *Achille* which was burnt and blew up, amongst them was a young French woman about five and twenty and the wife of one of the Main Topmen – when the *Achille* was burning she got out of the gun room port and sat on the rudder chains till some melted lead ran down her, and forced her to strip and leap off; she swam to a spar where several men were, but one of them bit and kicked her till she was obliged to quit and get to another, which supported her till she was taken up by the *PICKLE* and sent on board the *REVENGE*. Amongst the men she was lucky enough to find her husband – We were not wanting in civility to the lady; I ordered her two Pursers shirts to make a petticoat.

Curiously, the *BRITANNIA* also appears to have rescued a woman with a similar story from the wreckage of the *Achille* as the 20-year-old Second Lieutenant Lawrence Halloran, Royal Marines, recorded it in his journal. That the anecdote got around the fleet to be claimed by other ships is supported by this anonymous account from *VICTORY*. The ship did receive 'from the *PICKLE* 18 French prisoners, which was part of the men she saved out of the *Achille*', but Jeanette could not have been one of them if she had been received by the *REVENGE*!

We received 19 French men and one French woman from the wreck of the *Achilles* [*sic*]. The woman it appeared stripped herself and jumped overboard[.] The men of the Wreck gave her a pair of trousers and a shirt. she did not appear much concerned . . . after she was on board she amused herself working up a hair into watch springs. she was supplied with dresses from play actors drapes which we had on board. She was the wife of a Serg't Major on board *Achilles*.

DEPARTED HEROES

For a long time it was believed that very few women were aboard ships of the line. The Royal Navy did not officially sanction their presence, and they do not appear in the muster books. However, a substantial number went to sea, often the wives of petty officers or crew. In action they helped the surgeon or those waiting to see him, although there was no triage, which meant many more died than might have done. 'Jack Nastyface' Robinson gave an account from the *REVENGE*, which recorded 28 killed and 51 wounded:

> We were now called to clear the decks, and here might be witnessed an awful and interesting scene, for as each officer and seaman would meet, (oh what an opportunity for the Christian and man of feeling to meditate on the casualty of fate in this life,) they were inquiring for their messmates. Orders were now given to fetch the dead bodies from the after cockpit and throw them overboard. These were the bodies of the men who were taken down to the doctor during the battle, badly wounded, and who by the time the engagement was ended were dead. Some of these perhaps could not have recovered, while others might, had timely assistance been rendered, which was impossible; for the rule is, as order is requisite, that every person shall be dressed in rotation as they are brought down wounded, and in many instances some have bled to death
>
> The next call was 'all hands to splice the main brace' which is the giving out a gill of rum to each man, and indeed they much needed it, for they had not ate or drank from breakfast time.

Even in the most battered of ships, such as the *BELLEISLE*, there was the opportunity for a brief moment for refreshment during the day's horrors, although this example from Lieutenant Paul Nicholas illustrates the emptiness inside their minds.

About five o'clock the officers assembled in the captain's
cabin to take some refreshment. The parching effects
of the smoke made this a welcome summons, although
some of us had been fortunate in relieving our thirst
by plundering the captain's grapes which hung round
his cabin; still four hours exertion of body with the
energies incessantly employed, occasioned a lassitude,
both corporeally and mentally, from which the victorious
termination now so near at hand, could not arouse us;
moreover there sat a melancholy on the brows of some
who mourned the messmates who had shared their perils
and their vicissitudes for many years. Then the merits of
the departed heroes were repeated with a sigh, but their
errors sunk with them into the deep.

It was nevertheless a great victory, which was succinctly and
comprehensively summed up by an unknown officer in the
CONQUEROR:

The mode of attack, adopted with such success in the
Trafalgar action, appears to me to have succeeded from
the enthusiasm inspired throughout the British Fleet from
their being commanded by their beloved Nelson; from
the gallant conduct of the leaders of the two divisions;
from the individual exertions of each ship after the attack
commenced, and the superior practice of the guns in the
English fleet.
It was successful also from the consternation spread
through the combined fleet on finding the British so
much stronger than was expected; from the astonishing
and rapid destruction which followed the attack of the
leaders, witnessed by the whole of the hostile fleets,
inspiring the one and dispiriting the other and from the
loss of the admiral's ship early in the action.

Oblivious to the momentous events of the day and its impact on all those who had taken part, bones weary from an afternoon of fighting, blood and thirst, Captain Francis Austen, in the *CANOPUS*, returned to his single large sheet of notepaper addressed to his beloved Mary Gibson. In his neat handwriting, which was very like that of Jane Austen herself, he vented his frustrations:

October 21. – And after having been so many months in a
state of constant and unremitting fag, to be at last cut out
by a parcel of folk just come from their homes, where some
of them were sitting at their ease the greater part of last war,
and the whole of this, till just now, is particularly hard and
annoying.

You, perhaps, may not feel this so forcibly as I do, and
in your satisfaction at my having avoided the danger of
battle may not much regret my losing the credit of having
contributed to gain a victory; not so myself!

I do not profess to like fighting for its own sake, but if
there have been an action with the combined fleets I shall
ever consider the day on which I sailed from the squadron as
the most inauspicious one of my life.

9

'THAT UNHAPPY GALE'

The sun set on a scene very different from the one upon which it had risen that morning. Hideousness had replaced beauty. The wind was moderate but slowly increasing in strength from the west-south-west, blowing the lingering swirls of smoke into the night. The storm that Nelson had anticipated was rising to batter equally the ships of three nations some seven to eight miles off Cape Trafalgar.

After the battle, Collingwood decided not to anchor as Nelson had intended. It was no longer an order, now that he was commander in chief. Instead he took the fleet out to sea. He has been heavily criticized for this decision, particularly since of the 17 prizes the British had captured at the end of the battle he got only four to Gibraltar. Apart from being unable to explain an initial hesitation prior to his decision, a number of important factors indicate that he *did* know what he was doing. It is most probable that many of the ships could not anchor because their anchors and cables had been shot to pieces. If he were to go anywhere it would be to the safety of Gibraltar. However, in spite of the decisiveness of the battle his first priority was to maintain the blockade on Cadiz. He knew that Villeneuve's replacement, Admiral Rosily, was due there any time and that he would find at least 12 ships of the line with which he could sail north to reinforce Rear Admiral Ganteaume at Ushant. Collingwood had to remain on station to prevent this since such an outcome would create a force superior to Admiral Cornwallis's protecting the Channel. Moreover, even if he had tried to get to the Straits, the contrary winds blowing from the south-west would have made the attempt impracticable. His battered ships and prizes would have to endure whatever nature threw at them. It turned out to be a 'Great Storm' that blew powerfully for five days.

The majority of ships were far from being in a seaworthy condition, even in fine weather. Among the British ships the most seriously damaged, or bearing the highest casualties, were the COLOSSUS (40 killed and 160 wounded), the BELLEROPHON (27 killed and 150 wounded), the ROYAL SOVEREIGN (47 killed and 94 wounded), the VICTORY (57 killed and 102 wounded), and the BELLEISLE (33 killed and 93 wounded). Henry Mason in the PRINCE, with no casualties, still wrote, 'It came on to blow, and we had to look out for ourselves on a lee shore, with rigging and masts damaged, though all standing'; and Lieutenant Frederick Hoffman illustrated the seriousness of the problem in his description of the TONNANT (26 killed and 50 wounded) and how the British crews immediately set about looking after their damaged ships. Observers were amazed at the energy men who had just fought a battle put into this task:

> We were drifting like a pig upon a grating, and as helpless
> as a sucking shrimp, when the signal was made to repair
> damages. We soon cut away all that was useless, and in twenty
> minutes under topsails as courses, and top-gallant sails as
> topsails. The carpenters had cobbled up one of the cutters,
> in which I was sent on board the ROYAL SOVEREIGN to
> report our condition and to request the assistance of one of
> the fleet to tow us, as in consequence of our rudder being so
> much shattered by shot it was rendered unserviceable. The
> DEFIANCE was ordered to take us in tow.

'Jack Nastyface' Robinson in the REVENGE explained:

> We had now a good night's work before us; all our yards,
> masts and sails were sadly cut, indeed the whole of the
> sails were obliged to be unbent, being rendered completely
> useless and by the next morning we were partly jury-rigged:
> we now began to look for our prizes, as it was coming on

to blow hard on the land, and Admiral Collingwood made signals for each ship that was able, to take a prize in tow, to prevent them drifting into their own harbour, as they were complete wrecks and unmanageable.

At the battle, the *MINOTAUR* under the command of Captain Charles Mansfield had engaged Captain Don Cayetano Valdés's *Neptuno*, one of Dumanoir's squadron. The Spanish ship surrendered after an hour's struggle. This is how 26-year-old volunteer William Thorpe from Coventry, on board the *MINOTAUR*, described it in his notes:

Oct 21st   The 2nd Lieut. of Marines & 48 men on board the *Neptuno* – at 1/2 past 5 p.m. took possession of the ship – sent the first Lieut of the *Neptuno* on board the *MINOTAUR* to deliver his Captain's sword who was killed in the action and the second badly wounded. Also sent 25 men on board who then seized the other prisoners fire arms and magazines – Afterward found she was very leaky, – having no shot plug on board, – sent on board the *MINOTAUR* for some, received six and proceeded to plug up the shot holes that appeared most dangerous, – Whe where [*sic*] obliged to make the Prisoners ply at the Pump as at this time she had 5 1/2 feet water in her hold.

22nd   At day light began to clear away the wreck, got the Mizen Mast Fore Yard and Main top Gallt Mast over board and cut away a number loass [loose?] spars and rigging – at half past three p.m. the *MINOTAUR* took us in tow the wind continued to increase to a hard gale, – soon after the Hawzer broke, whe where now left to the mercy of the waves the Gale continued to increase the ship a mere wreck on a lee shore possessed by the enemy . . .

Throughout Tuesday 22 October the southerly wind increased in strength, reaching gale force by the evening. The logs of a selection of the British ships give a good account of what was happening.

Log of *EURYALUS*:

> A.M. At 8, Strong gales and rain. Fleet and prizes much
> scattered. P.M. At 8, ditto gales with heavy squalls and rain.

Log of *AJAX*:

> At 8 strong breezes and squally, with rain. *BRITANNIA* with
> a prize in tow near us ... Carpenter stopping shot holes
> between wind and water. Prize in tow.

Log of *MARS*:

> A.M. At 8 strong breezes and heavy rain ... Lost the yellow
> cutter by the painter breaking; could not hoist her up. At
> 5, took in fore topsail, and set storm staysails. P.M. At 5.30,
> committed the body of Captain Duff to the deep. At 12,
> strong gales and heavy rain.

Log of *AGAMEMNON*:

> A.M. Ship making four feet water per hour. P.M. Fresh gales
> and squally with rain. Ship makes three feet of water per hour.

Log of *ORION*:

> A.M. At 8, hove down to a Spanish ship dismasted [the
> *Bahama*], and took her in tow with two 8-inch hawsers on
> end. Very squally. P.M. At 6, strong gales and squally.

Log of *DREADNOUGHT*:

> A.M. At 9, took French ship *Swiftsure* in tow ... Shifted the
> foretopsail, the greatest part of the body of it being blown
> away. P.M. At 8, strong breezes and squally.

Log of *SPARTIATE*:

Noon. Fresh gales and thick rainy weather. *TONNANT* in tow. P.M. 2.10 Reefed the foresail. Pumped the ship out.

Log of *DEFIANCE*:

P.M. Strong gales and squally, with heavy rain. Boats endeavouring to get a hawser on board *l'Aigle*. Found every attempt ineffectual.

Log of *NAIAD*:

A.M. *BELLEISLE* still in tow. P.M. Fresh gales with rain.

Log of *PRINCE*:

A.M. Hauled down fore topmast staysail to repair shot holes ... Victualled 145 prisoners. P.M. Came on to blow very hard ... Came on a hard gale.

Log of *PHOEBE*:

Lost three whole hawsers and 100 fathoms of rope endeavouring to take *l'Aigle* and *Fouguex*, two French line of battleships, in tow.

Log of *PICKLE*:

A.M. At 10, reefed the mainsail, foresail and middle jib. The jolly boat employed carrying prisoners on board different ships. All the prizes in tow. P.M. At 6, strong gales and squally. The fleet very much separated. Several ships not in tow.

While this test of seamanship was challenging the ships' crews, news of the battle reached Cadiz. Commodore Alcalá-Galiano's son was there and captured the atmosphere, unaware that his father had been killed:

> The night came. It was a time of horrifying uncertainty. The 22nd of October began with a terrible look: heavy rain and strong winds came from the South West and mountainous waves pounded the sea walls of the harbour. Then the City received the bad news. The mole was crowded. We saw horrible scenes. We heard stories of suffering and heroism. The beach was covered with wreckage of ships, rigging, masts, even the hulls of ships and boats. Every so often you could see corpses. Little by little more news arrived. The English officers who came to Cadiz with the flag of truce were received courteously and accommodated in Mr. James Duff's house, the former Consul of this Nation before the war.

On 23 October, during what transpired to be only a lull in the fierce weather, the remnants of the Combined Fleet, led by the able, determined and aggressive Breton, Commodore Baron de Cosmao-Kerjulien, made a brief sortie out of harbour to face the enemy that had the day before defeated them. This counterattack was totally unexpected. Cosmao-Kerjulien, in command of the *Pluton*, had somehow managed to assemble an effective squadron consisting of the *Neptune*, *Rayo* (100), *Indomptable* and the *San Francisco de Asís* (74), together with the five French frigates and two brigs that had been at the battle. As an example of leadership it was superb. His aim was to attempt the recapture of some of the prizes. The relatively undamaged British ships, which had by now many of these in tow, were forced to cast them adrift in order to form a defensive line of battle. However, Cosmao-Kerjulien had no intention of engaging them, and set about retaking the *Neptuno* and *Santa Ana*. Unfortunately, on the following day he lost the *Rayo*, *Indomptable* and the *San Francisco de Asís* to the worsening weather. Nevertheless, his bold action prevented the British from saving most of their prizes, since by the time they were able to attend to them again they had drifted too close to the Spanish shore for the tows to be re-established. Instead, Collingwood issued the order to 'sink, burn or destroy' those most damaged.

William Thorpe, one of the prize crew sent on board the Spanish *Neptuno,* found himself a prisoner of war when the ship was retaken by her Spanish crew, and was set to work alongside the Spaniards to help pump ship and save the ship from foundering. However, the fierce weather drove her on to the Spanish coast where she was smashed to pieces. Thorpe was one of those aboard lucky enough to escape. He was imprisoned and eventually exchanged in a cartel for Spanish prisoners of war held by the British. He gave a direct account of his experience:

23rd At 12 Night the Main Mast whent by the board, stove in the Poop and Quarter Deck, – killed one of our seamen and the Spanish Capn of Marines who was lying asleep in his cot. – Whe then shoared up the Quarter Deck and the broken beams to prevent the Deck falling in upon us, – about three oclock cleard away the best Bower Anka on account of seeing Cadiz light show close under our lee, having only 18 Fathoms water, at ½ past 3 oclock let go the anka and brought her up. Veered the whole Cable service in the Hawze and remained in that situation till Daylight. Whe then saw a squadron in shore consisting of 5 sail of the line, 3 Frigates and a Brig which proved to be the Enemy, – Thus situated whe expected assistance from our own fleet but looked in vain, – at 10 oclock, rigged a spar to the stump of the main mast and an other to the [mizen] set a top Gallant upon each and got an other the Fore Mast, in lieu of a fore sail, – at 3 oclock cut our cable and stood toward our own Fleet with all sail whe could set, – but the enemy was gaining upon us fast from Cadiz, – whe cleared away our sternchasers and the magazine, – The prisoners observing this rose upon our people and retook the ship – in doing which they met with little opposition – indeed it would a been madness to resist, a slight resistance was made by some who narrowly escaped with their lives, – They now wore ship & stood toward Cadiz at 4 p.m. *Le Hermione* French Frigate of 44 Guns took us in tow and towd us to the Harbour Mouth where whe brought up amongst some of their disabled ships

24th ... and rode till 3 oclock following Day when we parted from our Ankors and not having an other Cable bent to bring her up they let her drive ashore, near St Martins bay – at this time the confusion on board is inexpressible it becoming Dark, and ignorant what part of the coast whe where cast upon, – expecting the Ship every moment to go to Pieces, the Spaniards naturally dispirited now showed every simptom of Dispair they run about in wild Disorder nor made the last effort to extricate themselves from the Danger that threatened them at Daylight our people conveyed three ropes on those, one from the Cat Head, one from the Bowspirit and another from the Fore Mast head, – by the assistance of wich, a number of men got safe on shore whilst others where imployd constructing a raft for more expeditously landing, as well as to convey such as where unwilling to risk themselves by the ropes, when the raft was completed 20 men ventured on board and arrived safe on the shore, but the raft was Driven so far upon the rocks that it was found impossible to get it of again, – those on board seeing this sad Disaster, far from giving way to dispair immediately set about making an other, which certainly was our last resource, as whe had not any more spars fit for that purpose, when finished whe launched it over board and 20 men embarked on board it who arrived safe one Spaniard excepted who was washed off by the surf, – then made fast a rope to the raft on shore and there being one already fast from the ship, the People Dragged It of to the ship, when 28 men embarkd on board, all of whom arrived safe on shore, the raft was again Dragged on board and 28 men imbarkd 6 of whom was washd from the raft, (Spaniards) by the surf

and perished, – The raft was much damaged upon the Rocks
it was again dragged of to ship but Fate had decreed that
all who remained on board should perish – the raft laden
shoved off from the Ships side but ere it gained the shore
apart and every soul perished, – no further attempt could
be made to save those unfortunate men who remained on
board, all perished. Whe where marchd Prisoners to Port
St Marys being about 4 miles from St Martins Port where
whe where wreckd, whe where lodged in Prison and treated
kindly by the Spaniards tho our lodging was on the ground,
– whe remained here 3 days.

LOSS OF THE *SANTISSIMA TRINIDAD*

For many others, the aftermath of battle was also an ordeal of survival
lasting several days. The great *Santissima Trinidad*'s difficulties were
described by her captain, Francisco Xavier de Uriarte:

As soon as the firing had ceased it was found that we
had more than 60 inches of water in the hold and all the
attention possible was given to the working of the pumps.
   The English three-decked ship *PRINCE* took possession of
the *Trinidad* and towed her with great difficulty, but it not
being possible to keep the water under – it amounting to 15
feet in the hold and people being exhausted after manning
the pumps day and night without cessation – at midday on
the 24th of the same month the English suddenly resolved
to leave her to founder, 3 or 4 ships of their nation taking
the people off between them which they were not able to
do entirely in spite of much assistance, for all the activity
they displayed they were obliged to abandon in this great
extremity a large number of wounded and disabled, who
went down in the *Trinidad* at dawn, at a distance of 7 or 8
leagues south of Cadiz.

Lieutenant John Edwards went aboard the former pride of the Spanish navy. He had joined the *PRINCE* on St Valentine's Day 1805, the eighth anniversary of the *Santissima Trinidad*'s engagement with the British at the battle of Cape St Vincent. He could not have imagined then that eight months later he would be helping to rescue her crew:

> We had the *Santissima Trinidad*, the largest ship in the world, in tow. 'Tis impossible to describe the horrors the morning presented, nothing but signals of distress flying in every direction. The signal was made to destroy the prizes. We had no time before to remove the prisoners; but what a sight when we came to remove the wounded, of which there were between three and four hundred. We had to tie the poor mangled wretches round their waists, and lower them down into a tumbling boat, some without arms, others no legs, and lacerated all over in the most dreadful manner.

For many others going into a prize was a shocking experience. Midshipman William Badcock, from the *NEPTUNE*, was also sent aboard the *Santissima Trinidad* to assist in rescuing the wounded men. The *NEPTUNE* had listed 44 casualties, only ten of whom had been killed. Badcock was ill-prepared for the carnage wrought by British guns on the enemy. He wrote to his father in London:

> I was on board our prize the *Trinidada* getting the prisoners out of her, she had between 3 and 400 killed and wounded, her Beams were covered with Blood, Brains, and peices [*sic*] of Flesh, and the after part of her Decks with wounded, some without Legs and some without an Arm; what calamities War brings on, and what a number of Lives where put an end to on the 21st.

He later described her as:

. . . a magnificent ship, and ought now to be in Portsmouth harbour. Her top-sides, it is true, were perfectly riddled by our beautiful firing, and she had, if I recollect right, 550 killed and wounded, but from the lower part of the sills of the lower deck ports to the waters edge, few shot of consequence had hurt her between wind and water, and those were all plugged up. She was built of cedar, and would have lasted for ages, a glorious trophy of the battle; but 'sink, burn and destroy' was the order of the day, and after a great deal of trouble, scuttling her in many places, hauling up her lower-deck ports – that when she rolled in the heavy sea might fill her decks, – she did at last go unwillingly to the bottom.

'Jack Nastyface' Robinson also conveyed the awfulness of the slaughter, illustrated the desperation of the Spanish aboard their stricken ship and provided a moving anecdote of the rescue of a father and son:

Some of our men were sent on board the Spanish ship before alluded to, in order to assist at the pumps, for she was much shattered in the hull, between wind and water. The slaughter and havoc our guns had made, rendered the scene of carnage horrid to behold; there were a number of their dead bodies piled up in the hold; many, in a wounded or mutilated state, were found lying amongst them; and those who were so fortunate as to escape our shot, were so dejected and crest-fallen, that they could not, or would not, work at the pumps and of course the ship was in a sinking state.

The gale at this time was increasing so rapidly, that manning the pumps was of no use, and we were obliged to abandon our prize, taking away with us all our men, and as many of the prisoners as we could. On the last boat's load leaving the ship, the Spaniards who were left on board appeared on the gangway and the ship's side, displaying their bags of dollars and doubloons, and eagerly offering them as a reward for saving them from the expected and unavoidable wreck; but, however well inclined we were, it was not in our power to rescue them, or it would have been effected without the proffered bribe.

Here a very distressing and affecting scene took place; it was struggle between inclination and duty. On quitting the ship, our boats were overloaded in endeavouring to save all the lives we could, that it is a miracle they were not upset. A father and his son came down the ship's side to get one board on of our boats; the father seated himself, but the men in the boat, thinking, from the loud and boisterous weather, that all their lives would be in peril, could not think of taking the boy; as the boat pulled off, the lad, as though determined not to quit his father, sprung from the ship into the water, and caught hold of the gunwale of the boat; but his attempt was resisted, as it risked all their lives, and some of the men resorted to their cutlasses to cut his fingers off, in order to disentangle the boat from his grasp; at the same time the feelings of the father were worked upon, that he was about to leap overboard, and perish with his son: Britons could face an enemy, but could not witness such a scene of self-devotion; as it were, a simultaneous thought burst forth from the crew, which said 'let us save both father and son, or die in the attempt.' The Almighty aided them in their design; they succeeded, and brought both father and son safe on board of our ship, where they remained, until, with other prisoners, they were exchanged at Gibraltar.

The *SWIFTSURE* took the *Redoubtable* in tow during the afternoon of 22 October. Her log records that 'at 5, the prize made a signal of distress to us'. Captain William Rutherford ordered his boats to the rescue but the weather was so bad that they could not complete the operation and 'at a quarter past 10, the *Redoubtable* sunk by the stern'. Midshipman George Alexander Barker from Bakewell in Derbyshire, aged 20, related the heart-wrenching episode as he and his companions witnessed the loss of so many souls:

On the 22nd it came on a most Violent gale of wind. The Prize in Tow, the *Redoubtable*, seem'd to weather it out tolerable well notwithstanding her shattered state until about three in the afternoon, when from her rolling so violently in a heavy sea, she carried away her fore Mast, the only mast she had standing. Towards the evening she repeatedly made signals of distress to us: we now hoisted our Boats. And sent them on board of her although there was a very high Sea and we were afraid the boats would be swampt alongside the Prize, but they happily succeeded in saving a great number. What added to the horrors of the night was the inability of our saving them all, as we could no longer endanger the lives of our people in open boats; at about 10 p.m. the *Redoubtable* sunk, and the hawser, by which we still kept her in tow, was carried away with the most violent shock.

Captain Edward Codrington of the *ORION* expressed his anguish at having to cast off the *Bahama*, in order to save his own ship, in a letter to his wife, dated 31 October. Fortunately, the people in the prize escaped with their lives.

For an hour and a half or two hours we dare not attempt to set even a storm stay-sail, although within about six miles of a lee shore where we must have been lost; and we therefore prepared to trust to our anchors, and cut away the masts; but the wind abating sufficiently for us to set our reef fore and main sail, after unwillingly making up my mind to cut the towrope, and sacrifice the unfortunate people in the prize, the *Bahama*, in spite of their signals of distress, I wore round, took advantage of the wind veering a little to the westward, and clawed off shore. It is a great comfort to me that the people in the prize were taken out by my launch, after all, on the 26th, and the vessel burned on the strand yesterday.

Detailed eye-witness accounts exist for three other prizes lost in the storm: the *Monarca, Intrépide* and the *Fougueux*. They are similar tales of courage as the crews struggled in vain to save their ships. Nine men led by a second lieutenant from the *BELLEROPHON* formed a party that took possession of the *Monarca*. One of them, a midshipman, left an account that told of how he was more frightened by the storm than by the battle, and recorded the end of the *Rayo*:

> We remained till the morning without further assistance,
> or we should most probably have saved her, though she had
> suffered much more than ourselves; we kept possession of
> her however for four days, in the most dreadful weather,
> when having rolled away all our masts, and being in danger
> of immediately sinking or running on shore, we were
> fortunately saved by the *LEVIATHAN*, with all but about 150
> prisoners, who were afraid of getting into the boats. I can
> assure you I felt not the least fear of death during the action
> which I attribute to the general confidence of victory which I
> saw all around me; but in the prize, when I was in danger of,
> and had time to reflect upon the approach of death, either
> from the rising of the Spaniards upon so small a number as
> we were composed of, or what latterly appeared inevitable
> from the violence of the storm, I was most certainly afraid,
> and at one time, when the ship made three feet of water in
> ten minutes, when our people were almost all lying drunk
> upon deck, when the Spaniards, completely worn out with
> fatigue, would no longer work at the only chain pump left
> serviceable; when I saw the fear of death so strongly depicted
> on the countenances of all around me, I wrapped myself in a
> union jack and lay down upon deck for a short time quietly
> awaiting the approach of death; but the love of life soon
> after again roused me, and after great exertions on the part
> of the British and Spanish officers, who had joined together
> for the mutual preservation of their lives, we got the Ship
> before the wind, determined to run her onshore: this was at

midnight, but at daylight in the morning, the weather being
more moderate, and having again gained upon the water,
we hauled our wind, perceiving a three-decker (*El Rayo*)
dismasted, but with Spanish colours up, close to leeward of
us: the *LEVIATHAN*, the first British ship we had seen for
the last thirty hours, seeing this, bore down, and firing a
shot ahead of us, the *Rayo*, struck without returning a gun.

MISFORTUNE AND THANKSGIVING

Sub-Lieutenant Gicquel des Touches decided to stay aboard the
Intrépide in order to be with one of his close comrades. His account
reveals one of a number of examples of how the strain of the battle
followed by the awfulness of the storm led to a breakdown in morale
and discipline:

> In the half darkness, while the tempest was still gathering
> its forces, we had to pass through a leeward gun port more
> than eighty wounded who were incapable of movement.
> With infinite trouble we did it, by means of a bed frame
> and capstan bars. We were then taken in tow by an English
> frigate [actually *AJAX*] which we followed, rolling from side
> to side and making water everywhere. At a certain point
> I noticed that the work of the pumps was slowing down,
> and I was told that the door of the storeroom had been
> forced and that everybody, French and English, had rushed
> there to get drunk. When I got to these men, reduced to
> the state of brutes, a keg of brandy had just been broken
> and the liquor was running along the deck and was lapping
> the base of a candle which had been stuck there. I only
> just had time to stamp out the flame, and in the darkness
> threatening voices were raised against me. With kicks
> and punches I made them get out of the storeroom,
> I barricaded the door, and reached an understanding

with the English officer to avert the danger which
seemed imminent.

I wished to stay on the *Intrépide* up to the last agonised
minute of one of my friends, who had been judged too badly
injured to be transferred. He was a sub-lieutenant named
Poullain, with whom I was closely connected, and who had
begged me not to leave him in the anguish of his last hour.

When I had heard the last sigh of my poor comrade, there
were just three of us alive on the *Intrépide* an artillery captain
and a midshipman who had not wished to leave me. Our
situation grew worse every minute. Among these bodies and
spilt blood, the silence was disturbed only by the sound of
the sea, and a dull murmur made by the water in the hold
as it rose and spread in the vessel. Night began to close in,
and the vessel settled deeper in the water, making it easy to
calculate that it would have disappeared before daybreak.
Having nothing more to do, I let myself fall asleep, but the
artillery officer, became nervous, heaped wooden debris up
on the deck and wanted to set fire to it, as he preferred a
quick death to the slow agony which was being prepared for
us. I saw his intention in time to oppose it absolutely. We
found a lantern which was fixed to the end of a rod, which
I advised him to wave. By lucky chance, the *ORION* passed
within hailing distance. We hailed her and a boat took us off.
Soon afterwards, the *Intrépide* disappeared beneath the waves.

Most unfortunate of all were those prizes driven on to the lee shore,
such as the *Indomptable* and *Fougueux*. The former was also carrying
survivors from the *Bucentaure* and more than 1,000 men were drowned
when she foundered on the rocks. Commander François Marie Bazin,
second in command of the *Fougueux*, which had already lost three-
quarters of her crew during the battle, was in Pierre Servaux's words
'in a terrible condition. The water had risen almost to the orlop deck.
Everywhere one heard the cries of the wounded and the dying.' Bazin,
while a prisoner in the *TÉMÉRAIRE*, wrote of her last moments. He

added that there was sixteen months' pay due to the crew, which makes her loyal performance at the battle remarkable!

> In the evening at 8 p.m. the *Fougueux* lost her mizenmast and at 10 p.m. requested assistance from the vessel, which was towing her, saying that she was sinking, and from 11 p.m. to 6 a.m. they were evacuating the ship. At 6 a.m. the *Fougueux* was abandoned by her enemies, who had taken off in the night about 40 Frenchmen, including several wounded, but were not able to save everybody. I have been able to question several of those who escaped from the wreck. From their report it would appear that the pumps were insufficient, that the abandoned ship was thrown ashore twenty-eight hours after she was captured and that only about 30 men got safely on shore who, added to those on board the English ship, could bring to 110–120 the number of men surviving from the crew of 682 on the day of departure.
>
> I must tell you of their position, at least of those who are in enemy hands. Several are wounded, and all are in the most frightful distress because they were almost entirely naked when they were rescued.

Cuthbert Collingwood observed humorously that, 'I have hardly a chair that has not a shot in it, and many have lost both legs and arms, without a hope of pension. My wine broke in moving, and my pigs were slain in battle; and these are heavy losses where they cannot be replaced.' He expressed his true feelings about the storm in a letter to his old friend Mrs Mary Moutray, whom he had met in Antigua in the early 1780s, and was described by Nelson 'as a treasure of a woman'. The pride it displays is justified, but the quote at the end, if true, cannot be taken literally, as these other accounts and Cosmao-Kerjulien's sortie demonstrate:

> After such a Battle, such a glorious fight, having nineteen of their Ships in our possession, to be so completely

dispersed by that unhappy gale! The condition of some
of our own Ships, too, was such that it was very doubtful
what would be their fate. Many a time would I have given
the whole group of our captures, to have endured our own.
But affairs were managed better for us. We saved four from
the general wreck. I can only say that in my life I never saw
such exertions as were made to save those Ships. It more
astonished the Spaniards than the beating they got; and one
of them said, when I assured him that none of our Ships
were lost 'How can we contend with such a people, on whom
the utmost violence of the elements has no effect?'

Collingwood ascribed his success to God and issued this general
order:

The Almighty God, whose arm is strength, having of his great
mercy been pleased to crown the exertions of His Majesty's
fleet with success, in giving them a complete victory over
their enemies on the 21st of this month; and that all praise
and thanksgiving may be offered up to the Throne of Grace,
for the great benefit to our country and mankind:
   I have thought proper that a day should be appointed
of general humiliation before God, and thanksgiving for
his merciful goodness, imploring forgiveness of sins, a
continuation of his divine mercy, and his constant aid to
us in the defence of our countries liberties and laws, and
without which the utmost efforts of man are nought; and
direct therefore that [space for date to be specified] be
appointed for this holy purpose.
   Given on board the *EURYALUS*, off Cape Trafalgar, 22nd
October, 1805
C. COLLINGWOOD
To the respective Captains and Commanders.
N.B. The fleet having been dispersed by a gale of wind, no
day has yet been able to be appointed for the above purpose.

HUMANITY AFTER HEROISM

The suffering and sorrow that follows the horror, death and mutilation of any battle generally leaves behind it a sickening sense of shame and revulsion. People ask themselves, 'Why?' Nelson, a devout Christian who nevertheless believed in the just nature of the cause entrusted to him to defend, had witnessed the dreadfulness of battle repeatedly. His last prayer written on the eve of Trafalgar had yearned for 'humanity after Victory' to 'be the predominant feature in the British Fleet'. It was. The green shoots of humanity were sprouting even before the battle was over. They continued to grow afterwards. The very special relationship that exists between those who go down to the sea in ships – ultimately they are all bound together by 'the fellowship of the sea' – made a huge contribution to this display, as did the impact of the great storm that followed the battle. It also owed something to the civility and chivalry of the age.

Collingwood exchanged formal courtesies with the Spanish authorities within a week of the battle, sending Captain Blackwood with a flag of truce and a tactfully worded letter to Marquis de la Solana, the Governor of Cadiz. It would have been sooner had it not been for the storm.

Hercules Robinson accompanied Blackwood, describing him at the time as 'rather short, but of extraordinary strength and finely made, well set up, a fresh complexion and small hands and feet'. Blackwood's character made a favourable impression on the Spaniards, as did his sartorial appearance: 'a gold-laced cocked hat, gold laced coat and epaulettes, white pantaloons and Hessian boots, a light crooked sabre and a great shirt frill'. Relations were immediately amicable. Blackwood was received with great courtesy and invited to both dine and sleep at the Governor's house. Robinson enjoyed pineapple and old sherry. On 31 October, Collingwood wrote home:

> To alleviate the miseries of the wounded as much as in my power, I sent a flag to the marquis Solana, to offer him his wounded. Nothing can exceed the gratitude expressed by

him for this act of humanity; all this part of Spain is in an uproar of praise and thankfulness to the English. Solana sent me a cask of wine, and we have a free intercourse with the shore. Judge of the footing we are on, when I tell you he offered me his hospitals. And pledged the Spanish honour for the care and cure of our wounded men. Our prize ships were most kindly treated: all the country was on the beach to receive them, the priests and women distributing wine, and bread, and fruit, amongst them. The soldiers turned out of their barracks to make lodging for them.

The cask of wine was followed up with a large quantity of fruit, including pomegranates, melons, grapes and figs and the promise of more to come. Collingwood returned the courtesy with a cask of porter and a cheddar cheese, the best things he had to offer at the time. This act of courtesy is reminiscent of a similar exchange of English beer and cheese in July 1797 between Commandant General Canaries Gutièrrez and Rear Admiral Sir Horatio Nelson, after the latter's failed attack on the town of Santa Cruz de Tenerife, when Nelson offered his 'sincerest thanks for your attention to myself and your humanity to those of our wounded'. Collingwood wrote:

> My Lord Marquis, I beg your Lordship will accept my very best thanks for your kind present of a cask of most excellent wine. As a token of your esteem, it is peculiarly grateful to me. I wish I had anything half so good to send your Excellency; but, perhaps, an English cheese may be a rarity at Cadiz; and I accordingly take the liberty of begging your Lordship's acceptance of one, and of a cask of porter.

As Collingwood wrote his letter, the debris and wreckage of the battle continued to wash up along the ten miles of beaches between Cape Trafalgar and Cape Roque, in the direction of Cadiz. Riders patrolled the beaches after every tide in search of bodies and numerous burial parties busied themselves digging holes in the sand for the countless dead. A merchant Englishman arriving in Cadiz after the battle has left us this moving account of the misery and horrible scenes that he saw:

Ten days after the battle, they were still employed bringing ashore the wounded; and spectacles were hourly displayed at the wharfs, and through the streets, sufficient to shock every heart not yet hardened to scenes of blood and human suffering. When, by the carelessness of the boatman, and the surging of the sea, the boats struck against the stone piers, a horrid cry, which pierced the soul, arose from the mangled wretches on board. Many of the Spanish gentry assisted in bringing them ashore, with symptoms of much compassion, yet as they were finely dressed, it had something of the appearance of ostentation at such a moment. It need not be doubted that an Englishman lent a willing hand to bear them up the steps to their litters, yet the slightest false step made them shriek out, and even yet shudder at the remembrance of the sound. On top of the pier the scene was affecting. The wounded were carried away to the hospitals in every shape of human misery, whilst crowds of Spaniards either assisted or looked on with signs of horror. Meanwhile, their companions, who had escaped unhurt, walked up and down with folded arms and downcast eyes, whilst women sat upon heaps of arms, broken furniture, and baggage, with their heads bent between their knees. I had no inclination to follow the litters of the wounded, yet I learned that every hospital in Cadiz was already full, and that convents and churches were forced to be appropriated to the reception of the remainder. If leaving the harbour, I passed through the town to the point, I still beheld the terrible effects of the battle. As far as the eye could reach, the sandy side of the isthmus bordering on the Atlantic was covered with masts and yards, the wrecks of ships, and here and there the bodies of the dead. Among others I noticed a topmast marked

with the name of the *Swiftsure*, and the broad arrow of
England, which only increased my anxiety to know how far
the English had suffered, the Spaniards still continuing to
affirm that they (the English) had lost their chief admiral,
and half their fleet. While surrounded by these wrecks,
I mounted on the cross-trees of a mast which had been
thrown ashore, and casting my eyes over the ocean, beheld
at a great distance, several masts and portions of wreck
floating about. As the sea was now almost calm, with a
light swell, the effect produced by these objects had in it
something of a sublime melancholy, and touched the soul
with the vicissitudes of human affairs. The portions of
floating wreck were visible from the ramparts, yet not a boat
dared to venture out to examine or endeavour to tow them
in, such were the apprehensions which still filled the minds
of the enemy.

The tides did not distinguish between friend or foe and many of the
victims washed ashore were British seamen, not so much casualties
of the battle but of the violent storm afterwards, which had wrecked
many of their prizes. Nevertheless, the Spanish treated them with
unstinting and unfailing courtesy, as a prize-crewman from the
SPARTIATE related:

We sent the prisoners ashore first, some of them had been
and seen their friends, and, as daylight came on, they
came down to assist us, which they did, for they brought
us some bread, and some figs, and some wine, to refresh
us, which we wanted very much, for we had scarcely tasted
anything the last twenty-four hours, and the Spaniards
behaved very kind to us. As for myself, after I had eaten
some bread and fruit, and drank some wine, I tried to
get up, but I could not, and one of the Spaniards, seeing
that state I was in, was kind enough to get two or three
more of his companions, and lifted me up in one of the

bullock-carts in which they had brought down the
provisions for us, and covered me up with one of their
great ponchos, and he tapped me on the shoulder, and
said, 'Bono English!' And being upon the cart, I was out
of the wind and rain – for it blew a heavy gale of wind –
and I felt myself quite comfortable, only my leg pained me
a good deal; but thanks be to God, I soon fell into a sound
sleep, and as I heard afterwards, the French soldiers came
down and marched the rest of my shipmates up to Cadiz,
and they put them into the Spanish prison. As for my part,
I was taken up to Cadiz, in the bullock-cart, and my kind
friend took me to his own house, and had me put to bed.
Where I found myself when I woke.

The Master of the *ORION*, Cass Halliday, a 39-year-old Yorkshire
man, was another prize-crewman rescued by the Spanish, and he also
marvelled at their kindness:

The poor Spaniards behaved very creditably indeed: they
not only sent boats for them (English and all) as soon as
the weather moderated, with bread and water for their
immediate relief; but when the boat, in which the Master
of the ship was sent, had got into Cadiz harbour a carriage
was backed into the water for him to step into from the
boat, all sorts of cordials and confectionery were placed
in the carriage for him, and clean linen, bed, etc. prepared
for him at a lodging on shore: added to which the women
and priests presented him with delicacies of all sorts as
the carriage passed along the streets. In short, he says and
with great truth, that had he been wrecked on any part of
the English coast he would never have received half the
attention which he did from these poor Spaniards, whose
friends we had just destroyed in such numbers.

Prisoner of war William Thorpe was treated with a similar civility:

On the 27th whe where marched 11 miles to a small town
in the Isle of Loyans Passed a little town calld point Royal
about nine miles from St Mary's whe where here lodged in
Prison and served with a pint of wine and some bread

The next day 28th, whe where marched to Cadiz distance
about nine miles where whe where again lodged in Prison
and received a Quarter Dollar per man to subsist us
twenty four hours the following day 29th they marchd us
to the Waterside and put us on board two Spanish gun
boats, and by them carried on board the *Hermione* French
Frigate, appointed to carry us to the Fleet, to be exchanged,
remained on board two nights when our allowance was
a Pint of Wine and Bread, the next day whe where put
on board the *SIRIUS* Frigate, and again shifted to the
SWIFTSURE 74 Guns – carryd to Gibraltar and Joined our
own ship to the great joy of us all our loss amounted to
four killed by the falling of the masts rigging and drowned,
– Tho the suffering of our People where great, yet no
instances of cruelty or even unkindness can be alleged to
the Spaniards those who arrived safe on shore looked upon
our men as their Deliverers and there where instances of
Grattitude and Kindness – that would do Honor to Any
Nation – It is with regret the Spaniard goes war with the
English who he wishes always to consider his Friends it is
from the unfortunate situation of affairs on the continent
he is compelled to act a part so foreign to his interest and
contrary to the Publick wish. Whoever therefore considers
the destructive consequences of war if his heart is not
callous to Humanity will feel for the sufferings of the
Widows Orphans and Friends of the brave Fellows who fell
on the 21st October 1805.

There are fewer examples of French civility and kindliness, the
animosity between them and the British being much stronger. The
Spanish, however, were almost thankful to have been beaten; it

relieved them of the political responsibility of supporting atheist France. A statement from 'an officer of the *EURYALUS*', published in the *Naval Chronicle*, stated that:

> . . . the Spaniards were very civil. Captain Blackwood examined the state of the hospitals which had been offered for our wounded men, but found them filled with the Spanish wounded, many of whom were hourly dying. The Spanish at Cadiz were not the least affected at their loss; they seemed to be glad of the circumstance that would deprive them of the French. They were sorry to lose the English and their commerce.

Within three years, their uncomfortable alliance with Napoleon was scrapped and they were fighting alongside the British to push the French out of their peninsula. Today, the Spanish regard Trafalgar as a glorious defeat, in much the same way as the British view Dunkirk. The Spanish had fought with courage. They had nothing to be ashamed of and they accepted their crushing defeat without rancour. Furthermore, the deeds of their heroes, among them Commodore Galiano, Captain Valdés, Commodore Churruca and Admiral Gravina, inflated their national pride. In retrospect, it is quite clear that Trafalgar prepared the foundations for Spain's subsequent declaration of independence in 1811, announced significantly from Cadiz.

The 'heroes' spent many weeks in the company of their opposite numbers. Many grew to like each other and they were not always Spanish. The scholarly Captain Edward Codrington of the *ORION* developed an affection for the rough and quite uneducated Captain Infernet of the French *Intrépide*, who according to one of the *Conqueror*'s officers had surrendered after 'one of the most gallant defences I ever witnessed . . . and it deserves to be recorded in the memory of those who admire true heroism'. Infernet swam to the *ORION* with his 10-year-old son, a midshipman, on his shoulders, their only possessions being the clothes they stood in. Codrington wrote to his wife:

> He is much like us in his open manner, is a good sailor,
> and I have no doubt a good officer, has more delicacy in his
> conduct, although, perhaps boisterous in his manner, than
> any Frenchman I have before met with: and endeavours
> to make himself agreeable to all in the ship. He fought
> most stoutly, and had I not had the advantage over him of
> position and a ready fire whilst he was engaged with others,
> we should not have escaped as well as we did.

Codrington advanced him £100. Captain Ben Hallowell, one of
Nelson's 'band of brothers' at the Nile, did the same, together with
a bed and a trunk packed full with two dozen shirts, stockings and
cloth for a coat, 'in acknowledgement of the great courtesy and
kindness that he himself had received from Admiral Gantheaume [sic]
and his officers, when a prisoner'. On Infernet's arrival in England as
a prisoner of war, Lady Codrington honoured him with an invitation
to stay as a guest at her husband's home.

Collingwood started a glowing and complimentary correspondence
with many of the senior Spaniards, congratulating Vice-Admiral
Álava, his opponent in the *Santa Ana*, on his recovery, and expressing
his genuine grief for Admiral Gravina when he heard that he died of
his wound four and half months after the battle.

The best officers of the service were also concerned for the other
victims of battle and they generally wrote appeals to Lloyd's Patriotic
Fund on behalf of their injured crew and their dependent families.
Collingwood did so on behalf of both the late Captain Cooke of the
BELLEROPHON and Captain Duff of the *MARS*. Captain Rotherham
did the same for the crew of his own ship, and William Pryce Cumby
made appeals on behalf of the *BELLEROPHON*'s crew. Cumby's
first letter to the Patriotic Fund included a list of the 156 killed
and wounded, provided by the ship's surgeon, and highlighted
the plight of:

> The widow and young family of Mr Thos. Robinson late
> boatswain of this ship, whose spirited conduct on the day

of battle was indeed worthy of the character of a British seaman; having been severely wounded in both hands towards the close of the action, he went down to be dressed, but finding the cockpit full of wounded, and the Surgeon with his Sole Assistant fully employed on cases which he deemed of greater danger than his own, he got the Purser's steward to bind up his hands and immediately returned to the deck, offering and entreating me to accept his services such as they then might be, wherever I thought them most useful; he was sent to Gibraltar Hospital where he died of wounds on 2nd November. His wife and two small children reside at No 19 Hanover Street, Portsea; and as I believe them to have been totally dependent on him for a livelihood I beg leave most earnestly to recommend them to your humane consideration.

Thomas Friend Robinson was 54 when he died from his wounds. Elizabeth, his widow, was granted £80 from the Fund. She also received her husband's prize money, £44 4s 6d, which had to be contested for, his bounty of £45 12s 6d, and a pension of £25 from the Charity for the Relief of Poor Widows of Commission and Warrant Officers of the Royal Navy. The children, Thomas William and Elizabeth, each received £15 6s 6d in trust.

Lloyd's Patriotic Fund had been established in July 1803 to provide charitable support on the one hand and reward on the other. The founders agreed that 'it behoves us to hold out every encouragement to our fellow-subjects, who may be in any way instrumental in repelling or annoying our implacable foe: and to prove to them that we are ready to drain both our purses and our veins in the greater cause which imperiously calls us to unite the duties of loyalty and patriotism'. Thus they resolved to establish 'a suitable Fund for their comfort and relief – for the purpose of assuaging the anguish of their wounds, or palliating in some degree the more weighty misfortune of the loss of limbs – of alleviating the distress of the widow and orphan – of smoothing the brow of sorrow for the fall of dearest relations – and of granting pecuniary rewards, or honourable badges of distinction, for successful exertions of valour or merit'.

Cumby wrote regularly to the Fund. Another beneficiary was a 13-year-old Volunteer First Class, George Pearson, who was wounded at the battle. He received £40 from the Fund.

> This youngster had joined the BELLEROPHON as his first ship just before we left England the preceding May. He was stationed on the Quarter-Deck and when he saw Captain Cooke fall he ran to his assistance but was himself brought down by a splinter in the thigh. As I was coming to take command of the ship I met on the quarter-deck ladder little Pearson in the arms of a Quarter-Master who was carrying him to The Surgeon in the Cockpit. Three days afterwards 10 sail of the line came out of Cadiz in good condition and made a demonstration of attacking some of our crippled ships and prizes who had been driven near Cadiz in a gale. When the signal was made to prepare for battle and our drums had beat to quarters for the purpose, the first person that caught my eye on the Quarter-deck was little Pearson dragging with difficulty one leg after another. I said to him, 'Pearson, you had better go below.' 'I should be very sorry to be below at a time like this.' I instantly said, 'Indeed I will not order you down and if you live you'll be a second Nelson.' Poor fellow he did live to be a lieutenant and then died of fever.

Like many other Royal Navy officers, Cumby himself received a tribute from the Fund, a sword, on which was the following inscription: 'From the Patriotic Fund at Lloyds to William Pryce Cumby, Captain of HMS BELLEROPHON, for his meritorious services in contributing to the signal victory obtained over the combined fleets of France and Spain off Cape Trafalgar on 21st October 1805.'

Captain Henry William Bayntun of the LEVIATHAN wrote to the Patriotic Fund on 23 October with the following 'trifling anecdote' about the captain of the forecastle, Thomas Main, 'as it will serve to show the enthusiasm of a British seaman when fighting with the enemies of his country'. Main was a 40-year-old Northumbrian, rated a Quarter Master's Mate. The anecdotes illustrate the detailed medical care that was a distinctive feature of the Royal Navy at the time:

> We had passed through the line, and had assisted in disabling and silencing the French Admiral's ship and the four-decker, *Santisima Trinidada*; we were much galled by a distant cannonade from a separated few of the enemy's ships; at last the *San Augustin*, of 74 guns, bearing the pendant of Commodore Cagigal, gave us an opportunity of closing with him, which was immediately embraced. While this was doing, a shot took off the arm of Thomas Main, when at his gun on the forecastle; his messmates kindly offered to assist him going to the Surgeon; but he bluntly said, 'I thank you, stay where you are; you will do more good there' he then went down by himself to the cockpit. The Surgeon (who respected him) would willingly have attended him, in preference to others, whose wounds were less alarming; but Main would not admit of it, saying, 'Avast, not until it comes to my turn, if you please.' The Surgeon soon after amputated the shattered part of the arm; near the shoulder; during which, with great composure, smiling, and with a steady clear voice, he sang the whole of 'Rule Britannia'. The cheerfulness of this rough son of Neptune has been of infinite use in keeping up the spirits of his wounded shipmates, and I hope this recital might be of service to him.

When the *LEVIATHAN* reached Plymouth Bayntun added a postscript dated 1 December: 'I am sorry to inform you, that the above-mentioned fine fellow died since writing the above, at Gibraltar Hospital, of a fever he caught, when the stump of his arm was nearly well.' The surgeon's log recorded:

Left arm shattered by a grape shot, which was amputated above the elbow joint. Nov. 5th he became feverish – prior to this he was walking about in good health & spirits & it was supposed his mess mates had incautiously given him too much to drink – an emetic was given him and as he grew worse blisters were applied to the temples & between the shoulder – febrifuge medicine.

Not everyone was fortunate enough to have such good mess-mates, or in the case of one young officer to get on with their men. Midshipman Edward Freeman Brooke, aged 14, from Wakefield, had joined the REVENGE from Chatham on 12 April 1805 as a Volunteer First Class. 'Jack Nastyface' Robinson described his fate.

We had a midshipman on board our ship of a wickedly mischievous disposition, whose sole delight was to insult the feelings of the seamen, and furnish pretexts to get them punished. His conduct made every man's life miserable that happened to be under his orders. He was a youth not more than twelve or thirteen years of age; but I have often seen him get on the carriage of a gun, call a man to him, and kick him about the thighs and body, and with his fist would beat him about the head; and these, although prime seamen, at the same time dared not murmur. It was ordained however, by Providence, that his reign of terror and severity should not last; for during the engagement he was killed on the quarter-deck by a grape-shot, his body greatly mutilated, his entrails being driven and scattered against the larboard side; nor were there any lamentations for his fate! – No! for when it was known that he was killed, the general exclamation was, 'Thank God, we are rid of the young tyrant!' His death was hailed as the triumph over an enemy.

10

'IT WAS THE DEATH HE WISHED'

Literally thousands of letters would have been written to wives, friends and loved ones after the battle. They would have been delivered at various times as the ships straggled home. The first would have started their journey when Collingwood's disabled ships had limped into Gibraltar. The *VICTORY*, towed by *NEPTUNE*, anchored there, in Rosia Bay, at seven in the evening on 28 October. Nelson's pendant was worn at half-mast from the jury-rig. The mood was melancholic and there was little sense of celebration. The letters generally reflect and sustain this mood. They recognize the importance of the victory but go on to convey relief that the writer has survived, probably embellished by an anecdote, and give various overviews of the battle – the basic details. Curiously, most of the letters also open in a similar way.

The 27-year-old Reverend John Greenly, from Hereford, was Chaplain to the *REVENGE*. He wrote to his father from 'Off Cadiz Oct 21st 1805':

> A glorious day in England
> Dear Father
> I have this day witnessed a scene, which I suppose you have
> discovered in the papers, yet I shall not lose the opportunity
> of a cutters' going to England from Lord Nelson; such news
> has not been heard since the Spanish Armada . . . I had a
> very narrow escape, a 42 pounder came within 6 inches of
> me, & entirely shattered a beam; the Captain ordered me off

twice, but I went up when I could from the wounded. We
had a dreadful carnage . . .

Captain Henry Blackwood in the *EURYALUS* had been so busy that
he had found no time to either change his clothes or write to his wife,
Harriet, since 19 October, but on 'Tuesday 22nd, 1 o'clock at night' he
finally put pen to paper and composed an account of the battle that is
overwhelmed by the shock and grief at Nelson's death:

> The first hour since yesterday morning that I could call my
> own is now before me, to be devoted to my dearest wife,
> who, thank God, is not a husband out of pocket. My heart,
> however, is sad, and penetrated with the deepest anguish.
> A Victory, such a one as has never been achieved, yesterday
> took place in the course of five hours; but at such an
> expense, in the loss of the most gallant of men, and best of
> friends, as renders it to me a Victory I never wished to have
> witnessed – at least, on such terms . . . To any other person,
> my Harriet, but yourself, I could not and would not enter so
> much into detail, particularly of what I feel at this moment.
> But you, who know and enter into all my feelings, I do not,
> even at the risk of distressing you, hesitate to say that in my
> life, I never was so shocked or so completely upset as upon
> my flying to the *VICTORY*, even before the Action was over,
> to find Lord Nelson was then at the gasp of death . . . What a
> horrid scourge is war!

Captain Eliab Harvey started to compose a letter to his wife, Louisa,
on 24 October 'to be forwarded without loss of time'. He was writing
from the *TÉMÉRAIRE* 'on her way to Gibraltar after the action of the
21st October 1805'.

> You will my Dear rejoice at the important events which I am
> about to relate and particularly so, as our Country will have
> the greatest reason to Triumph and that I am safe . . .

On 30 October Quarter-Master John Wells wrote to his parents living in Mason Street, Kingston upon Hull, from 'HM Ship *BRITANNIA* off Cadiz'. He was 23:

Dear Parents
Before you receive this I am afraid you will be uneasy at not hearing of my safety during our late glorious [encounter] with the Combined Fleets of France & Spain which took place on Monday the 21st of October, as follows . . . being on the Quarter Deck I had an opportunity of seeing the whole of the sport which I must own rather daunted me before the first or second broadside but after them I think I never should have been tired of drubbing the Jokers particularly when my Ship mates began to fall around me . . .

Christopher West, a 17-year-old volunteer from London, wrote to his brother on 16 November from the *MINOTAUR* at Gibraltar:

My Dear Brother,
I embrace this opportunity with pleasure to acquaint you that thank God, I am well, and have sent you an account of the action fought by the British Fleet under the command of Lord Nelson, and the combined Fleets, commanded by Admiral Villeneuve off Cape Trafalgar . . . This is conveyed to England by one of our crippled Ships, we had only 5 killed & 20 wounded, which was very few considering the time we were engaged. I never saw such a glorious day since I was born. I think they wont face us again for some time. We are now repairing our damages at Gibraltar. Lord Nelson poor man was killed, but he died in defence of his Country. The loss of the other Ships I don't know, but it must be immense.
    Let my Parents know that I am not hurt immediately. Adieu.

Quarter-Master Benjamin Stevenson, born in Berwick, Northumberland, a pressed man aged 24, wrote to his sister from *VICTORY* when she called in at Portsmouth before sailing, with Nelson's body still aboard, to Chatham. His letter is dated 5 November 1805:

> Dear Sister,
> I am happy to inform you of my being in good health and
> of A Verrey hard ingagement with the French and Spanish
> Fleet on 21st of Octber. Dear Sister we had Verrey hard
> ingagement with them indeed it lasted 4 hours and a half
> constant fire but thank god we had the great Fortune to
> gane the Victory . . . Dear Sister I shall say but little more
> abought it for it is two crual for your feelings sister but I
> Dare say you will here Anough of it in the Niewspapers but I
> am sorry to say that Lord Nelson fel in the Action. It would
> be A good thing for a great many of us if he had lived but it
> was god almightys pleasure to call upon him.

One of the more famous letters home was written about one week after the battle by 'Sam' from the *ROYAL SOVEREIGN*.

> Honoured Father . . . Our dear Admiral Nelson is killed! so
> we have paid pretty sharply for licking 'em. I never set eyes
> on him, for which I am both sorry and glad; for, to be sure,
> I should like to have seen him – but then, all the men in our
> ship who have seen him are such soft toads, they have done
> nothing but blast their eyes, and cry, ever since he was killed.
> God bless you! chaps that fought like the Devil, sit down
> and cry like a wench. I am still in the *ROYAL SOVEREIGN*,
> but the Admiral has left her for she is like a horse without
> a bridle, so he is in a frigate that he may be here and there
> and everywhere, for he's as cute and as bold as a lion, for all
> he can cry! I saw his tears with my own eyes, when the boat
> hailed and said my lord was dead.

Collingwood felt that the damage that *VICTORY* had sustained was sufficient cause to move Nelson's body to the *EURYALUS* for the journey home to England. The ship was making water and the pumps had to be constantly manned, but the crew of *VICTORY* thought otherwise and made such strong objections through one of the boatswain's mates that he gave way to their protest. Able Seaman James Bagley, writing to his sister, noted that 'they wanted to take Lord Nelson from us but we told Captain as we brought him out we would bring him home so it was so and he was put him into a cask of spirits'.

After some basic repairs *VICTORY* sailed on 4 November for England, accompanied by the *BELLEISLE*, rendezvoused with the rest of the fleet off Cadiz on 5 November and, after a slow and circuitous voyage in 'adverse winds and tempestuous weather', anchored at St Helen's exactly one month later.

Symbolically, the start of her long voyage coincided with a further defeat for the French of Rear Admiral Dumanoir le Pelley's squadron by Captain Sir Richard Strachan. Strachan's Action off Cape Vinano on 4 November resulted in the capture of the four French ships that had fled from the Battle of Trafalgar – the *Formidable*, *Duguay Trouin* (74), *Mont Blanc* (74) and *Scipion*. His victory was the coda to the Trafalgar campaign, and all of the prizes were quickly got and safely to Plymouth by 10 November. (Many in the South West of Britain heard about Strachan's Action before they heard about Trafalgar and may have even confused the reports of the two battles). The *VICTORY*'s departure also coincided with the landward dashes across southern England by Lieutenant Lapenotiere and Captain Sykes, bearing their separate versions of the news of Trafalgar. *VICTORY*'s log records:

> December 4th A.M. at 6 saw the Needles Light bearing
> N.N.E., five leagues standing for St Helens. Hoisted the Flag
> and Colours of the late Vice-Admiral Lord Viscount Nelson,
> K.B.   P.M. at 1.30 anchored in St Helens. 5th A.M. at 8.10
> weighed, and at 10 anchored at Spithead.

'DEATH COULD HAVE NO TERRORS IF FOLLOWED BY SUCH A FUNERAL'

Rumours were heard that Nelson was to be given a state funeral in London, and Hardy received orders for VICTORY to proceed to the Nore, the great naval anchorage at the mouth of the Thames. Furthermore, it seemed that there were plans prior to the funeral for Nelson to lie in state at Greenwich, his body exposed to the gaze of the public. Therefore, preparations were necessary. On inspecting the body, Beatty found:

> ... it exhibited a state of perfect preservation, without
> being in the smallest degree offensive. There were, however,
> some appearances that induced the Surgeon to examine
> the condition of the bowels; which were found to be much
> decayed, and likely in a short time to communicate the
> process of putrefaction to the rest of the body; the parts
> already injured were therefore removed. It was at this time
> the fatal ball was discovered: it had passed through the
> spine, and lodged in the muscles of the back, towards the
> right side, and a little below the shoulder-blade. A very
> considerable portion of the gold lace, pad, and lining
> of the epaulette, with a piece of the coat, was found
> attached to the ball: the lace of the epaulette was as firmly
> so, as if it had been inserted into the metal while in a
> state of fusion.

Hardy sailed for the Nore on 11 December. The weather continued foul and the VICTORY was forced to anchor off Dover for a few days.

A letter that appeared in the *Naval Chronicle* suggests that some people were rowed out to the ship and allowed aboard. Whoever they were, it is unlikely that they met Hardy or any others who had been close to Nelson, because the account has errors that they would not have been party to, for instance that Nelson 'lived about an hour'. Dated 16 December it read:

Mr Editor,

I am just come from on board the *VICTORY*: she is very much mauled, both in her hull and rigging; has upwards of 80 shot between wind and water: the foremast is very badly wounded indeed and though strongly fished, has sunk about six inches: the mainmast is also badly wounded, and very full of musket shots; she has a jury mizzen-mast, and fore and main-top-masts, and has a great many shot in her bowsprit and bows; one of the figures which support the arms has both legs shot off. I clearly ascertained that Lord Nelson was killed by a shot from the main-top of the *Redoubtable*: he was standing on the starboard side of the quarter-deck, with his face to the stern, when the shot struck him, and was carried down into the wings: he lived about one hour and was perfectly sensible until within five minutes of his death. When carrying down below, although in great pain, he observed the tiller ropes were not sufficiently tight, and ordered tackles to be got on them, which now remain; the ship he engaged was so close, that they did not fire their great guns on board the enemy, but only musketry, and manned the rigging on board, but nearly the whole that left the deck were killed; the ship had 25 guns dismounted with the *VICTORY*'s fire; a shot carried away four spokes from the wheel of the *VICTORY*, and never killed or wounded any of the men steering; temporary places have been fitted up between decks for the wounded men, which are warmed by stoves. R.J

At about noon on 22 December the Commissioner's yacht, *CHATHAM,* met the *VICTORY* crossing the flats from Margate. He confirmed that Nelson was to receive a grand state funeral. His yacht conveyed a macabre cargo: a coffin lined with white satin made from the main mast wreckage of *L'Orient,* which had blown up at the Battle of the Nile on 1 August 1797. Captain Benjamin Hallowell had presented it to a delighted Nelson who had been careful to preserve it. The brass plate affixed to it carried this inscription:

I do hereby certify, that every part of this coffin is made of
the wood and iron of *L'Orient*, most of which was picked
up by His Majesty's ship under my command, in the bay of
Aboukir. (signed) BENJ. HALLOWELL

In the space of a few weeks of the news of Trafalgar arriving in Britain
the atmosphere of the country had been transformed by the death
of Nelson. It had dampened the feelings of elation generated by
his victory. There was an immense outpouring of public grief, and
universally people 'from the highest to the lowest' felt as if they had
lost someone they knew personally – 'It might with truth be asserted
that the bosom of every Briton was a tomb in which the memory
of their favourite hero was embalmed.' The Poet Laureate, Robert
Southey, would later write that 'men started at the intelligence, and
turned pale, as if they had heard of the loss of a dear friend'. The
nation in mourning echoed the private feekings of Gilbert Elliot, Lord
Minto, conveyed in a letter to his wife:

My sense of this irreparable loss, as well as my sincere and
deep regret for so kind a friend, have hardly left room for
other feelings which belong, however, hardly less naturally
to this event. I was extremely shocked and hurt when I
heard it, and it has kept me low and melancholy all day. One
knows, on reflection, that such a death is the finest close,
and the crown, as it were of such a life; and possibly if his
friends were angels and not men, they would acknowledge
it as the last favour Providence could bestow a seal and
security for all the rest. His glory is certainly at its summit,
and could be raised no higher of life; but he might have
lived at least to enjoy it.

It was quickly realized that such intense national feeling could only be
assuaged by an extraordinary state funeral with elaborate ceremonies
lasting over five days. The College of Arms, under Garter King at
Arms, Sir Isaac Heard, was charged with making the arrangements.

He designed what was to be the last full heraldic funeral staged in Britain. It included a three-day lying in state at Greenwich Hospital in the magnificent hall painted by James Thornhill, a 'Grand River Procession' from Greenwich to Whitehall, a procession to the Admiralty and a vast funeral procession from the Admiralty to St Paul's Cathedral. London had seen nothing like it before (or since). The ceremonial was dominated by the army. Thousands of soldiers and cavalry took part. Heard made no provision for the crew of VICTORY, the proud veterans who had actually been at the battle. This led to an outcry by the popular press and Heard was humbled into changing the arrangements. 'A party of the brave crew of the VICTORY, armed with boarding pikes' assisted the guards at the Painted Hall, they took part in the river procession and in the funeral procession from the Admiralty to St Paul's Cathedral, when they carried their shot-torn colours and greatly impressed the crowds lining the route. Lady Elizabeth Hervey commented that, 'The show altogether was magnificent, but the common people, when the crew of the VICTORY passed, said, "We had rather see them than all the show!"'

Able Seaman John Brown, 25, a pressed man from Wakefield, was one of the crew. He wrote before the funeral from the 'VICTORY, Chatham, December 28':

> Whilst we expect to be drafted on board the new OCEAN as Lord Collingwood is going to have her (him that was Second in Command in Action) there has been great disputes between admirals and captains wanting this Ships company but government will let nobody but Lord Collingwood have them as he was Commander in chief when lord Nelson Fell. There is three hundred of us Pickt out to go to Lord Nelson Funral we are to wear blue Jackets white Trowsers and a black scarf round our arms and hats besides gold medal for the battle of Trafalgar Valued £7 1s. round our necks. That I shall care take of until I take it home and Shew it to you.

Over 20,000 took part in the funeral procession. Lord Nelson's 14-year-old nephew, George Matcham, was one of them and wrote this account in his journal:

Thursday Jan. 9th

Rose at 6. Put on our full dress and went to Clarges St. Took up the Boltons. Drove to the Earls, where breakfast was laid out. Saw the two sons of Lord Walpole, gentlemanly looking. Were not received at all by the Earl, not introduced to anybody. Put on there the Cloaks, etc.

About half past eight the Mourning Coaches came. Lords Merton and Nelson went in the first, drawn by six horses. My Father, Mr Bolton, Tom and myself in the second, and Messrs Barney, Walpole and Fielding (son to the great Fielding) went in the third as Relations. Went into St. James Park. Found there a vast number of carriages, waited for some time. Saw the Duke of York at the head of his Troops, a handsome man, but shorter than the rest of the Royal Family. He talked a good deal to the Aids de Camp. Saw Mr. Naylar as Herald, I thought his dress very ridiculous, his garment being covered with Armorial Bearings etc. Saw all the Captains and Admirals much confused, not being able to find their carriage.

From hence we moved by slow degrees and about one arrived at the Horse Guards, where the procession was joined by the Prince of Wales, and the Duke of Clarence. The body was then put into the Car, which represented the stern and bow of the VICTORY. [This description was taken from The Times.] The Case modelled at the ends in imitation of the hull of the VICTORY, its head towards the horses was ornamented with a figure of Fame, the Stern carved and painted in the naval style with the word 'Victory' in yellow raised letters on the lanthorn over the Poop. The Coffin with its head towards the Stern with an English Jack pendant over the Poop, and lowered half Staff. There was a Canopy over the whole supported by Pillars in the form of Palm Trees and partly covered with Black Velvet richly fringed, immediately above which in the front was inscribed in gold the word Nile at one end, on one side the following motto *HOSTE DEVICTO REQUIEVIT* behind the word *TRAFALGAR* and on the other side the motto of his arms *'Palmam qui meruit ferat'* [Let him who has deserved it bear the palm]. The Car was drawn by six led horses.

When the coffin was brought out of the Admiralty there seemed to be a general Silence, and everyone appeared to feel the Death of so noble and such a good Man. Poor Mr Scott came to our carriage and requested the Heralds to let him go in the same Coach with us. We were happy to receive him. After he had shaken us all heartily by hand, he said with Tears in his Eyes 'Ah poor Fellow! I remained with him as long as I could and then they turned me away.'

The procession moved on slowly, the soldiers lining the streets, and the Band playing the Dead March in Saul. At Temple Bar it was joined by the Mayor and suite, who took their place after the Prince of Wales. As it past the Regiments of the Dukes of York and Sussex, they stood still, and ordered that no salute should be made.

At St Paul's we got out, and walked in procession up the Passage. It was the most aweful [*sic*] sight I ever saw. All the Bands played. The Colours were all carried by the Sailors and a Canopy was held over the coffin, supported by Admirals. When we arrived at the Choir, the relations were placed at each side of the coffin on which was the Coronet placed on a Cushion. The service was read by the Bishop of Lincoln, but he did little justice to the occasion as his tone was monotonous and heavy. The Bishop of Chichester read the first lesson.

When the body was conveyed to the Dome for interment, the Prince of Wales passed close by us. He was dressed in the Order of the Garter. Next him was the Duke of York, and

he was followed by the Duke of Clarence, who shook my
Father by the hand, saying 'I am come to pay my last Duties
here, and I hope you and I shall never meet on such a like
occasion.' The organ played a Dirge meanwhile, the service
went on, the Body was lowered and the Herald declaring the
Titles of the Deceased broke the Staves and threw them into
the Grave.

There were 5 Dukes, besides the Royal Family. Mr Fox, Mr
Sheridan and Tierney were present. After waiting some time
we got to Clarges St. and went to Brompton about 8 with
Mr Scott.

Protocol prevented King George III from attending, but he asked for
the procession to go past St James's Palace so that at least he could
watch it from a window. Stunned into a long silence on hearing the
news of Nelson's death he had already declared that the battle should
be called Trafalgar and had very astutely reflected that 'It was the
death he wished.'

As the short January day came to an end and the light faded in St
Paul's Cathedral, large torches were lit in the choir and the galleries,
and the area under the dome where the coffin lay was illuminated
by a large lantern burning 130 candles. The service itself was very
simple and integrated into normal evensong. Only one piece of music
was composed specially for the occasion; a 'Grand Dirge', which was
played at the end by its composer, Thomas Attwood, the cathedral's
organist. After Sir Isaac Heard, the herald, had read out all the titles of
the deceased he added his own unscripted words: 'The hero, who in the
moment of Victory, fell covered with immortal glory.' The comptroller,
treasurer and steward of Nelson's household then broke their white
staves and gave them to the Garter who threw them into the grave as
the coffin was slowly lowered on a specially built mechanism into the
torch-lit crypt. At this moment 48 sailors from VICTORY were required
to reverently fold the shot-torn colours and place them on the coffin
as it disappeared from view. Quite unexpectedly they tore off a large
piece, ripped it into fragments and stuffed the pieces into their coats.

The marvellous spontaneity of the moment caught everyone's breath and the wife of Captain Edward Codrington of the ORION, one of the very few women at the service (none had been invited), expressed its meaning perfectly: 'That was *Nelson*: the rest was so much the Herald's Office.' The crew of *VICTORY* had indeed stolen the show.

As Nelson was invested with immortality his friend and second in command at Trafalgar was still at sea: Collingwood was now responsible for the Mediterranean command. Nelson's death had come as a shocking blow to Collingwood, which he referred to frequently as the 'most poignant grief'. He remained at sea for the next four years and then within days of receiving his notice of recall, died, worn out by the strain of his command. Lord Collingwood of Hethpole and Caldburne was laid to rest next to Nelson in St Paul's Cathedral, but he never saw his wife or precious daughters again, nor did he listen to the blackbirds in his beloved Northumbrian garden. He wrote to 'Lady Collingwood' for the last time from his flagship '*QUEEN*, off Carthagena, December, 1805':

> It would be hard if I could not find one hour to write a letter to my dearest Sarah, to congratulate her on the high rank to which she has been advanced by my success. Blessed may you be, my dearest love, and may you long live the happy wife of your happy husband!
>
> I suppose I must not be seen to work in my garden now; but tell old Scott that he need not be unhappy on that account. Though we shall never again be able to plant the Nelson potatoes, we will have them of some other sort, and right noble cabbages to boot, in great perfection.
>
> I am out of all patience with Bounce. The consequential airs he gives himself since he became a right honourable dog are insufferable. He considers it beneath his dignity to play with commoners' dogs, and truly thinks that he does them grace when he condescends to lift up his leg against them. This is, I think, carrying the insolence of rank to the extreme.

CHRONOLOGY

| 1758 | 29 September | Horatio Nelson born at Burnham Thorpe, Norfolk. |

1789 — French Revolution begins.

1793 1 February — Start of French Revolutionary War.

1797 14 February — Battle of Cape St Vincent.
24 July — Nelson's failed attack on
Santa Cruz de Tenerife. Loses arm.

1798 1 August — Battle of the Nile. Nelson destroys
French fleet at Aboukir Bay. Villeneuve escapes.

1801 2 April — Battle of Copenhagen. Nelson defeats Danish fleet.

1802 24 March — Treaty of Amiens ends French Revolutionary War.

1803 1 May — Work begins on new port and fortifications
at Boulogne.
16 May — Great Britain declares war on France
Start of Napoleonic War. Blockade of Brest resumes.
Nelson appointed C-in-C Mediterranean.
18 May — Nelson hoists flag in VICTORY.
23 May — Plans for invasion camps along Channel announced.
6 July — Nelson joins fleet off Toulon.

1804 — Nelson blockades French in Toulon.
16 May — Henry Dundas, Viscount
Melville named First Lord of the Admiralty.
2 July — Napoleon orders first invasion plan.
Cancelled on death of Admiral
Latouche-Tréville (19 August).
1 September — Napoleon crowned Emperor.
William Pitt Prime Minister again.
3 September — Admiral Villeneuve named to replace
Latouche-Tréville.
14 December — Spain declares war on Britain, creates
Combined Fleet.

1805 4 January — Franco-Spanish naval pact signed.
11 January — Admiral Missiessy breaks out
of Rochefort and sails for Caribbean.
16 January — Villeneuve returns to Toulon.

24 January	Great Britain declares war on Spain.
Jan-Feb	Nelson chases but fails to intercept Villeneuve's fleet.
28 March	Missiessy sails from Martinique for France.
30 March	Villeneuve sails from Toulon for Martinique.
4 April	Nelson hears that Villeneuve has again left Toulon.
8 April	Villeneuve breaks out into the Atlantic. Viscount Melville censured by Parliament and replaced by Lord Barham later in month.
10 April	Villeneuve with Gravina's squadron sails from Cadiz for Martinique.
12 May	Nelson sails for West Indies. Start of the Great Chase.
16 May	Villeneuve reaches Martinique.
20 May	Missiessy returns to Rochefort.
4 June	Nelson arrives at Carlisle Bay, Barbados.
7 June	Villeneuve learns of Nelson's arrival.
11 June	Villeneuve sails for France.
16 June	Nelson hears of Villeneuve's departure.
18 July	Nelson reaches Cape Spartel, Southern Spain.
22 July	Admiral Calder's action against Villeneuve off Cape Finisterre.
27 July	Villeneuve puts into Vigo Bay.
31 July	Villeneuve leaves Vigo Bay.
3 August	Napoleon arrives at Boulogne to await Villeneuve.
18 August	Nelson arrives at Portsmouth and returns to Merton.
21 August	The Combined Fleet reaches Cadiz.
26 August	*L'Armée d'Angleterre* breaks camp at Boulogne and marches to the Rhine. Invasion threat over.
14 September	Nelson rejoins the *VICTORY* at Portsmouth.
17 September	Napoleon names Admiral Rosily to replace Villeneuve.
28 September	Nelson takes command of the British fleet off Cadiz.
8 October	Captains of Combined Fleet revolt at Council of War.
14 October	Rosily leaves Madrid for Cadiz.

18 October	Villeneuve orders Combined Fleet to sail.
19 October	First ships leave Cadiz. Nelson orders 'General Chase'.
20 October	Remainder of Combined Fleet out of Cadiz by mid-afternoon, sailing for the Straits of Gibraltar. Napoleon defeats Austrians at Ulm.
21 October	**The Battle of Trafalgar.**

0600   Fleets in sight of each other.

0800   Villeneuve wears fleet to north.

1200   *Fougueux* opens fire on *ROYAL SOVEREIGN*.

1335   Nelson shot.

1600   Villeneuve captured.

1630   Death of Nelson.

1730   *Achille* blows up.

4 November	Rear Admiral Sir Richard Strachan captures Admiral Dumanoir's four ships off Cape Ortegal. *PICKLE* arrives off Falmouth. Lapenotiere leaves for London with dispatch.
6 November	News of Trafalgar arrives in London.
2 December	Napoleon crushes the Austrian and Russian armies at Battle of Austerlitz.
4 December	*VICTORY* arrives at Portsmouth with Nelson's body aboard.
5 December	Day of Thanksgiving for Trafalgar.
1806 8 January	Nelson's river-borne funeral procession.
9 January	Nelson's state funeral at St Paul's Cathedral.
22 April	Villeneuve commits suicide. 'I must die. How fortunate that I have no children to . . . be disgraced with the burden of my name.'

GLOSSARY

Aback 'The situation of the sails when their surfaces are flattened against the masts by the force of the wind' (Falconer) propelling the ship backwards (astern).

Abaft The stern or rear of a ship or any position towards the rear.

Able Seaman Skilled sailor.

Aboard On board, or the motion towards a ship.

About, go To change tack.

Admiral A flag rank. Admirals were eligible to command a fleet and fly a distinguishing flag. Flag ranks were divided into red, white and blue with blue being the junior rank.

Aft To the rear of the ship; behind.

Aloft The upper rigging, above generally.

Alongside Side by side.

Astern Behind a ship.

Back Trim sails to catch the wind on the wrong side so that they slow the ship down. Also means an anti-clockwise change in the wind direction.

Battleship A ship of the line carrying the heaviest guns. (See 'Ship of the line' and 'Rate'.)

Barge A type of ship's small boat, usually used by the captain.

Battery Relating to a ship, the heavy broadside guns mounted on a deck.

Bear up, Bear away Change course to run before the wind, i.e. downwind.

Beat To work a sailing ship to windward by successive tacking.

Berth Space for men to sleep or ships to anchor.

Between wind and water The waterline of a ship's hull. If ruptured here it would let in the sea.

Blockade A seaborne presence off an enemy coast to forbid movement of shipping and trade.

Bluejacket A Royal Marine term for sailors. Marines wore red tunics.

Blue light A fire signal made by pyrotechnics.

Board To go aboard a ship. Those attacking the enemy by boarding are known as boarders.

Boatswain (Bosun) A ship's officer responsible for the sails, rigging and working of the ship.

Bosun's call Whistle used to convey orders.

Bounty A sum of money paid as an inducement or a reward.

Bow Either side of the foremost part of a ship.

Bowsprit The mast or spar projecting from the bow of a sailing ship on which the jib-sails are set. Also, a stay for the foremast.

Breeching The rope attached to a heavy gun and the ship's side, preventing it from being run too far.

Brig A two-masted, square-rigged ship.

Breaking the line The act of passing through the line of battle of an opposing fleet so as to disrupt its formation.

Bulkhead A vertical partition in a ship.

Cable 1. Any large rope or hawser, usually more than 10 inches around. 2. A measure of distance: 120 fathoms. A cable's length is 200 yards.

Canister shot Projectile of lead balls in a tin container, resembling a giant shot-gun cartridge.

Carronade A short, heavy, large-calibre gun, usually 68lb, used on ships for firing canister at close range. Designed and founded by the Carron Iron Works, Scotland, in the early 1790s.

Cascabel The part behind the base ring at the rear of an artillery gun.

Chain shot A projectile where shot was linked by a bar or chain. Primarily designed to bring down spars and rigging.

Close-hauled When a ship is sailing as directly into wind as possible.

Copper bottom From the 1760s the Royal Navy sheathed the hulls of many of its ships to prevent

damage by the wood-boring teredo beetle. When clean it also meant the ship could move through the water more quickly.

Cockpit An area aft below the lower gun deck used by the surgeon in battle.

Cordage Rope or rigging.

Cot A bed strung up similar to a hammock.

Crapaud French word for toad. Used by British to describe Frenchmen generally.

Crosstrees Short transverse spars on a mast to which the topgallant mast is stayed.

Cutter 1. A type of ship's small rowing boat about 36ft long, with two step (demountable) masts and dipping lugsails. 2. Larger sailing vessel with fore and aft sails on a single mast.

Doubling Placing ships on either side of the enemy line at the same time.

Downwind Further from the source of the wind relative to another ship. Upwind is the opposite.

Enfilade Gunfire coming from the flank.

Ensign Flag flown aft of a ship to show its nationality.

Fathom Six feet.

First-rate The largest line

of sail battleship, carrying
100 guns or more.

Flintlock Gun discharged by a
spark produced from a flint.

Fore The front part of
a ship, forward.

Forecastle The deck built over the
forward part of the main deck.

Foremast The mast
nearest the bow.

Foresail The largest and lowest
square sail set on the foremast.

Fore-top The platform on
the foremast where the fore-
topmast was stepped.

Fore-topmast A separate spar
which extended the foremast upward
from which the foretopsail was set.

Foreyard The yard on which
the foresail was set.

Frigate A fifth- or sixth-rate three-
masted warship mounting 36–50
guns and 28–32 guns respectively
on a single deck. Frigates were
fast sailers. (see 'Rate'.)

Foretopsail The square sail set
on the fore-topmast yard.

Go aboard To place a ship
alongside an enemy ship.

Grape, Grape shot Iron balls
packed around an iron column
and held in place by canvas
and string that fly apart on
firing. Used at close range.

Grog Diluted spirits, usually rum.

Named after the grogram boatcloak
worn by Admiral Vernon, who
replaced the issue of brandy with
rum in 1740. The ration was 1:3,
rum to water, with ½ oz of lemon
juice and ½ oz of brown sugar,
served in halves twice a day.

Halliards, Halyards The rope
or tackle used to hoist a sail.

Haul To pull on a rope. To haul
down colours is surrendering.

Hawser A rope usually 5
inches or more around.

Helm The means of steering
a ship. The tiller. The order
given is the opposite direction
to the intended turn.

Holystone A block of sandstone
used to scour the decks. Large ones
were called bibles and small ones
were described as prayer books.

Jibboom An extension
of the bowsprit.

Jolly boat A ship's general
purpose small boat.

Jury-rig Improvised or replaced
masts, sails and rigging after
storm or battle damage.

Knot The speed of a ship through
the water was calculated by a 150
fathom log-line with knots tied at
fixed intervals. The number of knots
that ran out in the duration of a
sandglass gave the speed of the ship.

Larboard The older word for port. The left-hand side of the ship. The opposite of starboard.

Lay To aim or point a gun.

League A measure of distance equal to three miles.

Lee, Leeward The direction toward which the wind is blowing. The Lee Column at Trafalgar was downwind of the Weather Column.

Lee shore A coast facing an onshore wind.

Line abreast A formation where ships sail side by side rather than bow to stern.

Line ahead A formation where ships sail bow to stern, following each other. The line is divided into the van, the centre and the rear.

Line of battle The typical battle formation, which presented the broadside towards the enemy.

Linstock A short staff with a slowmatch (a slowly burning rope) at one end used to fire a gun.

Luff, Luff up, Luffing A method of losing way whereby the wind is spilled from the sails by turning the ship's bows into the wind.

Magazine A compartment in a warship for storing gunpowder.

Mast A vertical spar holding sails, yards and other spars.

Master A warrant sea officer responsible for the navigation and pilotage of the ship.

Mainmast The tallest mast in the ship (usually in the middle).

Mainsail The largest and lowest sail on the mainmast.

Midshipman A boy or young man hoping to become a commissioned officer.

Mizzen The aftermost mast of a ship.

Mizzen-top The platform on the mizzen mast sometimes used as a fighting platform. Nelson was hit by a shot from the mizzen-top of the *Redoubtable*.

Oakum Old rope teased into loose fibres used for caulking the seams of a ship.

Ordinary Seaman A sailor superior to a landsman but inferior to an Able Seaman.

Orlop deck The lowest deck in the ship, below the waterline.

Pinnace A type of ship's boat, oared.

Poop A short deck over the after end of the quarterdeck.

Powder monkey A young seaman who brought gunpowder cartridges from the magazine during battle.

Prize crew A crew put aboard a captured vessel in order to sail the prize to a friendly port.

Quarter The sides of the ship's stern.

Quarterdeck The deck above the rear half of the main deck. The usual station of the officers.

Quarter rail The rail around the quarterdeck.

Quoin A wedge inserted between the breech of a gun and the bed of the gun-carriage in order to adjust the elevation of the gun.

Rake Firing down the length of an enemy ship from ahead or astern.

Rate A ship's class according to a system introduced in Britain in the 1750s. There were six classes according to the number of guns. First-rates were 100 guns plus, second-rates had between 80 and 90 guns, third-rates mounted 74 guns and fourth-rates carried 64 guns.

Roundshot An iron ball, the most common form of projectile fired by smooth-bore heavy guns. Calibres used were 4, 6, 9, 12, 18, 24 and 32lb.

Run To sail downwind in the direction to which the wind is blowing.

Sail 'by the wind' To sail into the wind or with the wind at right-angles to the ship (abeam). When sailing 'on the wind' the ship had the wind behind.

Schooner A small sailing vessel fore- and aft-rigged on two masts.

Sheets Control ropes attached to the lower corners of the sails.

Ship of the line A warship large enough to form part of a line of battle. Typically 64 guns or more.

Shoal A sandbank, reef or area of shallow water.

Shot wads Wads of paper or material fibre rammed into a gun to hold the ball in place before firing.

Shroud A permanent stay supporting a mast from the side.

Slowmatch An impregnated length of smouldering cord used to detonate the gunpowder charge of a gun by touching it to the hole bored into the bore of the gun. (See 'Linstock'.)

Spar A mast, yard, pole, boom or gaff.

Splinter netting Netting erected over the deck areas prior to battle to protect the crew from falling rigging and splinters.

Spritsail A square sail set on a yard under the bowsprit.

Squadron A number of war ships, less than a fleet.

Square-rig An arrangement whereby square sails are fastened (bent) to yards lying horizontal to the masts.

Starboard The right-hand side of a ship.

Stern The back of a ship.

Stern chaser A gun pointing aft, usually through ports at the stern of the ship.

Strike (colours) To surrender a ship by lowering the national flag.

Studding sails, stunsails Lightweight square sails set outboard of the ordinary sails when the wind is light for extra speed.

Tack To turn a ship about by steering to windward. Beating to windward by successive tacks. In square-rigged ships the manoeuvre entailed changing the angle of the sails to the mast at the moment of turning.

Taffrail The rail running around the ship's stern.

Three-decker A ship of the line having three complete gun decks.

Topgallant 1. The highest of three wooden spars joined to make a mast. 2. The sail attached to the topgallant mast.

Tompion Protective plug placed in the muzzle of a gun when not in use.

Tumblehome The inward slope of a ship's side above the waterline.

Two-decker A ship of the line having two complete gun decks.

Upperworks The ship's superstructure. Not part of the hull.

Van The leading part of a line of ships, before the centre and the rear.

Veer 1. To alter course sharply. 2. To wear. 3. A clockwise change in the wind direction.

Victual, Victuals Foodstuffs, to supply foodstuffs.

Volunteer A person volunteering to serve, including a 'Boy First Class'.

Watch 1. A period of duty on a ship of four hours, except for two 'dog watches' of two hours between four and eight in the evening. 2. Division of the crew allowing half to rest while the other half work.

Way The movement of a ship through water.

Wear (wearing) To turn a ship about by moving its bow away from the source of the wind (i.e. to leeward). Slower but safer than tacking, but considered un-seamanlike.

Weather Relates to the direction from which the wind is blowing. 'When a ship under sail presents either of her sides to the wind, it is then called the weather-side' (Falconer). The opposite of Lee.

Weather gage (gauge) To get to windward of something. A fleet or ship having the weather gage of another is upwind of it.

Windward The direction from which the wind is blowing.

Yard A horizontal spar across the mast, from which sails are suspended.

Yardarm The ends of the yard.

THE COMBINED FLEET OF FRANCE AND SPAIN AT TRAFALGAR

(V) Vanguard   (C) Centre   (R) Rearguard
(SQO) Squadron of Observation

FRENCH SHIPS OF THE LINE

Ship	Guns	Fate	Casualties
Achille (SQO)	74	Caught fire and blew up on 21 Oct	480+
Aigle (SQO)	74	Engaged by *TONNANT*. Surrendered to *DEFIANCE*. Wrecked 23 Oct	270
Algésiras (SQO)	74	Struck to *TONNANT*. Retaken from prize crew. Escaped to Cadiz	216
Argonaute (SQO)	74	Engaged by *COLOSSUS* and *ACHILLE*. Escaped to Cadiz	160
Berwick (SQO)	74	Struck to *ACHILLE*. Wrecked 27 Oct	250
Bucentaure (C)	80	Struck to *CONQUEROR*. Wrecked 23 Oct	209
Duguay Trouin (R)	74	Escaped Trafalgar. Taken by Strachan on 4 Nov	0
Formidable (R)	80	Escaped Trafalgar. Taken by Strachan on 4 Nov	65
Fougueux (V)	74	Struck to *TÉMÉRAIRE*. Wrecked 22 Oct with prize crew	400
Héros (C)	74	Escaped to Cadiz	38
Indomptable (V)	80	Escaped. Took survivors of *Bucentaure*. Joined sortie 23 Oct. Sank 24 Oct	900+
Intrépide (V)	74	Struck to *ORION*. Burnt 24 Oct	306
Mont Blanc (R)	74	Escaped Trafalgar. Taken by Strachan on 4 Nov	0
Neptune (C)	84	Escaped. Joined sortie on 23 Oct	0
Pluton (V)	74	Escaped to Cadiz. Led sortie on 23 Oct	280

Redoubtable (C)	74	Struck to *TÉMÉRAIRE*. Foundered with prize crew on 23 Oct	544
Scipion (R)	74	Escaped Trafalgar. Taken by Strachan on 4 Nov	0
Swiftsure (SQO)	74	Struck to *COLOSSUS*. Prize. Became RN Ship. Broken up 1816	250

SPANISH SHIPS OF THE LINE

Argonauta (SQO)	80	Engaged by *ACHILLE*. Struck to *BELLEISLE*. Scuttled 29 Oct	305
Bahama (SQO)	74	Struck to *COLOSSUS*. Prize. Became RN ship. Broken up 1814	441
Monarca (V)	74	Struck to *BELLEROPHON*. Wrecked 25 Oct. *LEVIATHAN* saved crew	255
Montanes (SQO)	74	Escaped to Cadiz	49
Neptuno (R)	80	Struck to *MINOTAUR*. Retaken by sortie on 23 Oct. Wrecked. Burnt 31 Oct	89
Principe de Asturias (SQO)	112	Escaped to Cadiz	148
Rayo (R)	100	Escaped. Joined sortie. Struck to *DONEGAL*. Wrecked. Burnt on 31Oct	18
San Augustin (C)	74	Struck to *LEVIATHAN*. Burnt 30 Oct	385
San Francisco de Asis (R)	74	Escaped. Joined sortie on 23 Oct. Wrecked on 23 Oct	17
San Ildefonso (SQO)	74	Struck to *DEFENCE*. Prize. Became RN ship. Broken up 1816	160
San Juan Nepomuceno (SQO)	74	Struck to *DREADNOUGHT* (10 min fight). Prize. Became RN ship. Broken up 1818	250
San Justo (V)	74	Escaped to Cadiz	7
San Leandro (R)	64	Escaped to Cadiz	30
Santa Ana (V)	112	Struck to *ROYAL SOVEREIGN*. Retaken by sortie 23 Oct. Escaped to Cadiz	238

| Santissima Trinidad (C) | 140 | Struck to *PRINCE*. Scuttled 24 Oct | 427 |

Note: The exact number of casualties in the Combined Fleet will never be known. There are no official records.

Frigates and other ships

Argus	16	Lieutenant Taillard	0
Cornélie	40	Captain Chesneau	0
Furet	18	Lieutenant Dumay	0
Hermione	40	Captain Mahe	0
Hortense	40	Captain La Marre La Meillerie	0
Rhin	40	Captain Chesneau	0
Thémis	40	Captain Jugan	0

THE BRITISH FLEET AT TRAFALGAR

Ship	Guns	Commander	Casualties
Weather Column			
VICTORY	100	Vice Admiral Lord Nelson C-in-C (killed); Captain Thomas Masterman Hardy	159
TÉMÉRAIRE	98	Captain Eliab Harvey	123
NEPTUNE	98	Captain Thomas Fremantle	44
LEVIATHAN	74	Captain William Bayntun	26
BRITANNIA	100	Rear Admiral Earl of Northesk (3rd in command); Captain Charles Bullen	52
CONQUEROR	74	Captain Israel Pellew	12
AFRICA	64	Captain Henry Digby	62
AGAMEMNON	64	Captain Sir Edward Berry	10
AJAX	74	Lieutenant John Pilford	11
ORION	74	Captain Edward Codrington	24
MINOTAUR	74	Captain Charles Mansfield	25
SPARTIATE	74	Captain Sir Francis Laforey	23

Lee Column

ROYAL SOVEREIGN	100	Vice Admiral Cuthbert Collingwood (2nd in command); Captain Edward Rotherham	141
BELLEISLE	74	Captain William Hargood	130
MARS	74	Captain George Duff (killed); Lieutenant William Hennah	98
TONNANT	80	Captain Charles Tyler	76
BELLEROPHON	74	Captain John Cooke (killed); Lieutenant William Pryce Cumby	123
COLOSSUS	74	Captain James Nicoll Morris	200
ACHILLE	74	Captain Richard King	72
DREADNOUGHT	98	Captain John Conn	33
POLYPHEMUS	64	Captain Robert Redmill	6
REVENGE	74	Captain Robert Moorsom	79
SWIFTSURE	74	Captain William Rutherford	17
DEFIANCE	74	Captain Philip Durham	70
THUNDERER	74	Lieutenant John Stockham	16
DEFENCE	74	Captain George Hope	36
PRINCE	98	Captain Richard Grindall	0

Frigates and other ships

EURYALUS	36	Captain Henry Blackwood	0
NAIAD	38	Captain Thomas Dundas	0
PHOEBE	36	Captain Thomas Bladen Capell	0
SIRIUS	36	Captain William Prowse	0
PICKLE (schooner)	10	Lieutenant John Richards Lapenotiere	0
ENTREPENANTE (cutter)	8	Lieutenant Robert Young	0

BIBLIOGRAPHY

The sources for the majority of individual letters were:

The National Archives (formerly the Public Record Office)
  Kew Admiralty Papers (ADM), including ADM36, 37
  (Muster Books) and ADM51 (Captains' Logs)
National Maritime Museum, Greenwich
Admiralty and Royal Naval Museum Library, Portsmouth
The Colindale Newspaper Library
British Library: AddMss, Egerton
Royal Marines Museum, Southsea
Bedfordshire Record Office

The following bibliography lists the main books, articles and manuscripts consulted during the preparation of this book. It is not a comprehensive list.

Allen, Joseph (ed.): *Memoirs of the Life and Services of Admiral Sir William Hargood G.C.B.,G.C.H., Compiled from Authentic Documents Under the Direction of Lady Hargood by Joseph Allen Esq.* (Greenwich, 1841)
Ayshford, Pamela and Derek: *The Ayshford Trafalgar Roll* [CD-ROM] (Pamela & Derek Ayshford, 2004)
Beatty, Sir William, MD: *Authentic Narrative of the Death of Lord Nelson* (1807)
Bennett, Geoffrey: *Nelson The Commander* (BT Batsford, 1972)
    The Battle of Trafalgar (BT Batsford, 1977)
Broadley, AM and RG Bartelot: *Nelson's Hardy: His Life, Letters, and Friends* (London, 1909)
Charnock, John: *Biographical Memoirs of Lord Viscount Nelson &c* (London, 1806)
Clarke, James Stanier and John McArthur: *Life of Admiral Lord Nelson K.B., from his Lordship's manuscripts* (London, 1809)
Clarke, Richard: *The Life of Horatio Lord Viscount Nelson* (London, 1813)
Clayton, Tim, and Phil Craig: *Trafalgar: the Men, the Battle, the Storm* (Hodder & Stoughton, 2004)
Coleman, Terry, Corbett, Julian S: *The Campaign of Trafalgar* (London, 1910)
Cumby WP: The Battle of Trafalgar (an unpublished narrative), *The Nineteenth Century, A Monthly Review,* 46, pp. 717–28, (1899)
Desbrière, Édouard: *The Naval Campaign of 1805: Trafalgar,* trans. and ed. ConstanceEastwick (Oxford, 1933, 2 vols)
Des Touches, G: Souvenirs d'un marin de la République, *Revue des Deux Mondes,* 28, pp. 177–201 and 407–36 1905.

Dillon, WH (ed Michael Lewis): *A Narrative of My Professional Adventures 1790–1839*: vol. II, 1802-1839, Navy Records Society, 97 (London, 1956).

Fenwick, Kenneth: *HMS Victory* (Cassell, 1959)

Field, Colonel Cyril: *Britain's Sea Soldiers. A History of the Royal Marines and their predecessors and of their services in action, ashore and afloat, and upon sundry other occasions of moment*, Vol. 1, pp 25–258 (Liverpool, 1924)

Fraser, Edward: *The Enemy at Trafalgar: An account of the Battle from Eye-Witnesses' Narratives and Letters and Despatches from the French and Spanish Fleets* (Hodder & Stoughton, 1906)

Gardiner, Robert (ed): *The Campaign of Trafalgar 1803-1805* (Chatham, 1997)

Goodwin, Peter: *Nelson's Ships: A History of the vessels in which he served 1171–1805* (Conway, 2002).

Guimerá, Agustin: 'Commerce and shipping in Spain during the Napoleonic Wars, in Howarth', Stephen, ed., *Battle of Cape St Vincent 200 Years* (The 1805 Club, 1998). *Gravina y el liderazgo naval de su tiempo*, in Guimerá, A., A. Ramos, and G., Butrón, *Trafalgar y el mundo atlántico*, Madrid: Marcial Pons, Editores/Camara de Tenerife.

Harbron, John D: *Trafalgar and the Spanish Navy* (Conway, 1988)

Harris, David (ed): *The Nelson Almanac* (Conway, 1998)

Harrison, James: *Life of Viscount Nelson* (London, 1806)

Hoffman, Frederick (eds. A Beckford Bevan and HB Wolryche-Whitemore): *A Sailor of King George: The Journals of Captain Frederick Hoffman, R.N. 1793–1814* (London 1901)

Horne, Alistair: *How far from Austerlitz? Napoleon 1805–1815* (Macmillan, 1996)

Howarth, David: *Trafalgar: The Nelson Touch* (Collins, 1970)

Hughes, Edward (ed): *The Private Correspondence of Admiral Lord Collingwood* (Navy Records Society, 98, 1957)

Jackson, T. Sturges (ed): *Logs of the Great Sea Fights, 1794–1805* (Navy Records Society, Vol. 11)

Jackson, Hilary W., *A County Durham Man at Trafalgar, Cumby of the Bellerophon* (Durham County Local History Society)

James, William: *Naval History of Great Britain 1793–1820* (London, 7th edn 1886, 6 vols.)

Jennings, Louis J (ed): *The Correspondence and Diaries of the Late Right Honourable John Wilson Croker* (London, 1884, 3 vols.)

Keegan, John: *The Price of Admiralty, War at Sea from Man-of-War to Submarine* (London,1988)

Kerr, Mark: *The Sailor's Nelson* (Hurst and Blackett, 1932)

Lambert, Andrew: *War at sea in the Age of Sail 1650–1850* (Cassell, 2000)
Nelson: Britannia's God of War (Faber & Faber, 2004)

Lavery, Brian: *Nelson's Navy: The Ships, Men and Organisation 1793–1815* (Conway, 1989)

Nelson's Fleet at Trafalgar (National Maritime Museum, 2004)

Longford, Elizabeth: *Wellington, The Years of the Sword* (Weidenfeld & Nicholson, 1969)

Lovell, William Stanhope: *Personal Narrative of Events from 1799 to 1815, with Anecdotes* (Wm. Allen, 1879)

Mackenzie, Colonel Robert Holden, introd. Colin White: *The Trafalgar Roll: The Ships and the Officers* (rep. Chatham, 2004)

Mahan, Captain Alfred. T: *The Life of Nelson* (1897)

Influence of Sea Power upon the French Revolution and Empire (1892)

Marioné, Patrick: *The Complete Navy List of the Napoleonic Wars 1793–1815* [CD-ROM] (SEFF, 2003)

Matcham, M Eyre: *The Nelsons of Burnham Thorpe* (John Lane, The Bodley Head, 1911)

Moorhouse, E Hallam (ed): *Letters of the English Seaman 1587–1808* (London, 1910) *Naval Chronicle, The*, Vol. XIV; Vol. XV

Newbolt, Sir Henry: *The Year of Trafalgar* (1905)

Newnham Collingwood, GL: *A Selection from the Public and Private Correspondence of Vice-Admiral Lord Collingwood: Interspersed with Memoirs of his Life.* (London, 1829)

Nicolas, Sir H Nicholas (ed): *The Dispatches and Letters of Vice Admiral Lord Viscount Nelson* (London, 1844–5, 7 vols.; rep. Chatham, 1998)

Oman, Carola: *Nelson* (London, 1947)

Parsons, GS (ed, WH Long): *Nelsonian Reminiscences: Leaves from Memory's Log, A Dramatic Eye-Witness Account of the War at Sea 1795–1810* (Rep. 1998)

Pemberton, Charles Reece: *The Autobiography of Pel Verjuice by Charles Reece Pemberton, with an introduction on his life and work* (London,1929)

Perez Galdos, Benito: *Trafalgar: A Tale* (1873).

Pocock, Tom: *Horatio Nelson* (The Bodley Head, 1987)

The Terror before Trafalgar, Nelson, Napoleon and the Secret War (John Murray, 2002)

Pope, Dudley: *England Expects: Nelson and the Trafalgar Campaign* (London, 1959, rep. Chatham 1998)

Robinson, W: *The Nautical Economy or Recollections of Events During the Last War Dedicated to the Brave Tars of Old England by a Sailor politely called by the officers of the navy Jack Nastyface* (London, 1836)

Rodger, NAM: *The Wooden World: an Anatomy of the Georgian Navy* (Collins, 1986)

Russell, W Clark: *The Life of Admiral Lord Collingwood* (Methuen, 1895)

Schom, Alan: *Trafalgar, Countdown to Battle 1803–1805* (Michael Joseph, 1990)

Smith, DB: *The Defiance at Trafalgar*, Scottish Historical Review, 20, pp. 116–21 (1923)

Southey, Robert: *Life of Nelson* (1813)

Taylor, AH: *The Battle of Trafalgar*, Mariners' Mirror, 36, pp. 281–321 (Society for Nautical Research, 1950)

Terraine, John: *Trafalgar* (Sidgwick & Jackson, 1976)

Thursfield, Rear Admiral HG: *Five Naval Journals 1789–1817* (Navy Records Society, 1951)

Tracy, Nicholas: *Nelson's Battles:The Art of Victory in the Age of Sail* (Chatham, 1996)

Warner, Oliver: *A Portrait of Lord Nelson* (Chatto and Windus, 1958)
  Trafalgar (Batsford, 1959)
  Nelson's Battles (Batsford, 1965)

White, Colin: *1797 Nelson's Year of Destiny: Cape St Vincent and Santa Cruz de Tenerife* (RNM, Alan Sutton, 1998).
  The Nelson Encyclopaedia (Chatham 2002)
  (Ed) *The Nelson Companion* (RNM, Alan Sutton, 1995)

Zulueta, Julian de: *Trafalgar – The Spanish View*, Mariners' Mirror LXVI, pp 293–318, (Society for Nautical Research, 1980)

INDEX

Vessels of the Combined Fleet are
shown as Fr or Sp for French or Spanish

PICTURE CREDITS